The Rape
of the Mind

THE PSYCHOLOGY OF THOUGHT CONTROL, MENTICIDE, AND BRAINWASHING

by Joost A. M. Meerloo, M.D.

INSTRUCTOR IN PSYCHIATRY, COLUMBIA UNIVERSITY

LECTURER IN SOCIAL PSYCHOLOGY, NEW SCHOOL FOR SOCIAL RESEARCH

FORMER CHIEF, PSYCHOLOGICAL DEPARTMENT, NETHERLANDS FORCES

THE WORLD PUBLISHING COMPANY

CLEVELAND AND NEW YORK

Library of Congress catalog card number: 56-9252

— **SECOND PRINTING**

Permission to reprint has been granted by:

HARVARD UNIVERSITY PRESS, for the quotation on page 51 from *The New Man in Soviet Psychology* by R. A. Bauer, copyright 1952.

THE MACMILLAN COMPANY, for the quotation on page 29 from *The Cardinal's Story* by S. K. Swift, copyright 1949.

THE NEW YORK TIMES, for the quotation on pages 33 and 34 from The New York Times of February 27, 1955.

2HC157

CONTENTS

PART TWO

The Techniques of Mass Submission

PART THREE

Unobtrusive Coercion

CONTENTS

PART FOUR

In Search of Defenses

FOREWORD

And fear not them which kill the body,
but are not able to kill the soul.
     —MATTHEW 10:28

This book attempts to depict the strange transformation of the free human mind into an automatically responding machine—a transformation which can be brought about by some of the cultural undercurrents in our present-day society as well as by deliberate experiments in the service of a political ideology.

The rape of the mind and stealthy mental coercion are among the oldest crimes of mankind. They probably began back in prehistoric days when man first discovered that he could exploit human qualities of empathy and understanding in order to exert power over his fellow men. The word "rape" is derived from the Latin word *rapere,* to snatch, but also is related to the words to rave and raven. It means to overwhelm and to enrapture, to invade, to usurp, to pillage and to steal.

The modern words "brainwashing," "thought control," and "menticide" serve to provide a clearer conception of the actual methods by which man's integrity can be violated. When a concept is given its right name, it can be more easily recognized—and it is with this recognition that the opportunity for systematic correction begins.

In this book the reader will find a discussion of some of the imminent dangers which threaten free cultural interplay. It emphasizes the tremendous cultural implication of the subject of enforced mental intrusion. Not only the artificial techniques of coercion are important but even more the unobtrusive intrusion into our feeling and thinking. The danger of destruction of the spirit may be compared to the threat of total physical destruction through atomic warfare. Indeed, the two are related and intertwined.

My approach to this subject is based on the belief that it is only by looking at any problem from several angles that we are able to get at its heart.

According to Bohr's principle of complementarity, the rather simple phenomena of physics can be looked at from diverse viewpoints; different and seemingly contrasting concepts are needed to describe physical phenomena. For instance, for explanation of the behavior of electrons, both the concept of particle and the concept of wave are useful. The same is true for the even more complicated psychological and social interactions. We cannot look at brainwashing merely from a simple Pavlovian viewpoint. This book tries to do it also from the clinical descriptive view and from the Freudian concept of psychology; it tries to look at brainwashing from the standpoint that general mental coercion may belong to every human interaction.

Communication of any sort can almost be compared with trying to knock down a row of dolls in a throwing game. The more balls we throw, the greater is the probability that we may hit all the dolls. The more approaches we make to any problem, the greater chance we have of finding and grasping its essential core. Such detailed treatment will be impossible without some repetition in the text.

In this book we shall move from the specific subject of planned and deliberate mental coercion to the more general question of the influences in the modern world that tend to robotize and automatize man. The last chapters are devoted to the problem of inner backbone, as a first step in the direction of learning to maintain our mental freedom.

One of the great Dutch authors—Multatuli—wrote a letter to his friend excusing himself because the letter was so long: he had not had time enough to write a shorter one. In this paradox he expressed part of the problem of all search for expression and communication. It takes a long time to express an idea in a precise and communicable way. Yet being short and simple in one's descriptions is not always appreciated. Especially modern psychology is loaded with superlearnedness—with the secret intention of leaving the reading public awe-stricken. The man who tries to express himself in simple words, bypassing jargon, risks being called popular and unscientific. Nevertheless, I am aware of the fact that I have been so much steeped in psychological terminology that I cannot completely forego psychological language. The real test of psychological clarity is the way the layman absorbs and understands the ideas communicated. My aim has been to write for the general public, not to popularize but to bring some order to the chaos of our particular epoch.

Every word man speaks is a plagiarism. The task of an author is to absorb, incorporate, and transform the knowledge and emotional currents of his own epoch and to present them in his own personal way, enriched by his own experiences. I am grateful, indeed, to all those whose ideas I have been able to borrow, and especially to all those who inspired me to write down my own thoughts on this controversial subject.

J. A. M. M.

January, 1956

PART ONE

THE TECHNIQUES OF INDIVIDUAL SUBMISSION

THE FIRST PART OF THIS BOOK IS DEVOTED TO VARI-
OUS TECHNIQUES USED TO MAKE MAN A MEEK
CONFORMIST. IN ADDITION TO ACTUAL POLITICAL
OCCURRENCES, ATTENTION IS CALLED TO SOME IDEAS
BORN IN THE LABORATORY AND TO THE DRUG TECH-
NIQUES THAT FACILITATE BRAINWASHING. THE LAST
CHAPTER DEALS WITH THE SUBTLE PSYCHOLOGICAL
MECHANISMS OF MENTAL SUBMISSION.

CHAPTER ONE

You Too Would Confess

A fantastic thing is happening in our world. Today a man is no longer punished only for the crimes he has in fact committed. Now he may be compelled to confess to crimes that have been conjured up by his judges, who use his confession for political purposes. It is not enough for us to damn as evil those who sit in judgment. We must understand what impels the false admission of guilt; we must take another look at the human mind in all its frailty and vulnerability.

The Enforced Confession

During the Korean War, an officer of the United States Marine Corps, Colonel Frank H. Schwable, was taken prisoner by the Chinese Communists. After months of intense psychological pressure and physical degradation, he signed a well-documented "confession" that the United States was carrying on bacteriological warfare against the enemy. The confession named names, cited missions, described meetings and strategy conferences. This was a tremendously valuable propaganda tool for the totalitarians. They cabled the news all over the world: "The United States of America is fighting the peace-loving people of China by dropping bombs loaded with disease-spreading bacteria, in violation of international law."

After his repatriation, Colonel Schwable issued a sworn statement repudiating his confession, and describing his long months of imprisonment. Later, he was brought before a military court of inquiry. He testified in his own defense before that court: "I was never convinced in my own mind that we in the First Marine Air Wing had used bug warfare. I knew we hadn't, but the rest of it was real to me—the conferences, the planes, and how they would go about their missions."

"The words were mine," the Colonel continued, "but the thoughts were theirs. That is the hardest thing I have to explain: how a man can sit down and write something he knows is false, and yet, to sense it, to feel it, to make it seem real."

This is the way Dr. Charles W. Mayo, a leading American physician and government representative, explained brainwashing in an official statement before the United Nations: ". . . the tortures used . . . although they include many brutal physical injuries, are not like the medieval torture of the rack and the thumb-screw. They are subtler, more prolonged, and intended to be more terrible in their effect. They are calculated to disintegrate the mind of an intelligent victim, to distort his sense of values, to a point where he will not simply cry out 'I did it!' but will become a seemingly willing accomplice to the complete disintegration of his integrity and the production of an elaborate fiction."

The Schwable case is but one example of a defenseless prisoner being compelled to tell a big lie. If we are to survive as free men, we must face up to this problem of politically inspired mental coercion, with all its ramifications.

It is more than twenty years since psychologists first began to suspect that the human mind can easily fall prey to dictatorial powers. In 1933, the German Reichstag building was burned to the ground. The Nazis arrested a Dutchman, Marinus Van der Lubbe, and accused him of the crime. Van der Lubbe was known by Dutch psychiatrists to be mentally unstable. He had been a patient in a mental institution in Holland. And his weakness and lack of mental balance became apparent to the world when he appeared before the court. Wherever news of the trial reached, men wondered: "Can that foolish little fellow be a heroic revolutionary, a man who is willing to sacrifice his life to an ideal?"

During the court sessions Van der Lubbe was evasive, dull, and apathetic. Yet the reports of the Dutch psychiatrists described him as a gay, alert, unstable character, a man whose moods changed rapidly, who liked to vagabond around, and who had all kinds of fantasies about changing the world.

On the forty-second day of the trial, Van der Lubbe's behavior changed dramatically. His apathy disappeared. It became apparent that he had been quite aware of everything that had gone on during the previous sessions. He criticized the slow course of the procedure. He demanded punishment—either by imprisonment or death. He spoke about his "inner voices." He insisted that he had his moods in check. Then he fell back into apathy. We now recognize these symptoms as a combination of behavior forms which we can call a confession syndrome. In 1933 this type of behavior was unknown to psychiatrists. Unfortunately, it is very familiar today and is frequently met in cases of extreme mental coercion.

Van der Lubbe was subsequently convicted and executed. When the trial was over, the world began to realize that he had merely been a scapegoat. The Nazis themselves had burned down the Reichstag building and had staged the crime and the trial so that they could take over Germany. Still later we realized that Van der Lubbe was the victim of a diabolically clever misuse of medical knowledge and psychologic technique, through which he had been transformed into a useful, passive, meek automaton, who replied merely yes or no to his interrogators during most of the court sessions. In a few moments he threatened to jump out of his enforced role. Even at that time there were rumors that the man had been drugged into submission, though we never became sure of that.*

Between 1936 and 1938 the world became more conscious of the very real danger of systematized mental coercion in the field of politics. This was the period of the well-remembered Moscow purge trials. It was almost impossible to believe that dedicated old Bolsheviks, who had given their lives to a revolutionary movement, had suddenly turned into dastardly traitors. When, one after

* The psychiatric report about the case of Van der Lubbe is published by Bonhoeffer and Zutt. Though they were unfamiliar with the "menticide syndrome," and not briefed by their political fuehrers, they give a good description about the pathologic, apathetic behavior, and his tremendous change of moods. They deny the use of drugs.

another, every one of the accused confessed and beat his breast, the general reaction was that this was a great show of deception, intended only as a propaganda move for the non-Communist world. Then it became apparent that a much worse tragedy was being enacted. The men on trial had once been human beings. Now they were being systematically changed into puppets. Their puppeteers called the tune, manipulated their actions. When, from time to time, news came through showing how hard, rigid revolutionaries could be changed into meek, self-accusing sheep, all over the world the last remnants of the belief in the free community presumably being built in Soviet Russia began to crumble.

In recent years, the spectacle of confession to uncommitted crimes has become more and more common. The list ranges from Communist through non-Communist to anti-Communist, and includes men of such different types as the Czech Bolshevik Rudolf Slansky and the Hungarian cardinal, Joseph Mindszenty.

Mental Coercion and Enemy Occupation

Those of us who lived in the Nazi-occupied countries during the Second World War learned to understand only too well how people could be forced into false confessions, and into betrayals of those they loved. I myself was born in the Netherlands and lived there until the Nazi occupation forced me to flee. In the early days of the occupation, when we heard the first eyewitness descriptions of what happened during Nazi interrogations of captured resistance workers, we were frightened and alarmed.

The first aim of the Gestapo was to force prisoners under torture to betray their friends and to report new victims for further torture. The Brown Shirts demanded names and more names, not bothering to ascertain whether or not they were given falsely under the stress of terror. I remember very clearly one meeting held by a small group of resisters to discuss the growing fear and insecurity. Everybody at that meeting could expect to be mentioned and picked up by the Gestapo at some time. Should we be able to stand the Nazi treatment, or would we also be forced to become informers? This question was being asked by anti-Nazis in all the occupied countries.

During the second year of the occupation we realized that it was better not to be in touch with one another. More than two contacts were unsafe. We tried to find medical and psychiatric preventives to harden us against the Nazi torture we expected. As a matter of fact, I myself conducted some experiments to determine whether or not narcotics would harden us against pain. However, the results were paradoxical. Narcotics can create pain insensitivity, but their dulling action at the same time makes people more vulnerable to mental pressure. Even at that time we knew, as did the Nazis themselves, that it was not the direct physical pain that broke people, but the continuous humiliation and mental torture. One of my patients, who was subjected to such an interrogation, managed to remain silent. He refused to answer a single question, and finally the Nazis dismissed him. But he never recovered from this terrifying experience. He hardly spoke even when he returned home. He simply sat—bitter, full of indignation—and in a few weeks he died. It was not his physical wounds that had killed him; it was the combination of fear and wounded pride.

We held many discussions about ways of strengthening our captured underground workers or preventing them from final self-betrayal. Should some of our people be given suicide capsules? That could only be a last resort. Narcotics like morphine give only a temporary anesthesia and relief; moreover, the enemy would certainly find the capsules and take them away.

We had heard about German attempts to give cocaine and amphetamine to their air pilots for use in combat exhaustion, but neither medicament was reliable. These drugs might revive the body by making it less sensitive to pain, but at the same time they dulled the mind. If captured members of the underground were to take them, as experiments had shown, their bodies might not feel the effects of physical torture, but their hazy minds might turn them into easier dupes of the Nazis.

We also tried systematic exercises in mental relaxation and auto-hypnosis (comparable with Yogi exercises) in order to make the body more insensitive to hunger and pain. If an individual's attention is fixed on the development of conscious awareness of automatic body functions, such as breathing, the alert functioning of the brain cortex can be reduced, and awareness of pain will diminish. This state of pain insensitivity can sometimes be achieved through autohypnotic exercises. But very few of our people were able to bring themselves into such anesthesia.

Finally we evolved this simple psychological trick: when you can no longer outwit the enemy or resist talking, the best thing to do is to talk too much. This was the idea: keep yourself sullen and act the fool; play the coward and confess more than there is to confess. Later we were able to verify that this method was successful in several cases. Scatterbrained simpletons confused the enemy much more than silent heroes whose stamina was finally undermined in spite of everything.

I had to flee Holland after a policeman warned me that my name had been mentioned in an interrogation. I had twice been questioned by the Nazis on minor matters and without bodily torture. When they later caught up with me in Belgium, probably as the result of a betrayal, I had to undergo a long initial examination in which I was beaten, fortunately not too seriously. The interview had started pleasantly enough. Apparently, the Nazi officer in charge thought he would be able to get information out of me through friendly methods. Indeed, we even had a discussion (since I am a psychiatrist) about the methods used in interrogation. But when he found that the friendly approach was getting him nowhere, the officer's mood changed, and he behaved with all the sadistic characteristics we had come to expect from his type. Happily, I managed to escape from Belgium that very night before a more systematic and more torturous investigation could begin.

Arriving at the London headquarters after an adventurous trip through France and Spain, I became Chief of the Psychological Department of the Netherlands Forces in England. In this official position I was able to gather data on what was happening to the millions of victims of Nazi terror and torture. Later on I questioned and treated several escapees from internment and concentration camps. These people had become real experts in suffering. The variety of human reactions under these infernal circumstances taught us an ugly truth: the spirit of most men can be broken, men can be reduced to the level of animal behavior. Both torturer and victim finally lose all human dignity.

My government gave me the power to investigate a group of traitors and I also interrogated imprisoned Nazis. When I review all these wartime experiences, all the confusion about courage and cowardice, treason, morale, and mental fortitude, I must confess that my eyes were only really opened after a study of the Nuremberg trials of the Nazi leaders. These trials gave us the real story of the systematic coercive methods used by the Nazis. At about the same time we began to learn more about the perverted psychological strategy Russia and her satellites were using.

Witchcraft and Torture

The specific techniques used in the modern world to break man's mind and will and to extort confessions for political propaganda purposes are relatively new and highly refined. Yet enforced confession itself is nothing new. From time immemorial tyrants and dictators have needed these "voluntary" confessions to justify their own evil deeds. The knowledge that the human mind can be influenced, tamed, and broken down into servility is far older than the modern dictatorial concept of enforced indoctrination. The primitive shaman used awe-inspiring ritual to bring his victim into such a state of fright hypnosis that he yielded to all suggestions. The native on whom a spell of doom has been cast by the medicine man may become so hypnotized by his own fear that he simply sits down, accepts his fate, and dies (Malinowski).

Throughout history men have had an intuitive understanding that the mind can be manipulated. Elaborate strategies have been worked out to achieve this end. Ecstasy rituals, frightening masks, loud noises, eerie chants—all have been used to compel the crowd to accept the beliefs of their leaders. Even if an ordinary man at first resists a cruel shaman or medicine man, the hypnotizing ritual gradually breaks his will.

More painful methods are not new either. When we study the old reports of the Inquisition, or of the many witch trials, both in Europe and America, we learn a great deal about these methods. The floating test is one example. Those accused of witchcraft were thrown into the river, their feet and hands tied together. If the body did not sink, the victim was immediately pulled out of the water and burned at the stake. The fact that he did not sink was proof positive of his guilt. If, on the other hand, the accused obeyed the law of gravity and sank to the bottom of the river, the drowned body was ceremoniously removed from the river and proclaimed innocent. Not much choice was left to the victim!

Man has been tremendously inventive in developing means for inflicting suffering on his fellow man. With refined passion he has devised techniques which provoke the most exquisite pain in the most vulnerable parts of the human body. The rack and the thumbscrew are age-old instruments and have been used not only by primitive judges but also by so-called civilized dictators and tyrants.

In order better to understand modern mental torture, we must constantly keep in mind the fact that from the earliest days bodily anguish and the rack were never meant merely to inflict pain on the victim. They may not have expressed their understanding in sophisticated terms, but the medieval judge and hangman were nevertheless aware that there is a peculiar spiritual relationship and mental interplay between the victim and the rest of the community. Much painful torture and hanging had to be done as public demonstrations. After suffering the most intense pain, the witch would not only confess to shocking sexual debaucheries with the devil, but would herself gradually come to believe the stories she had invented and would die convinced of her guilt. The whole ritual of interrogation and torture finally compelled her to yield to the fantasies of her judges and accusers. In the end she even yearned for death. She wanted to be burned at the stake in order to exorcise the devil and expiate her sins.

These same judges and hangman realized, too, that their witch trials were intended not only to torture the witches, but even more to torture the bystanders, who, albeit unconsciously, identified themselves with the victims. This is, of course, one of the reasons burnings and hangings were held in public and became the occasion for great pageants. Terror thus became widespread, and many judges spoke euphemistically of the preventive action of such torture. Psychologically, we can see this entire device as a blackmailing of human sympathy and the general tendency to identify with others.

As far back as 1563 the courageous Dutch physician Johannes Wier published his masterwork, *De Praestigiis Daemonum (On the Delusions About Demons*), in which he states that the collective and voluntary self-accusation of older women—through which they exposed themselves to torture and death by their inquisitors—was in itself an act inspired by the devil, a trick of demons, whose aim it was to doom not only the innocent women but also their reckless judges. Wier was the first medical man to introduce what became the psychiatric concept of *delusion* and mental blindness. Wherever his book had influence, the persecution of witches ceased, in some countries more than one hundred and fifty years before it was finally brought to an end throughout the civilized world. His work and his insights became one of the main instruments for fighting the witch delusion and physical torture (Baschwitz). Wier realized even then that witches were scapegoats for the inner confusion and desperation of their judges and of the *Zeitgeist* in general.

The Refinement of the Rack

All knowledge can be used either for good or for evil, and psychology is not immune to this general law. Psychology has delivered up to man new means of torture and intrusion into the mind. We must be more and more aware of what these methods and techniques are if we are successfully to fight them. They can often be more painful and mentally more paralyzing than the rack. Strong personalities can tolerate physical agony; often it serves to increase stubborn resistance. No matter what the constitution of the victim, physical torture finally leads to a protective loss of consciousness. But to withstand mental torture leading to creeping mental breakdown demands an even stronger personality.

What we call brainwashing (a word derived from the Chinese *Hsi-Nao*) is an elaborate ritual of systematic indoctrination, conversion, and self-accusation used to change non-Communists into submissive followers of the party (Hunter). "Menticide" is a word coined by me and derived from *mens*, the mind, and *caedere*, to kill.* Both words indicate the same perverted refinement of the rack, putting it on what appears to be a more acceptable level. But it is

* Here I followed the etymology used by the United Nations to form the word "genocide," meaning the systematic destruction of racial groups.

a thousand times worse and a thousand times more useful to the inquisitor.

Menticide is an old crime against the human mind and spirit but systematized anew. It is an organized system of psychological intervention and judicial perversion through which a powerful dictator can imprint his own opportunist thoughts upon the minds of those he plans to use and destroy. The terrorized victims finally find themselves compelled to express complete conformity to the tyrant's wishes. Through court procedures, at which the victim mechanically reels off an inner record which has been prepared by his inquisitors during a preceding period, public opinion is lulled and thrown off guard. "A real traitor has been punished," people think. "The man has confessed!" His confession can be used for propaganda, for the cold war, to instill fear and terror, to accuse the enemy falsely, or to exercise a constant mental pressure upon others.

One important result of this procedure is the great confusion it creates in the mind of every observer, friend or foe. In the end no one knows how to distinguish truth from falsehood. The totalitarian potentate, in order to break down the minds of men, first needs widespread mental chaos and verbal confusion, because both paralyze his opposition and cause the morale of the enemy to deteriorate—unless his adversaries are aware of the dictator's real aim. From then on he can start to build up his system of conformity.

In both the Mindszenty and the Schwable cases, we have documented reports of the techniques of menticide as it has been used to break the minds and wills of courageous men.

Let us look first at the case of Cardinal Mindszenty, accused of misleading the Hungarian people and collaboration with the enemies, the United States. In his exposé on Cardinal Mindszenty's imprisonment, Stephen K. Swift graphically describes three typical phases in the psychological "processing" of political prisoners. The first phase is directed toward extorting confession. The victim is bombarded with questions day and night. He is inadequately and irregularly fed. He is allowed almost no rest and remains in the interrogation chamber for hours on end while his inquisitors take turns with him. Hungry, exhausted, his eyes blurred and aching under unshaded lamps, the prisoner becomes little more than a hounded animal.

> . . . when the Cardinal had been standing for sixty-six hours [*Swift reports*], he closed his eyes and remained silent. He did not even reply to questions with denials. The colonel in charge of the shift tapped the Cardinal's shoulder and asked why he did not respond. The Cardinal answered: "End it all. Kill me! I am ready to die!" He was told that no harm would come to him; that he could end it all simply by answering certain questions.
>
> . . . By Saturday forenoon he could hardly be recognized. He asked for another drink and this time it was refused. His feet and legs had swollen to such proportions that they caused him intense pain; he fell down several times.

To the horrors the accused victim suffers from without must be added the horrors from within. He is pursued by the unsteadiness of his own mind, which cannot always produce the same answer to a repeated question. As a human being with a conscience he is pursued by possible hidden guilt feelings, however pious he may have been, that undermine his rational awareness of innocence. The panic of the "brainwashee" is the total confusion he suffers about all concepts. His evaluations and norms are undermined. He cannot believe in anything objective any more except in the dictated and indoctrinated logic of those who are more powerful than he. The enemy knows that, far below the surface, human life is built up of inner contradictions. He uses this knowledge to defeat and confuse the brainwashee. The continual shift of interrogators makes it ever more impossible to believe in consecutive thinking. Hardly has the victim adjusted himself to one inquisitor when he has to change his focus of alertness to another one.

Yet, this inner clash of norms and concepts, this inner contradiction of ideologies and beliefs is part of the philosophical sickness of our time!

As a social being the Cardinal is pursued by the need for good human relationships and companionship. The constantly reiterated suggestion of his guilt urges him toward confession. As a suffering individual he is blackmailed by an inner need to be left alone and undisturbed, if only for a few minutes. From within and without he is inexorably driven toward signing the confession prepared by his persecutors. Why should he resist any longer? There are no visible witnesses to his heroism. He cannot prove his moral courage and rectitude after his death. The core of the strategy of menticide is the taking away of all hope, all anticipation, all belief in a future. It destroys the very elements which keep the mind alive. The victim is utterly alone.*

If the prisoner's mind proves too resistant, narcotics are given to confuse it: mescaline, marihuana, morphine, barbiturates, alcohol. If his body collapses before his mind capitulates, he receives stimulants: benzedrine, caffein, coramine, all of which help to preserve his consciousness until he confesses. Many of the narcotics and stimuli which ultimately help to induce mental dependency and enforced confusion also can create an amnesia, often a complete forgetting of the torture itself. The torture techniques achieve the desired effect, but the victim forgets what has actually happened during the interrogation. The clinicians who do therapeutic work with amphetamine derivatives, which when injected into the blood stream help patients to remember long-forgotten experiences, are familiar with the drug's ability to bring soothing forgetfulness of the period during which the patient was drugged and questioned.†

Next the victim is trained to accept his own confession, much as an animal is trained to perform tricks. False admissions are reread, repeated, hammered into his brain. He is forced to reproduce in his memory again and again the fantasied offenses, fictitious details which ultimately convince him of his criminality. In the first stage he is forced into mental submissiveness by others. In the second stage he has entered a state of autohypnosis, convincing himself of fabricated crimes. According to Swift: "The questions during the

---

* This continual attack on human conscience and guilt by unconscious self-accusations is brilliantly depicted by Franz Kafka in *The Trial*. In this novel the victim never knows of what he is accused but his inner guilt leads him to conviction. Kafka anticipated the age of blackmailing into confession. His novel was written before the 1930's. The same theme has been treated from a psychological point of view by Theodor Reik in his *Confession Compulsion and the Need for Punishment*.
† See Chapter Three.

interrogation now dealt with details of the Cardinal's 'confession.' First his own statements were read to him; then statements of other prisoners accused of complicity with him; then elaborations of these statements. Sometimes the Cardinal was morose, sometimes greatly disturbed and excited. But he answered all questions willingly, repeated all sentences—once, twice, or even three times when he was told to do so." (Lassio)

In the third and final phase of interrogation and menticide the accused, now completely conditioned and accepting his own imposed guilt, is trained to bear false witness against himself and others. He doesn't have to convince himself any more through autohypnosis; he only speaks "his master's voice." He is prepared for trial, softened completely; he becomes remorseful and willing to be sentenced. He is a baby in the hands of his inquisitors, fed as a baby and soothed by words as a baby.*

Menticide in Korea

Now let us take a look at the Schwable case. In its general outline it is similar to the Mindszenty story; it differs only in details. As an officer of the United States Marine Corps, fighting with the United Nations in Korea, he is taken prisoner by the enemy. The colonel expects to be protected by international law and by the regulations regarding officer prisoners of war, which have been accepted by all countries. However, it slowly dawns on him that he is being subjected to a kind of treatment very different from what he expected. The enemy looks on him not as a prisoner of war, but as a victim who can be used for propaganda purposes.

He is subjected to slow but constant pressures devised to break him down mentally. Humiliation, rough, inhuman treatment, degradation, intimidation, hunger, exposure to extreme cold—all have been used to crumble his will and to soften him. They need to wangle military secrets out of him and to use him as a tool in their propaganda machine. He feels completely alone. He is surrounded by filth and vermin. For hours on end he has to stand up and answer the questions his interrogators hurl at him. He de-

* A more extended survey of the different psychological stages in menticide and brainwashing will be given at the end of Chapter Four.

velops arthritic backache and diarrhea. He is not allowed to wash or shave. He doesn't know what will happen to him next. This treatment goes on for weeks. Then the hours of systematic and repetitious interrogation and oppression increase. He no longer dares to trust his own memory. There are new teams of investigators every day, and each new team points out his increasing errors and mistakes. He cannot sleep any more. Daily his interrogators tell him they have plenty of time, and he realizes that in this respect at least they are telling the truth. He begins to doubt whether he can resist their seductive propositions. If he will just unburden himself of his guilt, they tell him, he will be better treated. The inquisitor is treacherously kind and knows exactly what he wants. He wants the victim captured by the influence of a slowly induced hypnosis. He wants a well-documented confession that the American army used bacteriological warfare, that the captive himself took part in such germ warfare. The inquisitor wants this confession in writing because it will make a convincing impression and will shock the world. China is plagued by hunger and epidemics; such a confession will explain the high disease rate and exculpate the Chinese government, whose popularity is at a low ebb. So the colonel has to be prepared for a systematic confession, made before an international group of Communist experts. Mentally and physically he is weakened, and every day the Communist "truths" are imprinted on his mind.

The colonel has in fact become hypnotized; he is now able to reproduce for his jailers bits and pieces of the confession they want from him. It is a well-known scientific fact that the passive memory often remembers facts learned under hypnosis better than those learned in a state of alert consciousness. He is even able to write some of it down. Eventually, all the little pieces fit, like a jigsaw puzzle, into a complete, well-organized whole; they form part of a document which was in fact prepared beforehand by his captors. This document is placed in the colonel's hands, and he is even allowed to make some minor changes in the phrasing before he signs it.

By now, the colonel has been completely broken. He has given in. All sense of reality is gone; identification with the enemy is complete. For weeks after signing the confession he is in a state of depression. His only wish is the wish to sleep, to have rest from it all.

A man will often try to hold out beyond the limits of his endurance because he continues to believe that his tormentors have some basic morality, that they will finally realize the enormity of their crimes and will leave him alone. This is a delusion. The only way to strengthen one's defenses against an organized attack on the mind and will is to understand better what the enemy is trying to do and to outwit him. Of course, one can vow to hold out until death, but even the relief of death is in the hands of the inquisitor. People can be brought to the threshold of death and then be stimulated into life again so that the torments can be renewed. Attempts at suicide are foreseen and can be forestalled.

In my opinion hardly anyone can resist such treatment. It all depends on the ego strength of the person and the exhaustive technique of the inquisitor. Each man has his own limit of endurance, but that this limit can nearly always be reached and even surpassed is supported by clinical evidence. Nobody can predict for himself how he will handle a situation when he is called to the test. The official United States report on brainwashing* admits that "virtually all American P.O.W.'s collaborated at one time or another in one degree or another, lost their identity as Americans . . . thousands lost their will to live," and so forth. The British report† gives a statistical survey about the abuse of their P.O.W.'s. According to this report one third of the soldiers absorbed enough indoctrination to be classified as Communist sympathizers.

The same report describes in a more extended way some of the sadistic means used by the enemy:

> If a prisoner accepted Communist doctrines, his life became easier, according to the men's stories. But if a prisoner resisted Communist doctrines, the Chinese considered him a criminal and reactionary deserving of any brutalities. The tortures applied to the "reactionaries" included:
> Making a prisoner stand at attention or sit with legs outstretched in complete silence from 4:30 A.M. to 11 P.M. and constantly waking him during the few hours allowed for sleep.

* The New York Times, August 18, 1955.
† The New York Times, February 27, 1955.

Keeping prisoners in solitary confinement in boxes about five by three by two feet. A private of the Gloucester Regiment spent more than six months in one of these.

Withholding liquids for days "to help self-reflection."

Binding a prisoner with a rope passed over a beam, one end fixed as a hangman's noose round his neck and the other end tied to his ankles. He was then told that if he slipped or bent his knees he would be committing suicide.

Forcing a prisoner to kneel on jagged rocks and hold a large rock over his head with arms extended. It took a man who had undergone this treatment days to recover the ability to walk.

At one camp North Korean jailers pushed a pencil-like piece of wood or metal through a hole in the cell door and made the prisoner hold the inner end in his teeth. Without warning a sentry would knock the outer end sidewise, breaking the man's teeth or splitting the sides of his mouth. Sometimes the rod was rammed inward against the back of the mouth or down the throat.

Prisoners were marched barefooted to the frozen Yalu River, water was poured over their feet and they were kept for hours with their feet frozen to the ice to "reflect" on their "crimes."

Time, fear, and continual pressure are known to create a menticidal hypnosis. The conscious part of the personality no longer takes part in the automatic confessions. The brainwashee lives in a trance, repeating the record grooved into his mind by somebody else. Fortunately, this, too, is known: as soon as the victim returns to normal circumstances, the panicky and hypnotic spell evaporates, and he again awakens into reality.

This is what happened to Colonel Schwable. True, he confessed to crimes he did not commit, but he repudiated his confession as soon as he was returned to a familiar environment.

When, during the military inquiry into the Schwable case, I was called upon to testify as an expert on menticide, I told the court of my deep conviction that nearly anybody subjected to the treatment meted out to Colonel Schwable could be forced to write and sign a similar confession.

"Anyone in this room, for instance?" the colonel's attorney asked me, looking in turn at each of the officers sitting in judgment on this new and difficult case.

And in good conscience I could reply, firmly: "Anyone in this room."

It is now technically possible to bring the human mind into a condition of enslavement and submission. The Schwable case and the cases of other prisoners of war are tragic examples of this, made even more tragic by our lack of understanding of the limits of heroism. We are just beginning to understand what these limits are, and how they are used, both politically and psychologically, by the totalitarians. We have long since come to recognize the breast-beating confession and the public recantation as propaganda tricks; now we are beginning to see ever more clearly how the totalitarians use menticide: deliberately, openly, unashamedly, as part of their official policy, as a means of consolidating and maintaining their power, though, of course, they give a different explanation to the whole procedure—it's all confession of real and treacherous crimes.

This brutal totalitarian technique has at least one virtue, however. It is obvious and unmistakable, and we are learning to be on our guard against it, but as we shall see later, there are other subtler forms of mental intervention. They can be just as dangerous as the direct assault, precisely because they are more subtle and hence more difficult to detect. Often we are not aware of their action at all. They influence the mind so slowly and indirectly that we may not even realize what they have done to us.

Like totalitarian menticide, some of these less obvious forms of mental manipulation are political in purpose. Others are not. Even if they differ in intent, they can have the same consequences.

These subtle menticidal forces operate both within the mind and outside it. They have been strengthened in their effect by the growth in complexity of our civilization. The modern means of mass communication bring the entire world daily into each man's home; the techniques of propaganda and salesmanship have been refined and systematized; there is scarcely any hiding place from the constant visual and verbal assault on the mind. The pressures of daily life impel more and more people to seek an easy escape from responsibility and maturity. Indeed, it is difficult to withstand these pressures; to many the offer of a political panacea is very tempting, to others the offer of escape through alcohol, drugs, or other artificial pleasures is irresistible.

Free men in a free society must learn not only to recognize this stealthy attack on mental integrity and fight it, but must learn also what there is inside man's mind that makes him vulnerable to this attack, what it is that makes him, in many cases, actually long for a way out of the responsibilities that democracy and maturity place on him.

☙

CHAPTER TWO

Pavlov's Students as Circus Tamers

☙

Before asking ourselves what the deeper mental mechanisms are of brainwashing, false confession, and conversion into a collaborator, let us try to see things from the standpoint of the totalitarian potentates. What is their aim? What terms do they use to describe the behavior of their prisoners? What do they want from the Schwables and the Mindszentys?

The totalitarian jailers don't speak of hypnosis or suggestion; they even deny the fact of imposed confession. They think about human behavior and human government in a much more mechanical way. In order to understand them we have to give more attention to their adoration of simplified Pavlovian concepts.

The Salivating Dog

In the latter part of the nineteenth century the Russian Nobel-prize winner Ivan Petrovich Pavlov conducted his famous experiments with a bell and a dog. He knew that salivation is associated with eating, and that if a dog was hungry, its mouth would water each time it saw food. Pavlov took advantage of this useful inborn reflex, which serves the digestive process, to develop in his experimental animal the salivating response in answer to a stimulus which would not ordinarily create it. Each time Pavlov fed the dog, he rang a bell, and at each feeding the dog's mouth watered. Then after many repetitions of the combined food-bell stimulus, Pavlov rang the bell but did not feed the dog. The animal reacted to the bell alone just as it had previously reacted to the sight of food—its mouth watered. Thus the scientist had found out that the dog could be induced to salivate involuntarily in response to an arbitrary signal. It had been "conditioned" to respond to the ringing of the bell as if that sound were the smell and taste of food.

From this and other experiments, Pavlov developed his theory of the conditioned reflex, which explains learning and training as the building up of a mosaic of conditioned reflexes, each one based on the establishment of an association between different stimuli. The greater the number of learned complex responses—also called patterns—the greater the number of conditioned reflexes developed. Because man, of all the animals, has the greatest capacity for learning, he is the animal with the greatest capacity for such complicated conditioning.

Pavlov's experiments were of great value in the study of animal and human behavior, and in the study of the development of neurotic symptoms. However, this knowledge of some of the mechanisms of the human mind can be used as we have seen already, like any other knowledge, either for good or for evil. And unfortunately, the totalitarians have used their knowledge of how the mind works for their own purposes. They have applied some of the Pavlovian findings, in a subtle and complicated way and sometimes in a grotesque way, to try to produce the reflex of mental and political conditioning and of submission in the human guinea pigs under their control. Even though the Nazis employed these methods before the Second World War, they can be said to have reached their full flower in Soviet Russia. Through a continued repetition of indoctrination, bell ringing and feeding, the Soviet man is expected to become a conditioned reflex machine, reacting according to a prearranged pattern, as did the laboratory dogs. At least, such a simplified concept is roaming around in the minds of some of the Soviet leaders and scientists (Dobrogaev).

In accordance with one of Stalin's directives, Moscow maintains a special "Pavlovian Front" (Dobrogaev) and a "Scientific Council on Problems of Physiological Theory of the Academician I. P. Pavlov" (London). These institutions, part of the Academy of Science, are dedicated to the political application of the Pavlovian theory. They are under orders to emphasize the purely mechanical aspects of Pavlov's findings. Such a theoretical view can reduce all human emotions to a simple, mechanistic system of conditioned reflexes. Both organizations are control agencies dealing in research problems, and the scientists who work on them explore the ways in which man can theoretically be conditioned and trained as animals are. Since Pavlovian theory is proclaimed by the obdurate totalitarian theoreticians as the gospel of animal and human behavior, we have to grapple with the facts they adduce to prove their point, and with their methods and theoretical explanations.

What the Pavlovian council tries to achieve is the result of an oversimplification of psychology. Their political task is to condition and mold man's mind so that its comprehension is confined to a narrow totalitarian concept of the world. It is the idea that such a limitation of thinking to Lenin-Marxist theoretical thinking must be possible for two reasons: first, if one repeats often enough its simplification, and second, if one withholds any other form of interpretation of reality.

This concept is based on the naive belief that one can permanently suppress any critical function and verification in human thinking. Yet, through taming and conditioning of people, during which period errors and deviations must continually be corrected, unwittingly a critical sense is built up. True, at the same time the danger of using this critical sense is brought home to the students. They know the dangers of any dissent, but even this promotes the development of a secondary and more refined critical sense. In the end, human rebellion and dissent cannot be suppressed; they await only one breath of freedom in order to awake once more. The idea that there exist other ways to truth than those he sees close at hand lives somewhere in everybody. One can narrow his pathways of research and expression, but a man's belief in adventurous new roads elsewhere is ever present in the back of his mind.

The inquisitive human mind is never satisfied with a simple recital of facts. As soon as it observes a set of data, it jumps into the area of theory and offers explanations, but the way a man sees a set of facts, and the way he juggles them to build them into a theory is largely determined by his own biases and prejudices. Let me be the first to confess that I am affected by my own subjectivities. Even the words we use are loaded with implications and suggestions. The word "reflex," for example, so important in Pavlovian theory, is a perfect instance of this. It was first used by the seventeenth-century philosopher Descartes, in whose philosophical system a parallel was made between the actions of the human body and those of a machine. For example, in the Cartesian view, the automatic reaction of the body to certain painful stimuli (e.g., withdrawing the hand after it has come into contact with fire) is compared with the automatic physical reflection of light from a mirror. The nervous system, according to Descartes, reflects its response just as the mirror does. Such a simple explanation of behavior, and the very words used to describe it, immediately denies the whole organism taking part in that response. Yet man is not only a mirror, but a thinking mirror. According to the old mechanical view, actions are associated only with the part of the body which performs them, and they have no relationship whatsoever to the purposeful behavior of the organism as a whole. But man is not a machine composed of independently functioning parts. He is a whole. His mind and body interact; he acts on the outside world and the outside world acts on him. The innate reflexes, of which this hand withdrawal is one example, are part of a whole system of adaptive responses which serve to help the individual, as an entity, to adjust to changed circumstances. They can be described as the result of an inborn adaptation tendency. The only real difference between the innate reflexes and the conditioned reflexes is that the former supposedly have developed in the entire race over the millions of years of the evolutionary process, while the latter are developed during the life span of the individual as a result of the gradual automatization of acquired responses. If you analyze any one of the complicated actions you may perform during the course of a single day (driving an automobile, for example), you will see that it occurs outside your conscious management. And yet, before the process could be automatized, the actions, purposefully directed toward the satisfaction of some goal, had to be consciously learned and managed. You were not born with the innate reflex of jamming on the brake to stop a car quickly in an emergency. You had to learn to do it, and in the process of learning and driving, this response became automatic. If, after you have learned to drive, you see a child running across the path of your car, you put the brake on immediately, by reflex, without thinking.

The Conditioning of Man

Pavlov's research on the machinery of the mind taught us how all the animals—including man—learn adjustment to existing limitations through linking the signs and signals of life to body reactions. The mind creates a relationship between repeated simultaneous occurrences, and the body reacts to the connections the mind forms. Thus the bell, rung each time the dog was fed, became a signal to the animal to prepare for digestion, and the animal began to salivate.

Recent experiments conducted by Dr. Gregory Razran of Queens College show how men may develop these same kinds of responses. Dr. Razran treated a group of twenty college students to a series of free luncheons at which music was played or pictures shown. After the final luncheon, these twenty students were brought together with another group who had not been luncheon guests. At this meeting, as at the luncheons, music was played and pictures shown, and all the students were asked to tell what the music and pictures made them think of. The music and the pictures generally reminded the first group of something related to eating, but had no such associations for the second group. There was obviously a temporary connection in the minds of the luncheon guests between the music and pictures on the one hand and eating on the other.

The Chinese did their mass conditioning in an even simpler way. After having taught the prisoners for days to write down all possible nonsense and political lies—in an atmosphere of utter confusion and stress—they were ripe to sign collectively the lie of having taken part in germ warfare (Winokur).

All conditioned reflexes are involuntary temporary adjustments to pressures which create an apparent connection between stimuli which may be in fact totally unrelated. For this reason, the conditioned reflex is not necessarily permanently imprinted on the individual, but can gradually disappear. If, after the dog's conditioned reflex to the bell has been developed, the bell is rung over and over again and no food is presented to the animal, the salivating reflex disappears. Doubtless Dr. Razran's students will not always think of food when they hear music.

We could describe the conditioned reflex another way: it is a selected response of the mind-body unit to a given stimulus. The ways in which the stimulus and the response are connected vary considerably—they may have been associated in time, in place, or by coincidence, or by a common aim—and thus they may form a special conditioned complex in our mental and physical attitude. Some of these complex responses, or patterns, are more autonomous than others, and will act like the innate patterns. Some are flexible and are continually changing. Analysis of some of the psychosomatic diseases, for example, shows us how our inner emotional attitudes can intensify or even change a conditional response. Stomach ulcers is an example of such a psychosomatic disease. It may arise when the body manufactures too much hydrochloric acid, which is necessary for the digestion of food. The stomach ulcer patient is a person who reacts to strong emotions, especially repressed hostility, with an excessive secretion of hydrochloric acid. The innate secretion reflex, favorable for the digestion in case of hunger, grows into an unfavorable conditioned reflex where hunger and aggression mutually increase the hydrochloric acid secretion. Gradually more and more of the sour fluid is manufactured until finally the patient finds himself suffering from ulcers. The stomach consumes, as it were, its own tissue. This same paradox may be seen in many educational processes. The mother who puts her child on a too rigid feeding schedule may change the child's favorable response to hunger into a stubborn reaction against feeding.

For our purpose we have to be aware that conditioning takes place throughout all our lives in the most subtle and in the most obvious ways. We discover that the molding of our personalities may occur in a thousandfold ways through such matters as these: the meal training given in early childhood; the harshness or the musical tone of the words spoken to us; the sense of haste in our surroundings; the steadiness of family habits or the chaos of neurotic parents; the noises of our machines; the reservedness of our friends; the discipline of our schools and the competitiveness of our clubs. We are even conditioned by such things as the frailty of our toys and the cosiness of our houses, the steadiness of traditions or the chaos of a revolution. The artist and the engineer, the teacher and the friend, the uncle or aunt and the servant—they all give shape to our behavior.

Isolation and Other Factors in Conditioning

Pavlov made another significant discovery: the conditioned reflex could be developed most easily in a quiet laboratory with a minimum of disturbing stimuli. Every trainer of animals knows this from his own experience; isolation and the patient repetition of stimuli are required to tame wild animals. Pavlov formulated his findings into a general rule in which the speed of learning is positively correlated with quiet and isolation. The totalitarians have followed this rule. They know that they can condition their political victims most quickly if they are kept in isolation. In the totalitarian technique of thought control, the same isolation applied to the individual is applied also to groups of people. This is the reason the civilian populations of the totalitarian countries are not permitted to travel freely and are kept away from mental and political contamination. It is the reason, too, for the solitary confinement cell and the prison camp.

Another of Pavlov's findings was that some animals learned more quickly if they were rewarded (by affection, by food, by stroking) each time they showed the right response, while others learned more quickly when the penalty for not learning was a painful stimulus. In human terms, the latter animals could be described as learning in order to avoid punishment. These different reactions in animals may perhaps be related to an earlier conditioning by the parents, and they find their counterparts among human beings. In some people the strategy of reward and flattery is a stimulus to learning, while pain evokes all their resistance and rebellion; in others retribution and punishment for failure can be a means of training them into the desired pattern. Before he can do his job effectively, the brainwasher has to find out to which category his victim belongs. There are people more amenable to brainwashing than others. Part of the response may be innate or related to earlier conditioning to conformity.

Pavlov also distinguished between the weaker type of involuntary learning, in which the learned response was lost as soon as some disturbance occurred, and the stronger type, in which training was retained through all kinds of changed conditions. As a matter of fact, Pavlov described more types of learning than this, but for our purposes it is only important to know that there are some types of people who lose their conditioned learning easily, while others, the so-called "stronger" types, retain it. This, by the way, is another example of how our choice of words reflects our bias. The descriptions "strong" and "weak" depend completely on the aim of the experimenter. For the totalitarian, the "weak" P.O.W. is the man who stubbornly refuses to accept the new conditioning. His "weakness" may be, in fact, a resistance, the result of a previous strong conditioning to loyalty to antitotalitarian principles. We never know how strongly conditioning and initial learning are impressed on the personality. Rigid dogmatic behavior has its roots in early conditioning—and so may submissiveness based on ignorance rather than knowledge.

Pavlov showed, too, how internal and external factors interact in the conditioning process. If, for example, a new laboratory assistant was brought in to work with the animals, all of their newly acquired patterns could easily be inhibited because of the animals' emotional reactions to the newcomer. Pavlov explained this as a disruptive reaction caused by the animals' investigatory reflexes, which led them to sniff around the stranger. Current psychology tends to interpret it as the result of the changed emotional rapport between the animal and its trainers. We can easily expand the implications of this more modern view into the field of human relations. It points up the fact that there are some persons who can create such immediate rapport with others that the latter will soon give up many old habits and ways of life to conform with new demands. There are inquisitors and investigators whose personalities so deeply affect their victims that the victims speedily yield their secrets and accept entirely new ways of thinking. We can see the same thing in psychotherapy, where the development of an emotional rapport between doctor and patient is the most important factor leading to cure. In some cases rapport can be established immediately, in others rapport cannot be built up at all, in most cases it develops gradually during the course of the therapy. It is not difficult for a psychologist to test a man's "softness" and willingness to be conditioned, and as a matter of fact the Pavlovians have developed simple questionnaires through which they can easily determine a given individual's instability and adaptability to suggestion and brainwashing.

Pavlov found that all conditioning, no matter how strong it had been, became inhibited through boredom or through the repetition of too weak signals. The bell could no longer arouse salivation in the experimental dogs if it was repeated too often or its tone was too soft. A process of unlearning took place. The result of such internal inhibition of conditioning and the loss of conditioned reflex action is sleep. The inhibition spreads over the entire activity of the brain cortex; the organism falls into a hypnotic state. This explanation of the process of inhibition was one of the first acceptable theories of sleep. An interesting psychological question is whether too much official conditioning causes boredom and inhibition, and whether that is the reason why the Stakhanovite movement in Russia was necessary to counteract the loss of productivity of the people.

We can make a comparison with what happened to our prisoners of war in Korea. Under the daily signal of dulling routine questions—for every word can act as a Pavlovian signal—their minds went into a state of inhibition and diminished alertness. This made it possible for them to give up temporarily their former democratic conditioning and training. When they had unlearned and suppressed the democratic way, their inquisitors could start teaching them the totalitarian philosophy. First the old patterns have to be broken down in order to build up new conditioned reflexes. We can imagine that boredom and repetition arouse the need to give in and to yield to the provoking words of the enemy. Later I shall come back to the system of negative stimuli used in conditioning for brainwashing.

Mass Conditioning Through Speech

According to official Pavlovian psychology, human speech is also a conditioned reflex activity. Pavlov distinguished between stimuli of the first order, which condition men and animals directly, and stimuli of the second order, with weaker and more complicated conditioning qualities. In this so-called second signal system, verbal cues replace the original physical sound stimuli. Pavlov himself did not give much attention to this second signal system. It was especially after Stalin's publication in 1950 on the significance of linguistics for mass indoctrination (as quoted by Dobrogaev) that the Russian psychologists began to do work in this area. In his letter, Stalin followed Engel's theory that language is the characteristic human bit of adaptive equipment. That tone and sound in speech have a conditioning quality is something we can verify from our own experience in listening to or in giving commands, or in dealing with our pets. Even the symbolic and semantic meaning of words can acquire a conditioning quality. The word "traitor," for example, provokes direct feelings and reactions in the minds of those who hear it spoken, even if this discriminatory label is being applied dishonestly.

Through an elaborate study on speech reflexes written by one of the leading Russian psychologists, Dobrogaev, we get a fairly good insight into the ways in which speech patterns and word signals are used in the service of mass conditioning, by means of propaganda and indoctrination. The basic problems for the man tamer are rather simple: Can man resist a government bent on conditioning him? What can the individual do to protect his mental integrity against the power of a forceful collectivity? Is it possible to do away with every vestige of inner resistance?

Pavlov had already explained that man's relation to the external world, and to his fellow men, is dominated by secondary stimuli, the speech symbols. Man learns to think in words and in the speech figures given him, and these gradually condition his entire outlook on life and on the world. As Dobrogaev says, "Language is the means of man's adaptation to his environment." We could rephrase that statement in this way: man's need for communication with his fellow men interferes with his relation to the outside world, because language and speech itself—the verbal tools we use—are variable and not objective. Dobrogaev continues: "Speech manifestations represent conditioned-reflex functions of the human brain." In a simpler way we may say: he who dictates and formulates the words and phrases we use, he who is master of the press and radio, is master of the mind.

In the Pavlovian strategy, terrorizing force can finally be replaced by a new organization of the means of communication. Ready-made opinions can be distributed day by day through press, radio, and so on, again and again, till they reach the nerve cell and implant a fixed pattern of thought in the brain. Consequently, guided public opinion is the result, according to Pavlovian theoreticians, of good propaganda technique, and the polls a verification of the temporary successful action of the Pavlovian machinations on the mind. Yet, the polls may only count what people pretend to think and believe, because it is dangerous for them to do otherwise.

Such is the Pavlovian device: repeat mechanically your assumptions and suggestions, diminish the opportunity of communicating dissent and opposition. This is the simple formula for political conditioning of the masses. This is also the actual ideal of some of our public relation machines, who thus hope to manipulate the public into buying a special soap or voting for a special party.

The Pavlovian strategy in public relations has people conditioned more and more to ask themselves, "What do other people think?" As a result, a common delusion is created: people are incited to think what other people think, and thus public opinion may mushroom out into a mass prejudice.

Expressed in psychoanalytic terms, through daily propagandistic noise backed up by forceful verbal cues, people can more and more be forced to identify with the powerful noisemaker. Big Brother's voice resounds in all the little brothers.

News from Red China, as reported by neutral Indian journalists* tells us that the Chinese leaders are using this vocal conditioning of the public to strengthen their regime. Throughout the country, radios and loud-speakers are broadcasting the official "truths." The sugary voices take possession of people, the cultural tyranny traps their ears with loud-speakers, telling them what they may and may

* The New York Times, November 27, 1954.

not do. This microphone regimentation was foreseen by the French philosopher La Rochefoucauld, who, in the eighteenth century, said: "A man is like a rabbit, you catch him by the ears."

During the Second World War the Nazis showed that they too were very much aware of this conditioning power of the word. I saw their strategy at work in Holland. The radio constantly spread political suggestions and propaganda, and people were obliged to listen because the simple act of turning off one's radio was in itself suspicious. I remember one day during the occupation when I was taking a bicycle trip with some friends. We stopped off to rest at a café that, we later realized, was a true Nazi nest. When the radio, which had been on ever since we arrived, announced a speech by Hitler, everyone stood up in awe, and it was a must to take in the verbal conditioning by the *Fuhrer*. My friends and I had to stand up too, and were forced to listen to that raucous voice crackling in our ears and to summon all our resistance against that long, boring, repetitive attack on our eardrums and minds.

Throughout the occupation, the Nazis printed tons of propaganda, Big Lies, and distortions. They even went so far as to paint their slogans on the stoops of the houses and in the streets. Every week newly fabricated stereotypes ogled at us as if to convince us of the splendor of the Third Reich. But the Nazis did not know the correct Pavlovian strategy. By satisfying their own need to discuss and to vary their arguments in order to make them seem more logical, they only increased the resistance of the Dutch people. This resistance was additionally fortified by the London radio, on which the Dutch could hear the sane voice of their own legal government. Had the Nazis not argued and justified so much, and had they been able to prevent all written, printed, or spoken communication, the long period of boredom would have inhibited our democratic conditioning, and we might well have been more seduced by the Nazi oversimplifications and slogans.

Political Conditioning

Political conditioning should not be confused with training or persuasion or even indoctrination. It is more than that. It is taming. It is taking possession of both the simplest and the most complicated nervous patterns of man. It is the battle for the possession of the nerve cells. It is coercion and enforced conversion. Instead of conditioning man to an unbiased facing of reality, the seducer conditions him to catchwords, verbal stereotypes, slogans, formulas, symbols. Pavlovian strategy in the totalitarian sense means imprinting prescribed reflexes on a mind that has been broken down. The totalitarian wants first the required response from the nerve cells, then control of the individual, and finally control of the masses. The system starts with verbal conditioning and training by combining the required stereotypes with negative or positive stimuli: pain, or reward. In the P.O.W. camps in Korea where there was individual and mass brainwashing, the negative and positive conditioning stimuli were usually hunger and food. The moment the soldier conformed to the party line his food ration was improved: say yes, and I'll give you a piece of candy!

The whole gamut of negative stimuli, as we saw them in the Schwable case, consists of physical pressure, moral pressure, fatigue, hunger, boring repetition, confusion by seemingly logical syllogisms. Many victims of totalitarianism have told me in interviews that the most upsetting experience they faced in the concentration camps was the feeling of loss of logic, the state of confusion into which they had been brought—the state in which nothing had any validity. They had arrived at the Pavlovian state of inhibition, which psychiatrists call mental disintegration or depersonalization. It seemed as if they had unlearned all their former responses and had not yet adopted new ones. But in reality they simply did not know what was what.

The Pavlovian theory translated into a political method, as a way of leveling the mind (the Nazis called it *Gleichschaltung*) is the stock in trade of totalitarian countries. Some psychiatric points are of interest because we see that Pavlovian training can be used successfully only when special mental conditions prevail. In order to tame people into the desired pattern, victims must be brought to a point where they have lost their alert consciousness and mental awareness. Freedom of discussion and free intellectual exchange hinder conditioning. Feelings of terror, feelings of fear and hopelessness, of being alone, of standing with one's back to the wall, must be instilled.

The treatment of American prisoners of war in the Korean P.O.W. camps followed just such a pattern. They were compelled to listen to lectures and other forms of daily word barrage. The very fact that they did not understand the lectures and were bored by the long sessions inhibited their democratic training, and conditioned them to swallow passively the bitter doctrinal diet, for the prisoners were subjected not only to a political training program, but also to an involuntary taming program. To some degree the Communist propaganda lectures were directed toward retraining the prisoners' minds. This training our soldiers could reject, but the endless repetitions and the constant sloganizing, together with the physical hardships and deprivations the prisoners suffered, caused an *unconscious taming* and conditioning, against which only previously built-up inner strength and awareness could help.

There is still another reason why our soldiers were sometimes trapped by the Communist conditioning. Experiments with animals and experiences with human beings have taught us that threat, tension, and anxiety, in general, may accelerate the establishment of conditioned responses, particularly when those responses tend to diminish fear and panic (Spence and Farber). The emergency of prison-camp life and mental torture provide ideal circumstances for such conditioning. The responses can develop even when the victim is completely unaware that he is being influenced. Thus, many of our soldiers developed automatic responses of which they remained completely unconscious (Segal). But this is only one side of the coin, for experience has also shown that people who know what to expect under conditions of mental pressure can develop a so-called perceptual defense, which protects them from being influenced. This means that the more familiar people are with the concepts of thought control and menticide, the more they understand the nature of the propaganda barrage directed against them, the more inner resistance they can put up, even though inevitably some of the inquisitor's suggestions will leak through the barrier of conscious mental defense.

Our understanding of the conditioning process leads us also to an understanding of some of the paradoxical reactions found among victims of concentration camps and other prisoners. Often those with a rigid, simple belief were better able to withstand the continual barrage against their minds than were the flexible, sophisticated ones, full of doubt and inner conflicts. The simple man with deep-rooted, freely absorbed religious faith could exert a much greater inner resistance than could the complex, questioning intellectualist. The refined intellectual is much more handicapped by the internal pros and cons.

In the totalitarian countries, where belief in Pavlovian strategy has assumed grotesque proportions, the self-thinking, subjective man has disappeared. There is an utter rejection of any attempt at persuasion or discussion. Individual self-expression is taboo. Private affection is taboo.

Peaceful exchange of thoughts in free conversation will disturb the conditioned reflexes and is therefore taboo. No longer are there any brains, only conditioned patterns and educated muscles. In such a taming system neurotic compulsion is looked upon as a positive asset instead of something pathological. The mental automaton becomes the ideal of education.

Yet the Soviet theoreticians themselves are often unaware of this, and many of them do not realize the dire consequences of subjecting man to a completely mechanistic conditioning. They themselves are often just as frightened as we are by the picture of the perfectly functioning human robot. This is what one of their psychologists says: "The entire reactionary nature of this approach to man is completely clear. Man is an automaton who can be caused to act as one wills! This is the ideal of capitalism! Behold the dream of capitalism the world over—a working class without consciousness, which cannot think for itself, whose actions can be trained according to the whim of the exploiter! This is the reason why it is in America, the bulwark of present-day capitalism, that the theory of man as a robot has been so vigorously developed and so stubbornly held to." (Bauer)

Western psychology and psychiatry, although acknowledging its debt to Pavlov as a great pioneer who made important contributions to our understanding of behavior, takes a much less mechanical view of man than do the Soviet Pavlovians. It is apparent to us that their simple explanation of training ignores and rejects the concept of purposeful adaptation and the question of the goals to which this training is directed. Western experimental psychologists tend to see the conditioned reflex as developing fully only in the service of gratifying basic instinctual needs or of avoiding pain, that is, only when the whole organism is concerned in the activity. In that complicated process of response to the world, conscious, and especially unconscious, drives and motivations play a role, as Freud taught us.

All training, of which the conditioned response is only one example, is an automatization of actions which were originally consciously learned and thought over. The ideal of Western democratic psychology is to train men into independence and maturity by enlisting their conscious aid, awareness, and volition in the learning process. The ideal of the totalitarian psychology, on the other hand, is to tame men, to make them willing tools in the hands of their leaders. Like training, taming has the purpose of making actions automatic; unlike training, it does not require the conscious participation of the learner. Both training and taming are energy and timesaving devices, and in both the mystery of the psyche is hidden in the purposefulness of the responses. The automatization of functions in man saves him expenditure of energy but can make him weaker when encountering new unexpected challenges.

Cultural routinization and habit formation by local rules and myths make of everybody a partial automaton. National and racial prejudices are acted out unwittingly. Group hatred often bursts out almost automatically when triggered by slogans and catchwords. In a totalitarian world, this narrow disciplinarian conditioning is done more "perfectly" and more *ad absurdum*.

The Urge to Be Conditioned

One suggestion this chapter is not intended to convey is that Pavlovian conditioning as such is something wrong. This kind of conditioning occurs everywhere where people are together in common interaction. The speaker influences the listener, but the listener also the speaker. Through the process of conditioning people often learn to like and to do what they are allowed to like and do. The more isolated the group, the stricter the conditioning that takes place in those belonging to the group. In some groups one finds people more capable than others of conveying suggestion and bringing about conditioning. Gradually one can discern the stronger ones, the better-adjusted ones, the more experienced ones, and those noisier ones, whose ability to condition others is strongest. Every group, every club, every society has its leading Pavlovian Bell. This kind of person imprints his inner bell-ringing on others. He can even develop a system of monolithic bell-ringing: no other influential bell is allowed to compete with him.

Another subtle question belongs to these problems. Why is there in us so great an urge to be conditioned, the urge to learn, to imitate, to conform, and to follow the pattern of family and group? This urge to be conditioned, to submit to the communal pattern and the family pattern must be related to man's dependency on parents and fellow men. Animals are not so dependent on one another. In the whole animal kingdom man is one of the most helpless and naked beings. He remains like a monkey fetus, he never grows into the mature, hairy, fully covered state. In his persistent fetal state, he remains dependent on maternal care and paternal teaching and conditioning. But among the animals man has, relatively, the longest youth and time for learning. At least this is what Louis Bolk's fetalization theory tells us about man's retarded state and never-ending social dependency.

Puzzlement and doubt, which inevitably arise in the training process, are the beginnings of mental freedom. Of course, the initial puzzlement and doubt is not enough. Behind that there has to be faith in our democratic freedoms and the will to fight for it. I hope to come back to this central problem of faith in moral freedom as differentiated from conditioned loyalty and servitude in the last chapter. Puzzlement and doubt are, however, already crimes in the totalitarian state. The mind that is open for questions is open for dissent. In the totalitarian regime the doubting, inquisitive, and imaginative mind has to be suppressed. The totalitarian slave is only allowed to memorize, to salivate when the bell rings.

It is not my task here to elaborate on the subject of the biased use of Pavlovian rules by totalitarians, but without doubt part of the interpretation of any psychology is determined by the ways we think about our fellow human beings and man's place in nature. If our ideal is to make conditioned zombies out of people, the current misuse of Pavlovianism will serve our purpose. But once we become even vaguely aware that in the totalitarian picture of man the characteristic human note is missing, and when we see that in such a scheme man sacrifices his instinctual desires, his pleasures, his aims, his goals, his creativity, his instinct for freedom, his paradoxicality, we immediately turn against this political perversion of science. Such use of Pavlovian technique is aimed only at developing the automaton in man, not his free alert mind that is aware of moral goals and aims in life.

Even in laboratory animals we have found that affective goal-directedness can spoil the Pavlovian experiment. When, during a bell-food training session, the dog's beloved master entered the room, the animal lost all its previous conditioning and began to bark excitedly. Here is a simple example of an age-old truth: love and laughter break through all rigid conditioning. The rigid automaton cannot exist without spontaneous self-expression. Apparently, the fact that the dog's spontaneous affection for his master could ruin all the mechanical calculations and manipulations never occurred to Pavlov's totalitarian students.

CHAPTER THREE

Medication into Submission

As we have already seen in the preceding chapters, it is not only the political and Pavlovian pressure that may drag down man's mind into servile submissiveness. There are many other human habits and actions which have a coercive influence.

All kinds of rumors have been circulated telling how brain-washees, before surrendering to their inquisitor, have been poisoned with mysterious drugs. This chapter aims to describe what medical techniques—not only drugs—can do to reach behind man's inner secrets. Actually the thought-control police no longer need drugs, though occasionally they have been used.

I will touch upon another side to this problem as well, namely, our dangerous social dependence on various drugs, the problem of addiction, making it easier for us to slip into the pattern of submissiveness. The alcoholic has no mental backbone any more when you give him his drink. The same is true for the chronic user of sedatives or other pills. The use of alcohol or drugs may result in a chemical dependency, weakening our stamina under exceptional circumstances.

In the field of practical medicine, magic thinking is still rampant. Though we flatter ourselves that we are rational and logical in our choice of therapy, somewhere we know that hidden feelings and unconscious motivations direct the prescribing hand. In spite of the therapeutic triumphs of the last fifty years, the era of chemotherapy and antibiotics, let us not forget that the same means of medical victory can be used to defeat our purposes. No day passes that the mail does not flood the doctor's office with suggestions about what to use in his clinical practice. My desk overflows with gadgets and multicolored pills telling me that without them mankind cannot be happy. The propaganda campaign reaching our medical eyes and ears is often so laden with suggestions that we can be persuaded to distribute sedatives and stimulants where straight critical thinking would deter us and we would seek the deeper causes of the difficulties. This is true not only for modern pharmacotherapy; the same tendencies can also be shown in psychotherapeutic methods.

This chapter aims to approach the problem of mental coercion with the question: How compulsive can the use of medical drugs and medical and psychological methods become? In the former chapters on menticide I was able to describe political attempts to bring the human mind into submission and servility. Drugs and their psychological equivalents are also able to enslave people.

Dependency on the Drug Provider

Not long ago I was asked to give advice to a couple who had had marital difficulties for a long time. Although at the time of their marriage, the husband and wife were deeply in love, each had brought to his adventure of happiness the wrong emotional investment. She had expected him to be a kind of Hollywood hero, an eternal gallant, dedicated completely to her. He had been touched by her childlike dependency, but secretly he had hoped she would be mother, nurse, and companion to him. As might have been predicted, neither partner lived up to the other's expectations. Both were bitterly disappointed—and neither realized what was wrong. After a while, the wife became a whining, complaining nag; there were daily scenes, arguments, and recriminations. The husband began to seek solace away from home, with women he had known before his marriage. Soon thereafter, the wife found herself unable to sleep, and started to take barbiturates to bring herself the soothing forgetfulness of slumber. She became completely dependent on them and retreated into all kinds of vague bodily complaints which could be relieved temporarily by more drugs. When the husband first discovered this, he was appalled. But gradually he noticed that the drugs seemed to modify and ease the discord of their relationship. Under almost constant sedation, his wife was no longer a shrew. Indeed she was no longer even interested in him. He discovered that he had much more freedom and could spend his evenings and holidays as he chose, as long as he provided her with the wherewithal for those magic pills that had restored peace to their home. But one night the wife took an overdose of barbiturates, and it looked almost as if she had attempted suicide. This nearly fatal occurrence aroused all the husband's guilt feelings, and he sought medical and psychological help, in an effort to discover what had gone wrong in the marriage of two people who had felt so much initial love and good will.

This is only one of many cases in which the sleeping pill and drug habit covers up deep-seated, unspoken unhappiness. The growing dependency on easy escape into a soft and mild-appearing sedation and oblivion is an evil we must recognize. The general increase in the use of sleeping drugs is alarming, and the number of suicides resulting from barbiturates is growing every year. Nor can we look at such a phenomenon as simply a medical problem. Dependence on alcohol, barbiturates, drugs, or other soporifics indicates latent and overt social fear and anxiety, and the need to escape from reality. Drugs seem to their users to be miracle tablets which provide a passive and magic solution to all problems, and bring them to a point beyond the boundaries of the real world. The leader of a gang, who is able to provide such drugs for his members, is sure of their servility.

The Search for Ecstasy Through Drugs

Among drug addicts of all sorts we repeatedly encounter the yearning for a special ecstatic and euphoric mood, a feeling of living beyond everyday troubles. "Thou hast the keys of Paradise, O just, subtle, and mighty opium!" Thomas De Quincey says, in his *Confessions of an English Opium-Eater.* Although the ecstatic state is different for each person who experiences it, the addict always tells us that the drug takes him to the lost paradise he is looking for; it brings him a feeling of eternal euphoria and free elation that takes him past the restrictions of life and time.

In the ecstatic state, man rearranges the universe according to his own desires and, at the same time, seeks communion with the Higher Order of things. But the ecstatic state has its negative as well as its positive aspects. It may represent the Yogi's mystic feeling of unity with the universe, but it may also mean the chronic intoxicated state of the drunkard or the passion of some manic psychotic states. The feeling may express the intensified spiritual experience of a dedicated study group, but, on the other hand, it ·may be encountered in the lynch mob and the riot. There are many kinds of ecstasy—esthetic ecstasy, mystic ecstasy, and sick, toxic ecstasy.

The search for ecstatic experience is not only an individual search, it often reaches out to encompass whole groups. When moral controls become too burdensome, whole civilizations may give themselves up to uncontrolled orgies such as we saw in the Greek Bacchanalia and the contagious dance-fury of the Middle Ages. In these mass orgies, artificial stimulants are not necessarily used. The hypnotic influence of being part of the crowd can induce the same loss of control and sense of union with the outside world that we associate with drugs. In the mass orgy the individual loses his conscience and self-control. His sexual inhibitions may disappear; he is temporarily relieved of his deep frustrations and the burden of unconscious guilt. He endeavors to re-experience the blissful sensations of infancy, the utter yielding to his own body needs and desires.

The ecstatic participation in mass elation is the oldest psychodrama in the world. Taking part in some common action results in a tremendous emotional relief and catharsis for every individual in the group. This feeling of participation in the magic omnipotent group, of reunion and communion with the all-embracing forces in the world brings euphoria to the normal person and feelings of pseudo-strength to the weak. The demagogue who is able to provide such ecstatic release in the masses can be sure of their yielding to his influence and power. Dictators love to organize such mass rituals in the service of their dictatorial aims.

Ever since man has been a conscious being, he has tried from time to time to break down the inevitable tension between himself and the outside world. When mental alertness cannot be relaxed now and then, when the world is too much and too constantly with him, man may try to lose himself in the deep waters of oblivion. Ecstasy, drugged sleep, and its fantasies and swoons of mental exaltation temporarily take him beyond the burdensome effort of keeping his senses and ego alert and intact. Drugs can bring him to this state, and any addiction may be explained as a continuing need to escape. The body cooperates with the mind in this search for an evasion of life, and drugs gradually become a body need as well as an emotional necessity.

In criminal circles addicting drugs like cocaine or heroin are often given to members of the gang in order to make them more submissive to the leader who distributes them. The man who provides the drug becomes almost a god to the members of the gang. They will go through hell for him in order to acquire the drug they so desperately need.

In the hands of a powerful tyrant, this medication into dependency can become extremely dangerous. It is not unthinkable that a diabolical dictator might want to use addiction as a means of bringing a rebellious people into submission. In May, 1954, during a discussion in the World Health Organization, the fact was disclosed that Communist China, while forbidding the use of opium in her own country, was smuggling and exporting it in great quantities to her neighbors, who have consequently been compelled to carry on a constant struggle against opium addiction among their own people and against the passivity which results from use of the drug. At the same time, according to officials of Thailand who made the charge and who requested U.N. aid, Communist China has been sending all kinds of subversive propagandists into Thailand. Thailand charged that the Chinese were using every device they know to infect the Siamese people with their ideology: brain-weakening opium addiction, leaflets, radio, whispering campaigns, and so on.

The Nazis followed a similar strategy. During the occupation of Western Europe, they created an artificial shortage of normal medicaments by halting their usual export of healing drugs to the "inferior" countries. However, they made an exception in the case of barbiturates. In Holland, for example, these drugs were made readily available in many drugstores without doctors' prescriptions, a situation which was against customary Dutch law. Although the right therapeutic drugs were not made available for medical work, the drugs which created passivity, dependence, and lethargy were widely distributed.

The totalitarian dictator knows that drugs can be his helpers. It was Hitler's intention, in his so-called biological warfare, to weaken and subdue the countries that surrounded the Third Reich, and to break their backbones for good. Hunger and addiction were among his most valuable strategic tools.

What has all this to do with the growing addiction and alcoholism in our own country? I have already mentioned the alarming increases in death from barbiturates. But I would like to emphasize even more the psychological and political consequences. Democracy and freedom end where slavery and submission to drugs and alcohol begin. Democracy involves free, self-chosen activity and understanding; it means mature self-control and independence. Any man who escapes from reality through the use of alcohol and drugs is no longer a free agent; he is no longer able to exert any voluntary control over his mind and his actions. He is no longer a self-responsible individual. Alcoholism and drug addiction prepare the pattern of mental submission so beloved by the totalitarian brainwasher.

Hypnotism and Mental Coercion

From time immemorial those who wanted to know the inner workings of the other fellow's mind in order to exert pressure on him have used artificial means to find the hidden pathways to his most private thoughts. Modern brainwashers, too, have tried all kinds of drugs to arrive at their devious objectives. The primitive medicine man had several methods of compelling his victim to lose his self-control and reserve. Alcoholic drinks, toxic ointments, or permeating holy smoke which had a narcotizing effect, as used by the Mayas, for example, were used to bring people into such a state of rapture that they lost their self-awareness and restraint. The victims, murmuring sacred words, often revealed their self-accusing fantasies or even their deepest secrets. In the Middle Ages, so-called witch ointments were used either voluntarily or under pressure. These ointments were supposed to bring the anointed into touch with the devil. Since they contained opiates and belladonna in large quantities, which could have been absorbed by the skin, modern science can explain the ecstatic visions they evoked as the typical hallucination-provoking effect of these drugs.

One of the first useful techniques medicine delivered into the hands of the prier-into-souls was the knowledge of hypnosis, that intensified mental suggestion that makes people give up their own will and brings them into a strange dependency on the hypnotizer. The Egyptian doctors of three thousand years ago knew the technique of hypnosis, and ancient records tell us that they practiced it.

In the hands of an honest therapist, hypnosis can be extremely useful. Particularly in dealing with psychosomatic diseases and with physical pain—that bastard son of fantasy and reality—hypnosis, is the good Samaritan. But there are many quacks who practice hypnosis, not to cure their victims but to force them into submission, using the victim's unconscious ties and dependency needs in a criminal, profitable way. There are unconscious sexual roots in hypnosis, related to the passive yielding to the attacker, which the quack uses to give vent to his own passions. I once treated a girl after she had gone to such a "healer." It was only at the very last moment that she had been able to get out of her lethargic, submissive state and fight off his assault.

Not long ago I treated some teen-agers who had tried to hypnotize each other. They wanted to learn the intricacies of the technique in order to increase their mental power over other people. Inspired by some comic-book stories, they imagined that through the use of hypnosis they could influence girls to yield to their sexual advances. They expected to become supermen who could make other people instruments for the satisfaction of their own lust and will.

One of the most absorbing aspects of this whole problem of hypnosis is the question of whether people can be forced to commit crimes, such as murder or treason, while under a hypnotic spell. Many psychologists would deny that such a thing could happen and would insist that no person can be compelled to do under hypnosis what he would refuse to do in a state of alert consciousness, but actually what a person can be compelled to do depends on the degree of dependency that hypnosis causes and the frequency of repetition of the so-called posthypnotic suggestions. Actual psychoanalysis teaches that there even exist several other devices to live other people's lives. True, no hypnotizer can take away a man's conscience and inner resistance immediately, but he can arouse the latent murderous wishes which may become active in his victim's unconscious by continual suggestion and continual playing upon those deeply repressed desires. Actual knowledge of methods used in brainwashing and menticide proves that all this can be done. If the hypnotizer persists long enough and cleverly enough, he can be successful in his aim. There are many antisocial desires lying hidden in all people. The hypnotic technique, if cleverly enough applied, can bring them to the surface and cause them to be acted out in life. The mass criminality of the guards in concentration camps finds part of its explanation in the hypnotizing influence of the totalitarian state and its criminal dictator. Psychological study of criminals shows that their first violation of moral and legal codes often takes place under the strong influence and suggestion of other criminals. This we may look upon as an initial form of hypnosis, which is a more intensified form of suggestion.

True, the incitement to crime in a hypnotic state demands specially favorable conditions, but unfortunately these conditions can be found in the real and actual world.

Recently there has been much judicial discussion of the problem of the psychiatrist who uses his special knowledge of suggestion to force a confession from a defendant. Such a psychiatrist is going beyond the commonly accepted concepts of the limitations of psychiatry and beyond psychiatric ethics. He is misusing the patient's trust in the medical confidant and therapist in order to provoke a confession, which will then be used against the patient temporarily in his care. In so doing, the doctor not only acts against his Hippocratic oath, in which he promised only to work for the good of his patients and never to disclose his professional secrets, he also violates the constitutional safeguards accorded a defendant by the Fifth Amendment to the United States Constitution, which protects a man against self-incrimination.

What a defendant will reveal under hypnosis depends on his conscious and unconscious attitudes toward the entire question of magic influence and mental intrusion by another person. People are usually less likely to stand on their legal rights in dealing with a doctor than in dealing with a lawyer or a policeman. They have a yielding attitude because they expect magic help.

An interesting example of this can be seen in a case that was recently decided by the Supreme Court. In 1950, Camilio Weston Leyra, a man in his fifties, was arrested and accused by the police of the brutal hammer murder of his aged parents in their Brooklyn flat ("People v. Leyra"). At first, under prolonged questioning by the police, Leyra denied any knowledge of the crime and stated that he had not even been at his parents' home on the day of the murder. Later, after further interrogation by the police, he said he had been at their home that day, but he remained firm in his denial of the murder. He was detained in jail, and a psychiatrist was brought in to talk to him. Their conversation was recorded on tape. The psychiatrist told Leyra that he was "his doctor," although in fact he was not. Under slight hypnosis and after continued suggestion that Leyra would be better off if he admitted to having committed the murder in a fit of passion, Leyra agreed to confess to the crime. The police were called back in, and the confession was taken down.

During his trial, Leyra repudiated the confession, insisting that he had been under hypnosis. He was convicted, but the conviction was set aside on the grounds that the confession had been wrested from him involuntarily, and that his constitutional safeguards had been denied him. Later, Leyra was brought to trial and convicted a second time. Finally his case was appealed to the Supreme Court, which reversed the conviction in June, 1954, on the grounds that mental pressure and coercive psychiatric techniques had been used to induce the confession. The Supreme Court gave its opinion here, indirectly, of the responsibility of the brainwashed P.O.W.

For us, the question of Leyra's guilt or innocence is of less importance than the fact that under mental pressure he was induced to do what he would ordinarily have resisted doing, and that his confidence in the doctor, which led him to relax the defenses he would doubtless have put up against other investigators, was used to break him down.

Suggestion and hypnosis can be a psychological blessing, through which patients can solve emotional problems that resist conscious will, but they can also be the beginning of terror. Mass hypnosis, for example, can have a dangerous influence on the individual. Psychiatrists have found several times that public demonstrations of mass hypnosis may provoke an increased hypnotic dependency and submissiveness in many members of the audience that can last for years. Largely for this reason Great Britain has passed a law making séances and mass hypnotism illegal. Hypnosis may act as a trigger mechanism for a repressed infantile dependency need in the victim and turn him temporarily into a kind of waking sleep-walker and mental slave. The hypnotic command relieves him of his personal responsibility, and he surrenders much of his conscience to his hypnotizer. As we mentioned before, our own times have provided us with far too many examples of how political hypnosis, mob hypnosis, and even war hypnosis can turn civilized men into criminals.

Some personalities are more amenable to hypnosis than others. Strong egos can defend themselves for a long time against mental intrusion, but they too may have a point of surrender. There are overtly critical persons who are much less sensitive to suggestion from the outside than to images from within themselves. We can distinguish between heterosuggestive and autosuggestive person-alities, although quite a variety of reactions to hypnosis and sugges-tion could be distinguished. But even these autosuggestive types, if subjected to enough pressure, will gradually build up internal justi-fications for giving in to mental coercion.

Those "charming" characters who are easily able to influence others are often extremely susceptible to suggestion themselves. Some personalities with a tremendous gift for empathy and identi-fication provoke in others the desire to yield up all their secrets; they seem somehow to be the Father Confessor by the grace of God. Other emphatic types, by reflecting their own deceitful inner world, can more easily provoke the hidden lies and fantasies in their vic-tims. Still others make us close up completely. Why one man should inspire the desire to give in and another the desire to resist is one of the mysteries of human relationships and contact. Why do certain personalities complement and reinforce one another while others clash and destroy one another? Psychoanalysis has given new insight into those strange human relations and involvements.

Needling for the Truth

During the Second World War, the technique of the so-called truth serum (the popular name for narco-analysis) was developed to help soldiers who had broken down under the strain of battle. Through narco-analysis by means of injections of sedatives, they could be brought to remember and reveal the hyper-emotional and traumatic moments of their war experiences that had driven them into acute anxiety neurosis. Gradually a useful mental first-aid technique was developed which helped the unconscious to reveal its secrets while the patient was under the influence of the narcotic.

How does the truth serum work? The principle is simple: after an injection, the mind in a kind of half-sleep is unable to control its secrets, and it may let them slip from the hidden reservoirs of frustration and repression into the half-conscious mind. In certain acute anxiety cases, such enforced provocation may alleviate the anxieties and pressures that have led to breakdown. But narco-analysis often does not work. Sometimes the patient's mind resents this chemical intrusion and enforced intervention, and such a situation often obstructs the way for deeper and more useful psychotherapy.

The fear of unexpected mental intrusion and coercion may be pathological in character. When I first published my concept of menticide and brainwashing, I received dozens of letters and phone calls from people who were convinced that some outside person was trying to influence them and direct their thoughts. This form of *mental intrusion delusion* may be the early stage of a serious psychosis in which the victim has already regressed to primitive magic feelings. In this state the whole outside world is seen and felt as participating in what is going on in the victim's mind. There is, as it were, no real awareness of the frontiers between *I*, the person, and the world. Such fear-ridden persons are in constant agony because they feel themselves the victims of many mysterious influences which they cannot check or cope with; they feel continually endangered. Psychologically, their fear of intrusion from the outside can be partially explained as a fear of the intrusion of their own fantasies from the inside, from the unconscious. They are frightened of their own hidden, unconscious thoughts which they can no longer check.

It would be a vast oversimplification to stick an easy psychiatric label on all such feelings of mental persecution, for there are many real, outside mental pressures in our world, and there are many perfectly normal people who are continually aware of and disturbed by the barrage of stimuli directed at their minds through propaganda, advertising, radio, television, the movies, the newspapers—all the gibbering maniacs whose voices never stop. These people suffer because a cold, mechanical, shouting world is knocking continually at the doors of their minds and disturbing their feelings of privacy and personal integrity.

There is the further question of whether or not the drugs used in the truth serum always produce the desired effect of compelling the patient to tell the inner truth. Experiments conducted at Yale University in 1951 (J. M. MacDonald) on nine persons who received intravenous injections of sodium amytal—the so-called truth serum—showed interesting results, tending to weaken our faith in this drug. Each of the patients, prior to the injection, had been suggested a false story related to a historical period about which he was going to be questioned. The experimenters knew both the true and the false story. Let me quote from the report: "It is of interest that the three subjects diagnosed as normal maintained their [suggested] stories. Of the six subjects diagnosed as neurotic, two promptly revealed the true story; two made partial admissions, consisting of a complex pattern of fantasy and truth; one communicated what most likely was a fantasy as truth; and the one obsessive-compulsive individual maintained his cover story except for one parapraxia [faulty or blundering action]."

In several cases, American law courts have refused to admit as evidence the results of truth serum tests, largely on the basis of psychiatric conviction that the truth serum treatment is misnamed; that, in fact, narco-analysis is no guarantee of getting at the truth. It may even be used as a coercive threat in cases where victims are not aware of its limited action.

Still another danger, more closely related to our subject, is that a criminal investigator can induce and communicate his own thoughts and feelings to his victim. Thus the truth serum may cause the patient with a weak ego to yield to the interventionist's synthetically injected thoughts and interpretations in exactly the same way the victim of hypnosis may take over the suggestions implanted by the hypnotist.

Additionally, this method of inquisition by drugs contains some physical danger. I myself have seen cases of thrombosis develop as a result of intravenous medication of barbiturates.

Experiments with mescaline, which started thirty years ago, are suddenly fashionable again. Aldous Huxley in his recent book *The Doors of Perception* described the artificial chemical paradise which he experienced after taking the drug (also known as peyote). It can stimulate all kinds of pleasant, subjective symptoms, but these are, nevertheless, delusive in character. I do not want to start a clinical argument with an author I esteem, yet his own euphoric, ecstatic reactions to mescaline are not necessarily the same as those other people experience. Twenty-five years ago I myself experimented with mescaline in order to make a first-hand acquaintance with genuine pathological thoughts. I nearly collapsed as a result. Only a few people have had the ecstatic experiences Huxley describes. Mescaline is dangerous stuff when not used under medical control. And, anyway, why does Mr. Huxley want to sell artificial heavens?

There is a very serious social danger in all these methods of chemical intrusion into the mind. True, they can be used as a careful aid to psychotherapy, but they can also be frightening instruments of control in the hands of men with an overwhelming drive to power. In addition, they fortify more than ever in our *aspirin age* the fiction that we have to use miracle drugs in order to become free-acting agents. The propaganda for chemical elation, for artificial ecstasy and pseudo-nirvanic experience contains an invitation to men to become chemical dependents, and chemical dependents are weak people who can be made use of by any tyrannical political potentate. The actual propaganda carried on among general practitioners urging treatment of all kinds of anxieties and mental disturbances with new drugs has the same kind of dangerous implications.

The Lie-Detector

Hypnotism and narco-analysis are only two of the current devices that can be misused as instruments of enforced intrusion into the mind. The lie-detector, which has already been used as a tool for mental intimidation, is another. This apparatus, useful for psychobiological experimentation, can indicate—through writing down meticulously the changes in the psychogalvanic reflex—that the human guinea pig under investigation reacts more emotionally to certain questions than to others. True, this overreaction may be the reaction to having told a lie, but it may also be an innocent person's reaction to an emotion-laden situation or even to an increased fear of unjust accusation. The interpersonal processes between interrogator and testee have just as much influence on the emotional reactions and the changes in the galvanic reflex as feelings of inner guilt and confusion. This experiment only indicates inner turmoil and hidden repressions, with all their doubts and ambiguities. It is not in fact a lie-detector, although it is used as such (D. MacDonald). As a matter of fact, the pathological liar and the psychopathic, conscienceless personality may show less reaction to this experiment than do normal people. The lie-detector is more likely to become a tool of coercion in the hands of men who look more for a powerful magic in every instrument than a means of getting at the truth. As a result, even the innocent can be fooled into false confession.

The Therapist as an Instrument of Coercion

Medical therapy and psychotherapy are the subtle sciences of human guidance in periods of physical and emotional stress. Just as training requires the alert, well-planned participation of both student and teacher, so successful psychotherapy requires the alert, well-planned participation of both patient and doctor. And just as educational training, under special conditions, can degenerate into coercive taming, so therapy can degenerate into the imposition of· the doctor's will on his patient. The doctor himself need not even be conscious that this is happening. This misuse of therapy may show itself in the patient's submission to the doctor's point of view or in the patient's development of excessive dependency on his therapist. Such a dependency, and even increased dependency need, may extend not only far beyond the usual limits, but may continue even after the therapy has run its course.

I have seen quacks whose only knowledge was where to buy their couches. By calling themselves psychoanalysts they were able to gratify their own need to live other people's lives. Eventually the law will have to establish standards which can keep these dangerous intruders from psychotherapeutic practice. But even the honest, conscientious therapist has a serious moral problem to face. His profession itself continually encourages him, indeed obliges him, to make his patients temporarily dependent on him, and this may appeal to his own need for a sense of importance and power. He must be continually aware of the impact his statements and deductions have on his patients who often listen in awe to the doctor who is for them the omniscient magician. The therapist must not encourage this submissive attitude in his patients—though in some phases of the treatment it will help the therapy—for good psychotherapy aims toward educating man for freedom and maturity not for conforming submission.

The practitioners of psychology and psychiatry are now much more aware of the responsibility their profession imposes on them than they have ever been heretofore. The tools of psychology are dangerous in the hands of the wrong men. Modern educational methods can be applied in therapy to streamline man's brain and change his opinions so that his thinking conforms with certain ideological systems. Medicine and psychiatry may become more and more involved in political strategy as we have seen in the strategy of brainwashing, and for this reason psychologists and psychiatrists must become more aware of the nature of the scientific tools they use.

The emphasis on therapeutic techniques, on students knowing all the facts and the tricks, the overemphasis on psychotherapeutic diplomas and labels lead actual therapy toward conformism and rationalization of principles that are in contrast to the personal sensitivity needed. Our critical and rational faculty can be a destructive one, destroying or disguising our basic doubts and ambivalences born out of tragic despair, that creator of human sensitivity. The danger of modern psychotherapy (and psychology) is the tendency toward formalizing human intuition and empathy, and toward making an abstraction of emotion and spontaneity. It is a contradiction to attempt to mechanize love and beauty. If this were possible, we would find ourselves in a world where there is no inspiration and ecstasy but only cold understanding.

Every human relationship can be used for the wrong or the right aims, and this is especially true of the relationship of subtle unconscious ties which exists between psychotherapist and patient. This statement is equally true for medicine in general; the surgeon, too, thrives on strong ties with his patients and their willing submission to his surgical techniques. Freud gave us the first clear explanation of what happens in the mind during prolonged mental contact with a human being. He showed that in every intensive human relationship, each participant reacts at least partially in terms of the expectations and illusions he developed in his own childhood. As a result prolonged therapy—based on the principle of utter freedom of expression—provides as much opportunity for transference of private feelings for the doctor as for the patient. If the doctor is not careful, or if he does not understand this mutual transfer of hidden emotions, or if, in his compulsive zest to explain everything, he is too coercive, he may force the patient into acceptance of his point of view, instead of helping the patient to arrive at his own. This can become mental intrusion of a dangerous kind. Experiences in therapy have taught us that *faulty technique* can give the patient feelings of being bogged down. Sometimes patients feel as if they have to remain living in servile submission to the doctor. I have seen whole families and sects swear by such modern witch doctors.

No wonder that sound psychoanalytic instruction requires the therapist to submit himself for years to the technique he is about to apply to others, so that, armed with knowledge of his own unsound unconscious needs, he will not try to use his profession to mastermind other people's lives.

Various psychological agencies, with their different psychological concepts and techniques, such as family counseling, religious guidance, management counseling, and so forth, can easily be misused as tools of power. The good will that people invest in their leaders, doctors, and administrators is tremendous and can be used as a weapon against them. Even modern brain surgery for healing the mind could be misused by modern dictators to make zombies out of their competitors. Psychology itself may tend to standardize the mind, and the tendency among different schools of psychology to emphasize orthodoxy increases unwittingly the chance for mental coercion. ("If you don't talk my magic gobbledygook, I have to condition you to it.") It is easier to manipulate the minds of others than to avoid doing so.

A democratic society gives its citizens the right to act as free agents. At the same time, it imposes on them the responsibility for maintaining their freedom, mental as well as political. If, through the use of modern medical, chemical, and mechanical techniques of mental intrusion, we reduce man's capacity to act on his own initiative, we subvert our own beliefs and weaken our democratic system. Just as there is a deliberate political brainwashing, so can there be a suggestive intrusion masquerading under the name of justice or therapy. This may be less obtrusive than the deliberate totalitarian attack, but it is no less dangerous.

Medication into submission is an existing fact. Man can use his knowledge of the mind of a fellow being not to help him, but to hurt him and bog him down. The magician can increase his power by increasing the anxieties and fears of his victim, by exploiting his dependency needs, and by provoking his feelings of guilt and inferiority.

Drugs and medical techniques can be used to make man a submissive and conforming being. This we have to keep in mind in order to be able to make him really healthy and free.

CHAPTER FOUR

Why Do They Yield?

THE PSYCHODYNAMICS OF FALSE CONFESSION

Is there a bridge from the concept of Pavlovian conditioning to deeper psychological understanding? Only in those Pavlovian theoreticians who deny modern depth psychology does there exist a conflict between concepts. Pavlov himself acknowledged the presence of deeper, hidden motivations in man and the limitations of his study of animal behavior.

Our task is to go back to the brainwashee, asking ourselves: How can we better convey an understanding of what happened to him? What were the Pavlovian circumstances, and what were the inner motivations to yield to enforced political manipulation of the mind? Was it cowardice, was it a prison psychosis, was it the general loss of mental stamina in our world?

In the following observations and experiences I hope to make use of the clinical insight actually provided by modern depth psychology.

The Upset Philosopher

One day in 1672, the lonely philosopher of reason, Spinoza, had to be forcibly restrained by his friends and neighbors. He wanted to rush out into the streets and shout his indignation at the mob which had murdered his good friend Jan De Witt, noble statesman of the Dutch Republic, who had been falsely accused of treason.

But presently he calmed down and retreated to his room where, as usual, he ground optical lenses according to a daily and hitherto unbroken routine. As he worked, he thought back to his own behavior, which had been no more rational or sensible than the behavior of the rioting crowd which had killed De Witt. It was then that Spinoza realized the existence of the emotional beast hidden beneath human reason, which, when aroused, can act in a wanton and destructive fashion, and can conjure up thousands of justifications and excuses for its behavior.

For, as Spinoza sensed, and as the great psychologist Sigmund Freud later demonstrated, people are not the rational creatures they think they are. In the unconscious, that vast storehouse of deeply buried memories, emotions, and strivings, lie many infantile and irrational yearnings, which constantly influence the conscious acts. All of us are governed to some degree by this hidden tyrant, and by the conflict between our reason and our emotions.

To the extent that we are the victims of unchecked unconscious drives, to that extent we may be vulnerable to mental manipulation. And although there is a horrifying fascination in the idea that our mental resistance is relatively weak, that the very quality which distinguishes one man from another—the individual *I*—can be profoundly altered by psychological pressures, such transformations are merely extremes of a process we find operating in normal life. Through systematized suggestion, subtle propaganda, and more overt mass hypnosis, the human mind in its expressions is changed daily in any society. Advertising seduces the democratic citizen into using quackeries or one special brand of soap instead of another. Our wish to buy things is continually stimulated. Campaigning politicians seek to influence us by their glamour as well as by their programs. Fashion experts hypnotize us into periodic changes of our standards of beauty and good taste.

In cases of menticide, however, this assault on the integrity of the human mind is more direct and premeditated. By playing on the irrational child lying hidden in the unconscious and by sharpening the internal conflict between reason and emotion, the inquisitor can bring his victims to abject surrender.

All of the victims of deliberate menticide—the P.O.W.'s in Korea, the imprisoned "traitors" to the dictatorial regimes of the

Iron Curtain countries, the victims of the Nazi terror during the Second World War—are people whose ways of life had been suddenly and dramatically altered. They had been torn from their homes, their families, their friends, and thrown into a frightening, abnormal atmosphere. The very strangeness of their surroundings made them more vulnerable to any attack on their values and attitudes. When the dictator exploits his victim's psychological needs in a threatening, hostile, and unfamiliar world, breakdown is almost sure to follow.

The Barbed-Wire Disease

Already during the First World War, peculiar mental reactions, mixtures of apathy and rage, could be discerned in prisoners of war as a defensive adjustment against the hardships of prison life, the boredom, the hunger, the lack of privacy, the continual insecurity. The Korean War added to this situation the greater cruelty of the enemy, the prolonged fear of death, malnutrition, diseases, systematic attacks on the prisoner's mind, the lack of sanitation, and the lack of all human dignity.

Often improvement could be secured through acceptance of the totalitarian ideology. The psychological pressure not only led to an involvement with the enemy but caused mutual suspicion among the prisoners.

As I have already described, the barbed-wire disease begins with the initial apathy and despair of all prisoners. There is passive surrender to fate. In fact, people can die out of such despair; it is as if all resistance were gone.* Being anything but aloof and apathetic was even dangerous in a camp where the enemy wanted to debate and argue with you in order to tear down your mental resistance. Consequently a vicious circle was built up of apathy, not thinking, letting things go—a surrender to a complete zombie-like existence of mechanical dependency on the circumstances. Every sign of anger and alertness could be brutally punished by the enemy; that is why we did not find those sudden attacks of rage that were observed in the earlier prisoner-of-war camps during World Wars I and II. Results of psychological testing of the liberated

* See Chapter Nine on the action of fear.

soldiers from the Korean P.O.W. camps could indicate that this defensive apathy and retreat into secluded infantile dependency was likely to be found in nearly all of them. Yet, after being brought back into normal surroundings, alertness and activity returned rather soon, even in two or three days. Those few who remained anxious, apathetic, and zombie-like belong to the long chapter of war and battle neuroses (Strassman).

What are some of the factors which can turn a man into a traitor to his own convictions, an informer, a confessor to heinous crimes, or an apparent collaborator?

The Moment of Sudden Surrender

Several victims of the Nazi inquisition have told me that the moment of surrender occurred suddenly and against their will. For days they had faced the fury of their interrogators, and then suddenly they fell apart. "All right, all right, you can have anything you want."

And then came hours of remorse, of resolution, of a desperate wish to return to their previous position of firm resistance. They wanted to cry out: "Don't ask me anything else. I won't answer." And yet something in them, that conforming, complying being hidden deep in all of us, was on the move.

This sudden surrender often happened after an unexpected accusation, a shock, a humiliation that particularly hurt, a punishment that burned, a surprising logic in the inquisitor's question that could not be counterargued. I remember an experience of my own that illustrated the effect of such surprise.

After my escape from a Nazi prison in occupied Holland, I was able to reach neutral Switzerland via Vichy France. When I arrived, I was put in a jail where, at first, I was treated rather kindly. After three days, however, I was denied an officer's right to asylum and was told that I would be deported back to Vichy France. To this information, my jailers sneeringly added the comment that I should be happy I was not going to be deported back to the Germans. When I left to be transported to the border, I was asked to sign a paper stating that all my possessions (which had been taken from me on my imprisonment) had been returned.

I refused to sign because a few things—unimportant in themselves, but of great emotional value to me—were not included in the package my jailers handed me. One of the guards looked at me with contempt, the second tapped his foot impatiently and repeatedly demanded that I sign the paper, the third scolded and chattered in a French that was completely unintelligible to me. I continued firm in my refusal. Suddenly one of the officers started to slap me around the face and to beat me. Overwhelmed by surprise that they should display such fury over a bagatelle, I surrendered and signed the paper. (From the Vichy prison to which I was sent, I was permitted to write a letter of protest to the Swiss government. I still carry the official apology I received.)

This sudden change from a mood of defiant resistance to one of submission must be explained by the unconscious action of contrasting feelings. Consciously we tell ourselves to be strong, but from deep within us the desire to give in and to comply begins to disturb us and to affect our behavior. In psychology this is described as the innate ambivalence of all feelings.

The Need to Collapse

The vocabulary of psychopathology contains many sophisticated terms for the wish to succumb to mental pressure, such as "wish to regress," "dependency need," "mental masochism," "unconscious death wish," and many others. For our purposes, however, it is enough to state that every individual has two opposing needs which operate simultaneously: the need to be independent, to be oneself; and the need *not* to be oneself, *not* to be anybody at all, *not* to resist mental pressure. The need to be inconspicuous, to disappear, and to be swallowed up by society is a common one. In its simplest form we can see it all around us as a tendency to conform. Under ordinary circumstances the need for anonymity is balanced by the need for individuality, and the mentally healthy person is the one who can walk the fine line between them. But in the frightening, lonely situations in which the victims of menticidal terror find themselves—situations which have a nightmare quality, which are crammed with dangers so tremendous they cannot be grasped or understood because there is nobody to explain or reassure—the wish to collapse, to let go, to be not there, becomes almost irresistible.

This experience was reported by many concentration-camp victims. They had come into camp with one unanswered question burning in their minds: "Why has all this happened to me?" Their need for a sense of direction, for a feeling of purpose and meaning was unsatisfied, and hence they could not maintain their personalities. They let themselves go in what psychopathology calls a depersonalization syndrome, a general feeling of having lost complete control of themselves and their own existence. What Pavlovian conditioning can do in applying artificial confusion, can be done too by one shocking experience. "For what?" they asked themselves. "What is the meaning of all this suffering?" And gradually they sank dully into that paralyzed state of semi-oblivion we call depression: the self-destructive needs take over.

The Nazis were clever and unscrupulous in taking advantage of this need to collapse. The humiliation of concentration-camp life, the repeated suggestion that the Allies were as good as beaten—these conspired to convince the inmates that there would be no end to this pointless suffering, no victorious conclusion to the war, no future to their lives. The desire to break down, to give in, becomes almost insurmountable when a man feels that this horrible marginal existence is something permanent, that he cannot look toward a more personal goal, that he has to adjust to this dulling, degrading life forever.

At the moment faith and hope disappear, man breaks down. There are tragic stories of concentration-camp victims who fixed all their expectations on the idea that liberation would come on Christmas, 1944, and aimed their entire existence toward that date. When it passed and they were still incarcerated, many of them simply collapsed and died.

This tendency to collapse also serves as a protective device against danger. The victim seems to think, "If my torturer doesn't notice me, he will leave me alone." And yet this very feeling of anonymity, this sense of losing one's personality, of being useless, unnoticed and unwanted, also results in depression and apathy. Man's need to be an individual can never be completely killed.

The Need for Companionship

Not enough attention has been given to the psychology of loneliness, especially to the implications of enforced isolation of prisoners. When the sensory stimuli of everyday life are removed, man's entire personality may change. Social intercourse, our continual contact with our colleagues, our work, the newspapers, voices, traffic, our loved ones and even those we don't like—all are daily nourishment for our senses and minds. We select what we find interesting, reject what we do not want to absorb. Every day, every citizen lives in many small worlds of exchange of gratifications, little hatreds, pleasant experiences, irritations, delights. And he needs these stimuli to keep him on the alert. Hour by hour, reality, in cooperation with our memory, integrates the millions of facts in our lives by repeating them over and over.

As soon as man is alone, closed off from the world and from the news of what is going on, his mental activity is replaced by quite different processes. Long-forgotten anxieties come to the surface, long-repressed memories knock on his mind from inside. His fantasy life begins to develop and assume gigantic proportions. He cannot evaluate or check his fantasies against the events of his ordinary days, and very soon they may take possession of him.

I remember very clearly my own fantasies during the time I was in a Nazi prison. It was almost impossible for me to control my depressive thoughts of hopelessness. I had to tell myself over and over again: "Think, think. Keep your senses alert; don't give in." I tried to use all my psychiatric knowledge to keep my mind in a state of relaxed mobilization, and on many days I felt it was a losing battle.

Some experiments have shown that people who are deprived, for even a very short time, of *all* sensory stimuli (no touch, no hearing, no smell, no sight) quickly fall into a kind of hallucinatory hypnotic state. Isolation from the multitude of impressions that normally bombard us from the outside world creates strange and frightening symptoms. According to Heron, who performed experiments on a group of students at McGill University by placing each student in his own pitch-black, soundproof room, ventilated with filtered air, and encasing his hands in heavy leather mittens and his feet in heavy boots, "little by little their brains go dead or slip out of control." Even in twenty-four hours of such extreme sensual isolation, all the horror phantoms of childhood are awakened, and various pathological symptoms appear. Our instinct of curiosity demands continual feeding; if it is not satisfied, the internal hounds of hell are aroused.

The prisoner kept in isolation, although his isolation is by no means as extreme as in the laboratory test, also undergoes a severe mental change. His guards and inquisitors become more and more his only source of contact with reality, with those stimuli he needs even more than bread. No wonder that he gradually develops a peculiar submissive relationship to them. He is affected not only by his isolation from social contacts, but by sexual starvation as well. The latent dependency needs and latent homosexual tendencies that lie deep in all men make him willing to accept his guard as a substitute father figure. The inquisitor may be cruel and bestial, but the very fact that he acknowledges his victim's existence gives the prisoner a feeling that he has received some little bit of affection. What a conflict may thus arise between a man's traditional loyalties and these new ones! There are only a few personalities which are so completely self-sufficient that they can resist the need to yield, to find some human companionship, to overcome the unbearable loneliness.

During the World Wars, prisoners at first suffered from a peculiar, burning homesickness already called barbed-wire disease. Memories of mother, home, and family made the soldiers identify with babyhood again, but as they became more used to prison-camp life, thoughts of home and family also created positive values and helped make the prison-camp life less harrowing.

Even the prisoner who is not kept in isolation can feel lonely in the unorganized mass of prisoners. His fellow prisoners can become his enemies as easily as they can become his friends. His hatred of his guards can be displaced and turned against those imprisoned with him. Instead of suspecting the enemy, the victim may become suspicious of his companions in misery.

In the Nazi concentration camps and the Korean P.O.W. camps, a kind of mass paranoia often developed. Loneliness was increased because the prisoners cut themselves off from one another through suspicion and hatred. This distrust was encouraged by the guards. They constantly suggested to their victims that nobody cared for them and nobody was concerned about what was happening to them. "You are alone. Your friends on the outside don't know whether you're alive or dead. Your fellow prisoners don't even care." Thus all expectation of a future was killed, and the resulting uncertainty and hopelessness became unbearable. Then the guards sowed suspicion and spread terrifying rumors: "You are here because those people you call your friends betrayed you." "Your buddies here have squealed on you." "Your friends on the outside have deserted you." Playing on a man's old loyalties, making him feel deserted and alone, force him into submission and collapse.

The times that I myself wavered and entertained thoughts about joining the opposite forces always occurred after periods of extreme loneliness and deep-seated yearnings for companionship.* At such moments the jailer or enemy may become a substitute friend.

Blackmailing Through Overburdening Guilt Feelings

Deep within all of us lie hidden feelings of guilt, unconscious guilt, which can be brought to the surface under extreme stress. The strategy of arousing guilt is the mother's oldest tool for gaining dominance over her childrens' souls. Her warning and accusing finger or her threatening eyes give her a magic power over them and help to create deep-seated guilt feelings which may continue all through their adult lives. When we are children, we depend on our parents and resent them for just this reason. We may harbor hidden destructive wishes against those closest to us, and feelings of guilt about these wishes. There is no question that most men have a profound loyalty to their families, but the primitive in him hates those he loves, and this hatred makes him feel guilty. Buried deep in his unconscious is the knowledge that in his hostile fantasies he has felt himself capable of committing many crimes. Theodor Reik has drawn our attention to the unknown primitive murderer in all of us, whose compulsion to confess and to be punished may be easily provoked under circumstances of terror and

* I describe these phenomena of self-betrayal in Chapter Fourteen.

depression. This concept of concealed infantile hostility and destructiveness is often difficult for the layman to accept. But consider for a moment the popularity of the detective story. We may tell ourselves that we enjoy reading these tales because we identify with the keen and clever sleuth, but, as is clear from psychoanalytic experience, the repressed criminal in all of us is also at work and we also identify with the conscienceless killer. As a matter of fact our repressed hostilities make the reading of hostile acts attractive to us.

The method of systematically exploiting unconscious guilt to create submission is not too well known, but it may be better understood in the light of our investigation of the unconscious confession compulsion and the need for punishment. Guilt may be instilled early in life when the parent urges the child, too much and too early, to apologize for his disobedience, or uses other means to burden the child with a sense of guilt when he does not understand what was unmoral or wrong about a given act. Teaching the child to see right and wrong does not of necessity imply being conditioned with submissive and anxious anticipation of punishment to follow. In one of my cases the patient's mother cried after every little mistake the child made, "Look what you have done to me!" It took protracted therapy to relieve the patient of his hidden murderous impulses against his mother and his consequent burden of guilt.

In the political sphere, many such early child-rearing methods are symbolically repeated. Continual purges and confessions, as we encounter them in the totalitarian countries, arouse deeply hidden guilt feelings. The lesser sin of rebellion or subversion has to be admitted to cover personal thoughts of crime which are more deeply imbedded. The personal reactions of those who are continually interrogated and investigated give us a clue as to what happens. The very fact of prolonged interrogation can re-arouse the hidden and unconscious guilt in the victim. At a time of extreme emotion, after constant accusation and day-long interrogation, when he has been deprived of sleep and reduced to a state of utter despair, the victim may lose the capacity to distinguish between the real criminal act of which he is accused and his own fantasied unconscious guilt. If his upbringing burdened him with an almost pathological sense of guilt under normal circumstances, he will now be completely unable to resist the menticidal attack. Even normal people may be brought to surrender under such miserable conditions, and not only through the action of the inquisition, but also because of all the other weakening factors. Lack of sleep, hunger, and illness can create utter confusion and make any man vulnerable to hypnotic influence. All of us have experienced the mental fuzziness which comes with being overtired. Concentration-camp victims know how hunger, especially, induces a loss of mental control.* In the fantastic world of the totalitarian prison or camp, these effects are heightened and exaggerated.

The Nazis, through clever exploitation of their victims' unconscious guilt after poking into the back corners of their minds, were often able to convert courageous resistance fighters into meek collaborators. That they were not uniformly successful can be explained by two factors. The first is that most of the members of the underground were inwardly prepared for the brutality with which they were treated. The second is that, clever as the Nazi techniques were, they were not as irresistible as the methodical tricks of the Communist brainwashers are. When victims of Nazi brutality did break down, it was not torture but often the threat of reprisal against family which made them give in. Sudden acute confrontation with a long-buried childhood problem creates confusion and doubt. All of a sudden the enemy puts before you a clash of loyalties: your father or your friends, your brother or your fatherland, your wife or your honor. This is a brutal choice to have to make, and when the inquisitor makes use of your additional inner conflicts, he can easily force you into surrender. A clash between loyalties makes either choice a betrayal, and this arouses paralyzing doubt. This calculated but subtle attack on the weakest spots in man's mind, on a man's conscience, and on the moral system he has learned from the Judaeo-Christian ethics, paralyzes the reason

* The conversation in concentration camps usually revolved around food and memories of glorious gluttony. The mind could not work: it was fixed on eating and fantasies about food. A word grew up to express that constant possession by the idea of eating well once again: stomach masturbation (*Magen-onanie*). This kind of talk often took the place of all intellectual exchange.

and leads the victim more easily into betrayal. The inquisitor subtly tests his victim's archaic guilt feelings toward paternal figures, his friends, his children. He cleverly exploits the victim's early ambivalent ties with his parents. The sudden outbreak of hidden moral flaws and guilt can bring a man to tears and complete breakdown. He regresses to the dependency and submissiveness of the baby.

A very husky former hero of the Dutch resistance, known as King Kong because of his size and strength, became the treacherous instrument of the Nazis soon after his brother had been taken with him and the Nazis threatened to kill the youth. King Kong's final surrender to the enemy and his becoming their treacherous tool was psychiatrically recognizable as a defense mechanism against his deep guilt, arising from hidden feelings of aggression against his brother (Boeree).

Another example of breakdown is seen in the story of one young resistance fighter who, after the Nazis had threatened to torture his father, who was imprisoned with him, finally broke into childish tears and promised to tell them everything they wanted to know. After that he was taken back to his cell in order to be softened up again the following day. This was the routine of his interrogator. The inquisitors understood only too well the effectiveness of patient pursuit at repeated moments while intruding into a man's guilt feelings. Although both prisoners were liberated that night as a consequence of the Allied sweep through Belgium and the southwest part of Holland, the boy remained in his depression for a long time, tortured by his knowledge that he had nearly betrayed his best friends in the underground in order to save his father in spite of knowing, at the same time, that the promises of the enemy would not have protected his father. In the subsequent psychological exploration of the boy's breakdown and depression, his dreams gave us a clue to his long-buried aggressive fantasies against his father, whom he had symbolically killed in his dreams. The sense of guilt about this unconscious infantile hostility had weighed more heavily on his conscience than the possibility of being guilty toward his fellow partisans. A conscious understanding of what his difficulties had been, plus renewed military activity, did much to help him cope with the conflicts that tortured him, but other unwilling traitors were less fortunate. When finally they realized the enormity of their betrayal, several of them became psychotically depressed, and some even committed suicide.

The Law of Survival Versus the Law of Loyalty

The prisoners of war in Korea who gradually gave in to the systematic mental pressure of the enemy and collaborated in the production of materials that could be used for Communist propaganda—albeit tentatively and for only as long as they were in the orbit of the enemy—followed a peculiar psychological law of passive inner defense and inner deceit that when one cannot fight and defeat the enemy, one must join him (A. Freud). Later, a few of them were so taken in by totalitarian propaganda that they elected to remain in China and the totalitarian orbit. Some did it to escape punishment for having betrayed their comrades.

Man cannot become a turncoat without justifying his actions to himself. When Holland surrendered to the German army in 1940, I saw this general mechanism of mental surrender operating in several people who had been staunch anti-Nazis. "Maybe there is something good in Nazism," they told themselves as they saw the tremendous show of German strength. Those who were the victims of their own initial mental surrender and need to justify things, who could not stop and say to themselves "Hold on here; think this out," became the traitors and collaborators. They were completely taken in by the enemy's show of strength. The same process of self-justification and justifying the enemy started in the P.O.W. camps.

Experiences from the concentration camps give us some indication of how far this passive submission to the enemy can go. Because of the deep-seated human need for affection, many prisoners lived only for one thing: a friendly word from their guards. Each time it came, it fortified the delusion of grace and acceptance. Once these prisoners, mostly those who had been in the camps a long time, were accepted by the guards, they easily became the trusted tools of the Nazis. They started to behave like their cruel jailers and became torturers of their fellow campers. These collaborating prisoners, called *Kapos,* were even more cruel and vengeful than the official overseers. Because of misunderstood inner needs, the brainwasher and sadistic camp leader is direly in need of collaborators. They serve not only for the propaganda machine but also to exonerate their jailers from guilt.

When a man has to choose either hunger, death marches, and torture or a temporary yielding to the illusions of the enemy, his self-preservation mechanisms act in many ways like reflexes. They help him to find a thousand justifications and exculpations for giving in to the psychological pressure. One of the officers court-martialed for collaborating with the enemy in a Korean P.O.W. camp justified his conduct by saying that he followed this course of action in order to keep himself and his men alive. Is that not a perfectly valid, though not necessarily true, argument? The use of it serves to point up the fact that self-protective mechanisms are usually much stronger than ideological loyalty. No one who has not faced this same bitter problem can have an objective opinion as to what he himself would do under the circumstances. As a psychiatrist, I suggest that "most" people would yield and compromise when threat and mental pressure became strong enough.

Among the anti-Nazi undergrounds in the Second World War were physically strong boys who thought they could resist all pressure and would never betray their comrades. However, they could not even begin to imagine the perfidious technique of menticide. Repeated pestering, itself, is more destructive than physical torture. The pain of physical torture, as we have said, brings temporary unconsciousness and, consequently, forgetfulness, but when the victim wakes up, the play of anticipation begins. "Will it happen again? Can I stand it any more?" Anticipation paralyzes the will. Suicidal thoughts and identifications with death do not help. The foe doesn't let you die but drags you back from the very edge of oblivion. The anticipation of renewed torture increases internal anxieties. "Who am I to stand all this?" "Why must I be a hero?" Gradually resistance breaks down.

The surrender of the mind to its new master does not take place immediately under the impact of duress and exhaustion. The inquisitor knows that in the period of temporary relaxation of pressure, during which the victim will rehearse and repeat the torture experience to himself, the final surrender is prepared. During that tension of rumination and anticipation, the deeply hidden wish to give in grows. The action of continual repetition of stupid questions, reiterated for days and days, exhausts the mind till it gives the answers the inquisitor wants to have. In addition to the weapon of mental exhaustion, he plays on the physical exhaustion of the senses. He may use penetrating, excruciating noises or a constant strong flashlight that blinds the eyes. The need to close the eyes or to get away from the noises confuses the mental orientation of the victim. He loses his balance and feelings of self-confidence. He yearns for sleep and can do nothing else but surrender. The infantile desire to become part of the threatening giant machine, to become one with the forces that are so much stronger than the prisoner has won.

It is unequivocal surrender: "Do with me what you want. From now on I am you."

That only deprivation from sleep is able to produce various abnormal reactions of the mind was confirmed by Tyler in an experiment with 350 male volunteers. He deprived them of sleep for 102 hours. Forty-four men dropped out almost at once because they felt too anxious and irritated. After forty hours without sleep, 70 per cent of all subjects had already had illusions, delusions, hallucinations, and similar experiences. Those who had true hallucinations were dropped from the experiment. After the second night, sporadic disturbances of thinking were common to all subjects. The participants were embarrassed when they were informed later of their behavior.

The changes in emotional response had been most noticeable—euphoria followed by depression; dejection and restlessness; indifference to unusual behavior shown by other suspects. The experiment gave the impression that prolonged wakefulness causes some toxic substance to affect brain and mind.

Only the few strong, independent, and self-sufficient personalities, who have conquered their dependency needs, can stand such pressure or are willing to die under it.

The ritual of self-accusation and breast-beating and unconditional surrender to the rules of the elders is part of age-old religious rites. It was based on a more or less unconscious belief in a supreme and omnipotent power. This power may be the monolithic party state or a mysterious deity. It follows the old inner device of *Credo quia absurdum* ("I believe because it is absurd"), of faithful submission to a super-world stronger than the reality which confronts our senses.

Why the totalitarian and orthodox dogmatic ideology sticks to such a rigid attitude, with prohibition of investigation of basic premises, is a complicated psychological question. Somewhere the reason is related to the fear of change, the fear of the risk of change of habits, the fear of freedom, which may be psychologically related to the fear of the finality of death.

The denial of human freedom and equality lifts the authoritarian man beyond his mortal fellows. His temporary power and omnipotence give him the illusion of eternity. In his totalitarianism he denies death and ephemeral existence and borrows power from the future. He has to invent and formulate a final Truth and protective dogma to justify his battle against mortality and temporariness. From then on, the new fundamental certainty must be hammered into the minds of adepts and slaves.

What happens inside the human psyche under severe circumstances of mental and physical attack is clarified for us by Anna Freud in her book on the general mental defenses available to man; earlier, I myself tried in several publications to analyze the various ways people defend themselves against fear and pressure.

In the last phases of brainwashing and menticide, the self-humiliating submission of the victims serves as an inner defensive device annihilating the prosecuting inquisitor in a magic way. The more they accuse themselves, the less logical reason there is for *his* existence. Giving in and being even more cruel toward oneself makes the inquisitor and judge, as it were, impotent and shows the futility of the accusing regime.

We may say that brainwashing and menticide provoke the same inner defensive mechanisms that we observe in melancholic patients. Through their mental self-beatings, they try to get rid of fear and to avoid a more deeply seated guilt. They punish themselves in advance in order to overcome the idea of final punishment for some hidden, unknown, and worse crime. The victim of menticide conquers his tormentor by becoming even more cruel toward himself than the inquisitor. In this passive way, he annihilates his enemy.

The Mysterious Masochistic Pact

In Arthur Koestler's masterpiece, *Darkness At Noon,* he describes all the subtle intricacies, reasonings, and dialectics between the inquisitor and his victim. The old Bolshevik, Rubashov, preconditioned by his former party adherence, confesses to plotting against the party and the party line. He is partly motivated by the wish to render a last service: his confession is a final sacrifice to the party. I would explain the confession rather as part of that mysterious masochistic pact between the inquisitor and his victim which we encounter, too, in other processes of brainwashing.* It is the last gift and trick the tortured gives to his torturer. It is as if he were to call out: "Be good to me. I confess. I submit. Be good to me and love me." After having suffered all manner of brutality, hypnotism, despair, and panic, there is a final quest for human companionship, but it is ambivalent, mixed with deep despising, hatred, and bitterness.

Tortured and torturer gradually form a peculiar community in which the one influences the other. Just as in therapeutic sessions where the patient identifies with the psychiatrist, the daily sessions of interrogation and conversation create an unconscious transfer of feelings in which the prisoner identifies with his inquisitors, and his inquisitors with him. The prisoner, encaptured in a strange, harsh, and unfamiliar world, identifies much more with the enemy than does the enemy with him. Unwittingly he may take over all the enemy's norms, evaluations, and attitudes toward life. Such passive surrender to the enemy's ideology is determined by unconscious processes. The danger of communion of this kind is that at the end all moral evaluations disappear. We saw it happen in Germany. The very victims of Nazism came to accept the idea of concentration camps.

* The term "masochism" originally referred to sexual gratification received from pain and punishment, and later became every gratification acquired through pain and abjection.

In menticide we are faced with a ritual like that found in witch hunting during the Middle Ages, except that today the ritual has taken a more refined form. Accuser and accused—each affords the other assistance, and both belong together as collaborating members of a ritual of confession and self-denigration. Through their cooperation, they attack the minds of bystanders who identify with them and who consequently feel guilty, weak, and submissive. The Moscow purge trials made many Russians feel guilty; listening to the confessions, they must have said to themselves, "I could have done the same thing. I could have been in that man's place." When their heroes became traitors, their own hidden treasonable wishes made them feel weak and frightened.

This explanation may seem overly complicated and involved and perhaps even self-contradictory, but, in fact, it helps us to understand what happens in cases of menticide. Both torturer and tortured are the victims of their own unconscious guilt. The torturer projects his guilt onto some outside scapegoat and tries to expiate it by attacking his victim. The victim, too, has a sense of guilt which arises from deeply repressed childhood hostilities. Under normal circumstances, this sense is kept under control, but in the menticidal atmosphere of relentless interrogation and inquisition, his repressed hostilities are aroused and loom up as frightening phantasmagorias from a forgotten past, which the victim senses but cannot grasp or understand. It is easier to confess to the accusation of treason and sabotage than to accept the frightening sense of criminality with which his long-forgotten aggressive impulses now burden him. The victim's overt self-accusation serves as a trick to annihilate the inner accuser and the persecuting inquisitor. The more I accuse myself, the less reason there is for the inquisitor's existence. The victim's going to the gallows kills, as it were, the inquisitor too, because there existed a mutual identification: the accuser is made impotent the moment the victim begins to accuse himself and tomorrow the accuser himself may be accused and brought to the gallows.

Out of our understanding of this strange masochistic pact between accuser and accused comes a rather simple answer to the questions, Why do people want to control the minds of others, and why do the others confess and yield? It is because there is no essential difference between victim and inquisitor. They are alike. Neither, under these circumstances, has any control over his deeply hidden criminal and hostile thoughts and feelings.

It is obviously easier to be the inquisitor than the victim, not only because the inquisitor may be temporarily safe from mental and physical destruction, but also because it is simpler to punish others for what we feel as criminal in ourselves than it is to face up to our own hidden sense of guilt. Committing menticide is the lesser crime of aggression, which covers up the deeper crime of unresolved hidden hatred and destruction.

A Survey of Psychological Processes Involved in Brainwashing and Menticide

At the end of this chapter describing the various influences that lead to yielding and surrender to the enemy's strategy, it is useful to give a short survey of the psychological processes involved.

Phase I. ARTIFICIAL BREAKDOWN AND DECONDITIONING

The inquisitor tries to weaken the ego of his prisoner. Though originally physical torture was used—hunger and cold are still very effective—physical torture may often increase a person's stubbornness. Torture is intended to a much greater extent to act as a threat to the bystanders' (the people's) imagination. Their wild anticipation of torture leads more easily to *their* breakdown when the enemy has need of their weakness. (Of course, occasionally a sadistic enemy may find individual pleasure in torture.)

The many devices the enemy makes use of include: intimidating suggestion, dramatic persuasion, mass suggestion, humiliation, embarrassment, loneliness and isolation, continued interrogation, overburdening the unsteady mind, arousing more and more self-pity. Patience and time help the inquisitor to soften a stubborn soul.

Just as in many old religions the victims were humbled and humiliated in order to prepare for the new religion, so, in this case, they are prepared to accept the totalitarian ideology. In this phase, out of mere intellectual opportunism, the victim may consciously give in.

Phase II. SUBMISSION TO AND POSITIVE IDENTIFICATION
WITH THE ENEMY

As has already been mentioned, the moment of surrender may often arrive suddenly. It is as if the stubborn negative suggestibility changed critically into a surrender and affirmation. What the inquisitor calls the sudden inner illumination and conversion is a total reversal of inner strategy in the victim. From this time on, in psychoanalytic terms, a parasitic superego lives in man's conscience, and he will speak his new master's voice. In my experience such sudden surrender often occurred together with hysterical outbursts into crying and laughing, like a baby surrendering after obstinate temper tantrums. The inquisitor can attain this phase more easily by assuming a paternal attitude. As a matter of fact, many a P.O.W. was courted by a form of paternal kindness—gifts, sweets at birthdays, and the promise of more cheerful things to come.

Moloney compares this sudden yielding with the theophany or kenosis (internal conversion) as described by some theological rites. For our understanding, it is important to stress that yielding is an unconscious and purely emotional process, no longer under the conscious intellectual control of the brainwashee. We may also call this phase the phase of autohypnosis.

Phase III. THE RECONDITIONING TO THE NEW ORDER

Through both continual training and taming, the new phonograph record has to be grooved. We may compare this process with an active hypnosis into conversion. Incidental relapses to the old form of thinking have to be corrected as in Phase I. The victim is daily helped to rationalize and justify his new ideology. The inquisitor delivers to him the new arguments and reasonings.

This systematic indoctrination of those who long avoided intensive indoctrination constitutes the actual political aspect of brainwashing and symbolizes the ideological cold war going on at this very moment.

Phase IV. LIBERATION FROM THE TOTALITARIAN SPELL

As soon as the brainwashee returns to a free democratic atmosphere, the hypnotic spell is broken. Temporary nervous repercussions take place, like crying spells, feelings of guilt and depression. The expectation of a hostile homeland, in view of his having yielded to enemy indoctrination, may fortify this reaction. The period of brainwashing becomes a nightmare. Only those who were staunch Communists before may stick to it, but here, too, I have seen the enemy impose its mental pressure too well and convert their former comrades into eternal haters of the regime.

PART TWO

THE TECHNIQUES OF
MASS SUBMISSION

THE PURPOSE OF THE SECOND PART OF THIS BOOK IS
TO SHOW VARIOUS ASPECTS OF POLITICAL AND NON-
POLITICAL STRATEGY USED TO CHANGE THE FEELINGS
AND THOUGHTS OF THE MASSES, STARTING WITH
SIMPLE ADVERTISING AND PROPAGANDA, THEN SUR-
VEYING PSYCHOLOGICAL WARFARE AND ACTUAL
COLD WAR, AND GOING ON TO EXAMINE THE MEANS
USED FOR INTERNAL STREAMLINING OF MAN'S
THOUGHTS AND BEHAVIOR. PART TWO ENDS WITH
AN INTRICATE EXAMINATION OF HOW ONE OF THE
TOOLS OF EMOTIONAL FASCINATION AND ATTACK—
THE WEAPON OF FEAR—IS USED AND WHAT RE-
ACTIONS IT AROUSES IN MEN.

¥

CHAPTER FIVE

The Cold War Against the Mind

¥

Only blind wishful thinking can permit us to believe that our own society is free from the insidious influences mentioned in Part One. The fact is that they exist all around us, both on a political and a nonpolitical level and they become as dangerous to the free way of life as are the aggressive totalitarian governments themselves.

Every culture institutionalizes certain forms of behavior that communicate and encourage certain forms of thinking and acting, thus molding the character of its citizens. To the degree that the individual is made an object of constant mental manipulation, to the degree that cultural institutions may tend to weaken intellectual and spiritual strength, to the degree that knowledge of the mind is used to tame and condition people instead of educating them, to that degree does the culture itself produce men and women who are predisposed to accept an authoritarian way of life. The man who has no mind of his own can easily become the pawn of a would-be dictator.

It is often disturbing to see how even intelligent people do not have straight-thinking minds of their own. The pattern of the mind, whether toward conformity and compliance or otherwise, is conditioned rather early in life.

In his important social psychological experiments with students, Asch found out in simple tests that there was a yielding toward an *erring majority* opinion in more than a third of his test persons, and 75 per cent of subjects experimented upon agreed with the

majority in varying degrees. In many persons the weight of authority is more important than the quality of the authority.*

If we are to learn to protect our mental integrity on all levels,
we must examine not only those aspects of contemporary culture
which have to do directly with the struggle for power, but also
those developments in our culture which, by dulling the edge of
our mental awareness or by taking advantage of our suggestibility,
can lead us into the mental death—or boredom—of totalitarianism.
Continual suggestion and slow hypnosis in the wake of mechanical
mass communication promotes uniformity of the mind and may
lure the public into the "happy era" of adjustment, integration, and
equalization, in which individual opinion is completely stereotyped.

When I get up in the morning, I turn on my radio to hear the
news and the weather forecast. Then comes the pontifical voice
telling me to take aspirin for my headache. I have "headaches"
occasionally (so does the world), and my headaches, like everyone
else's, come from the many conflicts that life imposes on me. My
radio tells me not to think about either the conflicts or the headaches. It suggests, instead, that I should retreat into that old magic
action of swallowing a pill. Although I laugh as I listen to this
long-distance prescription by a broadcaster who does not know
anything about me or my headaches and though I meditate for a
moment on man's servility to the magic of chemistry, my hand has
already begun to reach out for the aspirin bottle. After all, I do
have a headache.

It is extremely difficult to escape the mechanically repeated suggestions of everyday life. Even when our critical mind rejects them,
they seduce us into doing what our intellect tells us is stupid.

The mechanization of modern life has already influenced man
to become more passive and to adjust himself to ready-made conformity. No longer does man think in personal values, following
his own conscience and ethical evaluations; he thinks more and
more in the values brought to him by mass media. Headlines in the
morning paper give him his temporary political outlook, the radio
blasts suggestions into his ears, television keeps him in continual
awe and passive fixation. Consciously he may protest against these

* In Chapter Ten, The Child Is Father to the Man, I will come back to this inner
urge toward conformity.

anonymous voices, but nevertheless their suggestions ooze into his system.

What is perhaps most shocking about these influences is that many of them have developed not out of man's destructiveness, but out of his hope to improve his world and to make life richer and deeper. The very institutions man has created to help himself, the very tools he has invented to enhance his life, the very progress he has made toward mastery of himself and his environment—all can become weapons of destruction.

The Public-Opinion Engineers

The conviction is steadily growing in our country that an elaborate propaganda campaign for either a political idea or a deep-freeze can be successful in selling the public any idea or object one wants them to buy, any political figure one wants them to elect. Recently, some of our election campaigns have been masterminded by the so-called public-opinion engineers, who have used all the techniques of modern mass communication and all the contemporary knowledge of the human mind to persuade Americans to vote for the candidate who is paying the public-relations men's salaries. The danger of such high-pressure advertising is that the man or the party who can pay the most can become, temporarily at least, the one who can influence the people to buy or to vote for what may not be in their real interest.

The specialists in the art of persuasion and the molding of public sentiment may try to knead man's mental dough with all the tools of communication available to them: pamphlets, speeches, posters, billboards, radio programs, and T.V. shows. They may water down the spontaneity and creativity of thoughts and ideas into sterile and streamlined clichés that direct our thoughts even although we still have the illusion of being original and individual.

What we call the will of the people, or the will of the masses, we only get to know after such collective action is put on the move, after the will of the people has been expressed either at the polls or in fury and rebellion. This indicates again how important it is who directs the tools and machines of public opinion.

In the wake of such advertising and engineering of consent, the citizen's trust in his leaders may become shaken and the populace may gradually grow more and more accustomed to official deceit. Finally, when people no longer have confidence in any program, any position, and when they are unable to form intelligent judgments any more, they can be more easily influenced by any demagogue or would-be dictator, whose strength appeals to their confusion and their growing sense of dissatisfaction. Perhaps the worst aspect of this slick merchandising of ideas is that too often even those who buy the experts, and even the opinion experts themselves, are unaware of what they are doing. They too are swayed by the current catchword "management of public opinion," and they cannot judge any more the tools they have hired.

The end never justifies the means; enough steps on this road can lead us gradually to Totalitaria.

At this very moment in our country, an elaborate research into motivation is going on, whose object is to find out why and what the buyer likes to buy. What makes him tick? The aim is to bypass the resistance barriers of the buying public. It is part of our paradoxical cultural philosophy to stimulate human needs and to stimulate the wants of the people. Commercialized psychological understanding wants to sell to the public, to the potential buyer, many more products than he really wants to buy. In order to do this, rather infantile impulses have to be awakened, such as sibling rivalry and neighbor envy, the need to have more and more sweets, the glamour of colors, and the need for more and more luxuries. The commercial psychologist teaches the seller how to avoid unpleasant associations in his advertising, how to stimulate, unobtrusively, sex associations, how to make everything look simple and happy and successful and secure! He teaches the shops how to boost the buyer's ego, how to flatter the customer. The marketing engineers have discovered that our public wants the suggestion of strength and virility in their products. A car must have more horsepower in order to balance feelings of inner weakness in the owner. A car must represent one's social status and reputation, because without such a flag man feels empty. Advertising agencies dream of *universitas advertensis,* the world of glittering sham ideas, the glorification of *mundus vult decipi,* the intensification of snob appeal, the expression of vulgar conspicuousness, and all this in order to push more sales into the greedy mouths of buying babies. In our world of advertising, artificial needs are invented by sedulous sellers and buyers. Here lies the threat of building up a sham world that can have a dangerous influence on our world of ideas.

This situation emphasizes the neurotic greed of the public, the need to indulge in private fancies at the cost of an awareness of real values. The public becomes conditioned to meretricious values. Of course, a free public gradually finds its defenses against slogans, but dishonesty and mistrust slip through the barriers of our consciousness and leave behind a gnawing feeling of dissatisfaction. After all, advertising symbolizes the art of making people dissatisfied with what they have. In the meantime it is evident man sustains a continual sneak attack on his better judgment.

In our epoch of too many noises and many frustrations, many "free" minds have given up the struggle for decency and individuality. They surrender to the *Zeitgeist,* often without being aware of it. Public opinion molds our critical thoughts every day. Unknowingly, we may become opinionated robots. The slow coercion of hypocrisy, of traditions in our culture that have a leveling effect— these things change us. We crave excitement, hair-raising stories, sensation. We search for situations that create superficial fear to cover up inner anxieties. We like to escape into the irrational because we dislike the challenge of self-study and self-thinking. Our leisure time is occupied increasingly by automatized activities in which we take no part: listening to piped-in words and viewing television screens. We hurry along with cars and go to bed with a sleeping pill. This pattern of living in turn may open the way for renewed sneak attacks on our mind. Our boredom may welcome any seductive suggestion.

Psychological Warfare as a Weapon of Terror

Every human communication can be either a report of straight facts or an attempt to suggest things and situations as they do not exist. Such distortion and perversion of facts strike at the core of human communication. The verbal battle against man's concept of truth and against his mind seems to be ceaseless. For example, if I can instill in eventual future enemies fear and terror and the suggestion of impending defeat, even before they are willing to fight, my battle is already half won.

The strategy of man to use a frightening mask and a loud voice to utter lies in order to manipulate friend and foe is as old as mankind. Primitive people used terror-provoking masks, magic fascination, or self-deceit as much as we use loudly spoken words to convince others or ourselves. They use their magic paints and we our ideologies. Truly, we live in an age of ads, propaganda, and publicity. But only under dictatorial and totalitarian regimes have such human habit formations mushroomed into systematic psychological assault on mankind.

The weapons the dictator uses against his own people, he may use against the outside world as well. For example, the false confessions that divert the minds of dictator's subjects from their own real problems have still another effect: they are meant (and sometimes they succeed in their aim) to terrorize the world's public. By strengthening the myth of the dictator's omnipotence, such confessions weaken man's will to resist him. If a period of peace can be used to soften up a future enemy, the totalitarian armies may be able in time of war to win a cheap and easy victory. Totalitarian psychological warfare is directed largely toward this end. It is an effort to propagandize and hypnotize the world into submission.

As far back as the early nineteenth century, Napoleon organized his Bureau de l'Opinion Publique in order to influence the thinking of the French people. But it fell to the Germans to develop the manipulation of public opinion into a huge, well-organized machine. Their psychological warfare became aggressive strategy in peacetime, the so-called war between wars. It was as a result of the Nazi attack on European morale and the Nazi war of nerves against their neighbors that the other nations of the world began to organize their own psychological forces, but it was only in the second half of the war that they were able to achieve some measure of success. The Germans had a long head start.

Hitler's psychological artillery was composed primarily of the weapon of fear. He had, for example, a network of fifth columnists whose main job was to sow rumors and suspicions among the citizens of the countries against which he eventually planned to fight. The people were upset not only by the spy system itself, but by the

very rumor of spies. These fifth columnists spread slogans of
and political confusion: "Why should France die for Engl
Fear began to direct people's actions. Instead of facing the real
threat of German invasion, instead of preparing for it, all of Europe
shuddered at spy stories, discussed irrelevant problems, argued
endlessly about scapegoats and minorities. Thus Hitler used the
rampant, vague fears to becloud the real issues, and by attacking
his enemies' will to fight, weakened them.

Not content with this strategic attack on the will to defend oneself, Hitler tried to paralyze Europe with the threat of terror, not
only the threat of bombing, destruction, and occupation, but also
the psychological threat implicit in his own boast of ruthlessness.
The fear of an implacable foe makes man more willing to submit
even before he has begun to fight. Hitler's criminal acts at home—
the concentration camps, the gas chambers, the mass murders, the
atmosphere of terror throughout Germany—were as useful in the
service of his fear-instilling propaganda machinery as they were a
part of his delusions.

There is another important weapon the totalitarians use in their
campaign to frighten the world into submission. This is the weapon
of psychological shock. Hitler kept his enemies in a state of constant
confusion and diplomatic upheaval. They never knew what this
unpredictable madman was going to do next. Hitler was never
logical, because he knew that that was what he was expected to be.
Logic can be met with logic, while illogic cannot—it confuses those
who think straight. The Big Lie and monotonously repeated nonsense have more emotional appeal in a cold war than logic and
reason. While the enemy is still searching for a reasonable counter-
argument to the first lie, the totalitarians can assault him with
another.

Strategical mental shocks were the instruments the Nazis used
when they entered the Rhineland in 1936 and when they concluded
their nonaggression pact with Russia in 1939. Stalin used the same
strategy at the time of the Korean invasion in 1950 (which he
directed), as did the Chinese and the North Koreans when they
accused the United States of bacteriological warfare. By acting in
this apparently irrational way, the totalitarians throw their logic-
minded enemies into confusion. The enemy feels compelled to deny

the propagandistic lies or to explain things as they really are, and these actions immediately put him in the weaker defensive position. For the galloping lie can never be overtaken, it can only be overthrown.

The technique of psychological shock has still another effect. It may so confuse the mind of the individual citizen that he ceases to make his own evaluations and begins to lean passively on the opinions of others. Hitler's destruction of Warsaw and Rotterdam —after the armistice in 1940, a complete violation of international law—immobilized France and shook the other democratic nations. Being in a paralysis of moral indignation, they became psychologically ill-equipped to deal with the Nazi horrors.

Just as the technological advances of the modern world have refined and perfected the weapons of physical warfare, so the advance in man's understanding of the manipulation of public opinion have enabled him to refine and perfect the weapons of psychological warfare.

The Indoctrination Barrage

The continual intrusion into our minds of the hammering noises of arguments and propaganda can lead to two kinds of reactions. It may lead to apathy and indifference, the I-don't-care reaction, or to a more intensified desire to study and to understand. Unfortunately, the first reaction is the more popular one. The flight from study and awareness is much too common in a world that throws too many confusing pictures to the individual. For the sake of our democracy, based on freedom and individualism, we have to bring ourselves back to study again and again. Otherwise, we can become easy victims of a well-planned verbal attack on our minds and consciences.

We cannot be enough aware of the continual coercion of our senses and minds, the continual suggestive attacks which may pass through the intellectual barriers of insight. Repetition and Pavlovian conditioning exhaust the individual and may seduce him ultimately to accept a truth he himself initially defied and scorned.

The totalitarians are very ingenious in arousing latent guilt in us by repeating over and over again how criminally the Western world has acted toward innocent and peaceful people. The totalitarians may attack our identification with our leaders by ridiculing them, making use of every man's latent critical attitude toward all leaders. Sometimes they use the strategy of boredom to lull the people to sleep. They would like the entire Western world to fall into a hypnotic sleep under the illusion of peaceful coexistence. In a more refined strategy, they would like to have us cut all our ties of loyalty with the past, away from relatives and parents. The more you have forsaken them and their so-called outmoded concepts, the better you will cooperate with those who want to take mental possession of you. Every political strategy that aims toward arousing fear and suspicion tends to isolate the insecure individual until he surrenders to those forces that seem to him stronger than his former friends.

And last but not least, let us not forget that in the battle of arguments those with the best and most forceful verbal strategy tend to win. The totalitarians organize intensive dialectical training for their subjects lest their doubts get the better of them. They try to do the same thing to the rest of world in a less obtrusive way.

We have to learn to encounter the totalitarians' exhausting barrage of words with better training and better understanding. If we try to escape from these problems of mental defense or deny their complications, the cold war will gradually be lost to the slow encroachment of words—and more words.

The Enigma of Coexistence

Is it possible to coexist with a totalitarian system that never ceases to use its psychological artillery? Can a free democracy be strong enough to tolerate the parasitic intrusion of totalitarianism into its rights and freedoms? History tells us that many opposing and clashing ideologies have been able to coexist under a common law that assured tolerance and justice. The church no longer burns its apostates.

Before the opposites of totalitarianism and free democracy can coexist under the umbrella of supervising law and mutual good will, a great deal more of mutual understanding and tolerance will have to be built up. The actual cold war and psychological warfare certainly do not yet help toward this end.

To the totalitarian, the word "coexistence" has a different meaning than it has to us. The totalitarian may use it merely as a catchword or an appeaser. The danger is that the concept of peaceful coexistence may become a disguise, dulling the awareness of inevitable interactions and so profiting the psychologically stronger party. Lenin spoke about the strategic breathing spell (*peredyshka*) that has to weaken the enemy. Too enthusiastic a peace movement may mean a superficial appeasement of problems. Such appeal has to be studied and restudied, lest it result in a dangerous letdown of defenses which have to remain mobilized to face a ruthless enemy.

Coexistence may mean a suffocating subordination much like that of prisoners coexisting with their jailers. At its best, it may imitate the intensive symbiotic or ever-parasitic relationship we can see among animals which need each other, or as we see it in the infant in its years of dependency upon its mother.

To those living freely in a democracy, coexistence must imply freedom and mutuality. The totalitarian concept of un-freedom can not mix with freedom. There are concepts and ideas that cannot coexist and that do not tolerate one another.

In order to coexist and to cooperate, one must have notions and comparable images of integration, of a sameness of ideas, of a belonging-together, of an interdependence of the whole human race, in spite of the existence of racial and cultural differences. Otherwise the ideology backed by the greater military strength will strangle the weaker one.

Peaceful coexistence presupposes on *both* sides a high understanding of the problems and complications of simple coexistence, of mutual agreement and limitations, of the diversity of personalities, and especially of the coexistence of contrasting and irreconcilable thoughts and feelings in every individual, of the innate ambivalence of man. It demands an understanding of the rights of both the individual and the collectivity. Using coexistence as a catchword, we may obscure the problems involved, and we may find that we use the word as a flag that covers gradual surrender to the stronger strategist.

CHAPTER SIX

Totalitaria and Its Dictatorship

There actually exists such a thing as a technique of mass brainwashing. This technique can take root in a country if an inquisitor is strong and shrewd enough. He can make most of us his victims, albeit temporarily.

What in the structure of society has made man so vulnerable to these mass manipulations of the mind? This is a problem with tremendous implications, just as brainwashing is. In recent years we have grown more and more aware of human interdependence with all its difficulties and complications.

I am aware of the fact that investigation of the subject of mental coercion and thought control becomes less pleasant as time goes on. This is so because it may become more of a threat to us here and now, and our concern for China and Korea must yield to the more immediate needs at our own door. Can totalitarian tendencies take over here, and what social symptoms may lead to such phenomena? Stern reality confronts us with the universal mental battle between thought control (and its corollaries) and our standards of decency, personal strength, personal ideas, and a personal conscience with autonomy and dignity.

Future social scientists will be better able to describe the causes of the advent of totalitarian thinking and acting in man. We know that after wars and revolutions this mental deterioration more easily finds an opportunity to develop, helped by special psychopathic personalities who only flourish on man's misery and confusion. It is also true that the next generation spontaneously begins to correct the misdeeds of the previous one because the ruthless system has become too threatening to them.

My task, however, is to describe some symptoms of the totalitarian process (which implies deterioration of thinking and acting) as I have observed them in our own epoch, keeping in mind that the system is one of the most violent distortions of man's consistent mental growth. No brainwashing is possible without totalitarian thinking.

The tragic facts of political experiences in our age make it all too clear that applied psychological technique can brainwash entire nations and reduce their citizens to a kind of mindless robotism which becomes for them a normal way of living. Perhaps we can best understand how this frightening thing comes about by examining a mythical country, which, for the sake of convenience, we shall call Totalitaria.

The Robotization of Man

First, let me utter a word of caution. We must not make the mistake of thinking that there is any one particular nation that can be completely identified with this hypothetical land. The characteristics to be discussed can come into existence here. Some of Totalitaria's characteristics were, of course, present in Nazi Germany, and they can today be found behind the Iron Curtain, but they exist to some extent in other parts of the world as well. Totalitaria is any country in which political ideas degenerate into senseless formulations made only for propaganda purposes. It is any country in which a single group—left or right—acquires absolute power and becomes omniscient and omnipotent, any country in which disagreement and differences of opinion are crimes, in which utter conformity is the price of life.

Totalitaria—the Leviathan state—is the home of the political system we call, euphemistically, totalitarianism, of which systematized tyranny is a part. This system does not derive from any honest political philosophy, either socialist or capitalist. Totalitaria's leaders may mouth ideologies, but these are in fact mainly catchwords used to justify the regime. If necessary, totalitarianism can change its slogans and its behavior overnight. For totalitarianism embodies, to me, the quest for total power, the quest of a dictator to rule the world. The words and concepts of "socialism" and "communism" may serve, like "democracy," as a disguise for the megalomaniac intention of the tyrant.

Since totalitarianism is essentially the social manifestation of a psychological phenomenon belonging to every personality, it can best be understood in terms of the human forces that create, foster, and perpetuate it. Man has two faces; he wants to grow toward maturity and freedom, and yet the primitive child in his unconscious yearns for complete protection and irresponsibility. His mature self learns how to cope with the restrictions and frustrations of daily life, but at the same time, the child in him longs to hit out against them, to beat them down, to destroy them—whether they be objects or people. Totalitarianism appeals to this confused infant in all of us; it seems to offer a solution to the problems man's double yearning creates. Our mythical Totalitaria is a monolithic and absolute state in which doubt, confusion, and conflict are not permitted to be shown, for the dictator purports to solve all his subjects' problems for them. In addition, Totalitaria can provide official sanction for the expression of man's most antisocial impulses. The uncivilized child hidden in us may welcome this liberation from ethical frustrations.

On the other hand, our free, mature, social selves cannot be happy in Totalitaria; they revolt against the restriction of individual impulses.

The psychological roots of totalitarianism are usually irrational, destructive, and primitive, though disguised behind some ideology, and for this reason there is something fantastic, unbelievable, even nightmarish about the system itself. There is, of course, a difference in the psychic experience of the elite, who can live out their needs for power, and the masses, who have to submit; yet the two groups influence each other. When a dictator's deep neurotic needs for power also satisfy some profound emotional need in the population of his country, especially in times of misery or after a revolution, he is more easily able to assume the power for which he longs. If a nation has suffered defeat in war, for example, its citizens feel shame and resentment. Loss of face is not simply a political abstraction, it is a very real and personal thing to a conquered people; every man, consciously or unconsciously, identifies with his native land. If a country suffers from prolonged famine or severe depression, its citizens become bitter, depressed, and resentful, and will more willingly accept the visions and promises of the aspiring dictator. If the complexity of a country's political and economic apparatus makes the individual citizen feel powerless, confused, and useless, if he has no sense of participation in the forces that govern his daily life, or if he feels these forces to be so vast and confusing that he can no longer understand them, he will grasp at the totalitarian opportunity for belonging, for participation, for a simple formula that explains and rationalizes what is beyond his comprehension. And when the dictator has taken over finally, he transfers his own abnormal fantasies, his rage and anger, easily to his subjects. Their resentments feed his; his pseudo-strength encourages them. A mutual fortification of illusions takes place.

Totalitarianism as a social manifestation is a disease of inter-human relations, and, like any other disease, man can best resist its corroding effects if, through knowledge and training, he is well immunized against it. If, however, he is unfortunate enough to catch the totalitarian bug, he has to muster all the positive forces in his mind to defeat it. The raging internal struggle between the irresponsible child and the mature adult in him continues until one or the other is finally destroyed completely. As long as a single spark of either remains, the battle goes on. And for as long as man is alive, the quest for maturity keeps on.

Cultural Predilection for Totalitarianism

In the battle against this dread disease, social factors as well as personal ones play an important role. We can see this more clearly if we analyze the ways in which the ideals of a culture as a whole affect its citizens' vulnerability to totalitarianism. The ethics of our own Western civilization are our strongest defenses against the disease, for the ideal of these ethics is to produce a breed of men and women who are strongly individualistic and who evaluate situations primarily in terms of their own consciences. We aim to develop in our citizens a sense of self-responsibility, a willingness to confront the world as it is, and an ability to distinguish between right and wrong through their own feelings and thoughts. Such men and women are impelled to action by their personal moral standards rather than by what some outside group sets up as correct. They are unwilling to accept group evaluations immediately unless these coincide with their own personal convictions, or unless they have been able to discuss them in a democratic way. People like this are responsible to their communities because they are first responsible to themselves. If they disagree, they will form a *loyal minority*, using their rights of convincing other people at appropriate times.

There are other cultures which emphasize attitudes and values that are different from these. The Eastern ideal of man, as we find it in China and some of the other Oriental countries, is in the first place that of *oneness*, of being one with the family, one with the fatherland, one with the cosmos—nirvana. The Oriental psyche looks for a direct esthetic contact with reality through an indefinable empathy and intuition. Eternal truth is behind reality, behind the veil of Maya. Man is part of the universe; his ideal is passive servility and nonirritability. His ideal of peace lies in rest and relaxation, in meditation, in being without manual and mental travail. The happiness of the Oriental psyche lies in the ecstasy of feeling united with the universal cosmos. Ascesis, self-redemption, and poverty are better realized ideals in Oriental culture than in our Western society. The classic Oriental culture pattern can best be described as a pattern of participation. In it the individual is looked upon as an integral part of the group, the family, the caste, the nation. He is not a separate, independent entity. In this culture, greater conformity to and acceptance of the collective rules are the ideals. An Oriental child may be trained from infancy into a pattern of submission to authority and to the rules of the group. Many primitive cultures also display this pattern. To a person raised in these cultures, the most acceptable standards, the best conceivable thoughts and actions, are those sanctioned by the group. The totalitarian world of mass actions and mass thoughts is far more comprehensible to the members of a participation-patterned and less individual-minded culture than it is to Western individualists. What is to us unbearable regimentation and authoritarianism may be to them comforting order and regularity.

An example of an intensified pattern of participation and thought control and mutual spying has been given by the anthropologist E. P. Dozier.* The Pueblo Indians of the Rio Grande area believe that wrongdoing or wrong thinking of one man in the tribe affects all members. He may upset the cosmic balance by ill feeling toward any one of his fellow men. The moral code of the village is group-centered. The individual who transgresses this jeopardizes the well-being of all. Epidemics, crop failures, droughts are interpreted as a result of "deviationism" of one member of the group. Village members are closely watched and spied on in order to discover the culprit or "witch." Gossip and accusations of witchcraft are rampant, and the Pueblo Indian is constantly searching in his own conscience for harmful thoughts and attitudes. It is as if we watch the ritual of the purge in the totalitarian state.†

Such forms of *creeping collectivism* and participation we may see in every group formation where tolerance for nonconformism ceases to exist. Wherever dogmatic partisanship dominates, the mind is coerced. We may even detect such encroaching tendencies in some scientific circles where there exists an overemphasis on group research, teamwork, membership cards, and a disdain for individual opinion.

The culture into which a man is born and his own psychological constitution interact to produce his personality in much the same way as his body and mind interact to produce his behavior. Our culture of individual freedom may offer us a partial immunity to the disease of totalitarianism, but at the same time our personal immaturities and repressed savageries can make us vulnerable to it. The participation type of culture may make men more susceptible in general to totalitarianism, although personal strivings toward maturity and individuality can offer them, too, some measure of protection against it.

* *The New York Times,* December 11, 1955; *Science News Letter,* December 3, 1955.
† See Chapter Seven.

Because of the interaction between these social and personal forces, no culture is completely safe from internal attack by totalitarianism and from the mental destruction it may create. As I said before, our Totalitaria is a mythical country, but the brutal truth is that any country can be turned into a Totalitaria.

The aims of the rulers of our fictitious country are simply formulated: despotism, the total domination of man and mankind, and the unity of the entire world under one dictatorial authority. At first glance, this idea of unity can be most attractive—the idea, oversimplified, of a brotherhood unity of nations under a central powerful agency. When the world is one, it would seem, there will be no more war, the tensions that face us will be eliminated, earth will become a paradise, but the simplified conception of a universal dictatorship is false and reflects the danger inherent in the totalitarian goal: all men are different, and it is the difference between them that creates the greatness, the variety, and the creative inspirations of life, as well as the tensions of social intercourse. The totalitarian conception of equalization can be realized only in death, when the chemical and physical laws that govern all of us take over completely. Death is indeed the great equalizer.

In life, all of us are different. Our bodies and minds interact with one another and with the outside world in different ways. Each man's personality is unique. True, all of us share certain basic human qualities with all the other members of the human race, but the differences in personality are also so many and so varied that no two men anywhere in the world or ever in all of human history can be said to be exactly alike. This uniqueness is as true of the citizen of Totalitaria as it is of anyone else. As a human being, he is not only different from us, he is different from his compatriots. However, to create man in the totalitarian image through leveling and equalization means to suppress what is essentially personal and human in him, the uniqueness and the variety, and to create a society of robots, not men. The noted social scientist, J. S. Brunner, in his introduction to Bauer's book on Soviet psychology has expressed this thought in a different way: "Man's image of the nature of man is not only a matter for objective inquiry; it is and has always been a prime instrument of social and political control. He who molds that image does so with enormous consequences for the society in which he lives."

Totalitaria fosters the illusion that everyone is part of the government, a voter; no one can be a non-voter or anti-voter. His inner pros and cons and doubts are not private problems of the individual himself any more; his thoughts belong to the state, the dictator, the ruling circle, the Party. His inner thoughts have to be controlled. Only those in power know what really lies behind national policy. The ordinary citizen becomes as dependent and obedient as a child. In exchange for giving up his individuality, he obtains some special gratifications: the feeling of belonging and of being protected, the sense of relief over losing his personal boundaries and responsibilities, the ecstasy of being taken up and absorbed in wild, uncontrolled collective feelings, the safety of being anonymous, of being merely a cog in the wheel of the all-powerful state.

The despotism of modern Totalitaria is very different from the lush, exotic personal tyrannies of ancient times. It is an ascetic, cold, mechanical force, aiming at what Hanna Ahrendt calls the "transformation of human nature itself." In our theoretical country, man has no individual ego any longer, no personality, no self. A leveling system is at work, and everything above the common level is trampled on and beaten down.

The Totalitarian Leader

The leaders of Totalitaria are the strangest men in the state. These men are, like all other men, unique in their mental structure, and consequently we cannot make any blanket psychiatric diagnosis of the mental illness which motivates their behavior. But we can make some generalizations which will help us toward some understanding of the totalitarian leader. Obviously, for example, he suffers from an overwhelming need to control other human beings and to exert unlimited power, and this in itself is a psychological aberration, often rooted in deep-seated feelings of anxiety, humiliation, and inferiority. The ideologies such men propound are only used as tactical and strategical devices through which they hope to reach their final goal of complete domination over other men. This domination may help them compensate for pathological fears and feelings of unworthiness, as we can conclude from the psychological study of some modern dictators.

Fortunately, we do not have to rely on a purely hypothetical picture of the psychopathology of the totalitarian dictator. Dr. G. M. Gilbert, who studied some of the leaders of Nazi Germany during the Nuremberg trials, has given us a useful insight into their twisted minds, useful especially because it reveals to us something about the mutual interaction between the totalitarian leader and those who want to be led by him.

Hitler's suicide made a clinical investigation of his character structure impossible, but Dr. Gilbert heard many eyewitness reports of Hitler's behavior from his friends and collaborators, and these present a fantastic picture of Nazism's prime mover. Hitler was known among his intimates as the carpet-eater, because he often threw himself on the floor in a kicking and screaming fit like an epileptic rage. From such reports, Dr. Gilbert was able to deduce something about the roots of the pathological behavior displayed by this morbid "genius." Hitler's paranoid hostility against the Jew was partly related to his unresolved parental conflicts; the Jews probably symbolized for him the hated drunken father who mistreated Hitler and his mother when the future *Fuhrer* was still a child. Hitler's obsessive thinking, his furious fanaticism, his insistence on maintaining the purity of "Aryan blood," and his ultimate mania to destroy himself and the world were obviously the results of a sick psyche. As early as 1923, nearly ten years before he seized power, Hitler was convinced that he would one day rule the world, and he spent time designing monuments of victory, eternalizing his glory, to be erected all over the European continent when the day of victory arrived. This delusional preoccupation continued until the end of his life; in the midst of the war he created, which led him to defeat and death, Hitler continued revising and improving his architectural plans.

Nazi dictator Number Two, Hermann Goering, who committed suicide to escape the hangman, had a different psychological structure. His pathologically aggressive drives were encouraged by the archaic military tradition of the German Junker class, to which his family belonged. From early childhood he had been compulsively and overtly aggressive. He was an autocratic and a corrupt cynic, grasping the Nazi-created opportunity to achieve purely personal gain. His contempt for the "common people" was unbounded; this was a man who had literally no sense of moral values.

Quite different again was Rudolf Hess, the man of passive yet fanatical doglike devotion, living, as it were, by proxy through the mind of his *Führer*. His inner mental weakness made it easier for him to live through means of a proxy than through his own personality, and drove him to become the shadow of a seemingly strong man, from whom he could borrow strength. The Nazi ideology gave this frustrated boy the illusion of blood identification with the glorious German race. After his wild flight to England, Hess showed obvious psychotic traits; his delusions of persecution, hysterical attacks, and periods of amnesia are among the well-known clinical symptoms of schizophrenia.

Still another type was Hans Frank, the devil's advocate, the prototype of the overambitious latent homosexual, easily seduced into political adventure, even when this was in conflict with the remnants of his conscience. For unlike Goering, Frank was capable of distinguishing between right and wrong.

Dr. Gilbert also tells us something about General Wilhelm Keitel, Hitler's Chief of Staff, who became the submissive, automatic mouthpiece of the *Führer,* mixing military honor and personal ambition in the service of his own unimportance.

Of a different quality is the S. S. Colonel, Hoess, the murderer of millions in the concentration camp of Auschwitz. A pathological character structure is obvious in this case. All his life, Hoess had been a lonely, withdrawn, schizoid personality, without any conscience, wallowing in his own hostile and destructive fantasies. Alone and bereft of human attachments, he was intuitively sought out by Himmler for this most savage of all the Nazi jobs. He was a useful instrument for the committing of the most bestial deeds.

Unfortunately, we have no clear psychiatric picture yet of the Russian dictator Stalin. There have been several reports that during the last years of his life he had a tremendous persecution phobia and lived in constant terror that he would become the victim of his own purges.

Psychological analysis of these men shows clearly that a pathological culture—a mad world—can be built by certain impressive psychoneurotic types. The venal political figures need not even comprehend the social and political consequences of their behavior. They are compelled not by ideological belief, no matter how much they may rationalize to convince themselves they are, but by the distortions of their own personalities. They are not motivated by their advertised urge to serve their country or mankind, but rather by an overwhelming need and compulsion to satisfy the cravings of their own pathological character structures. The ideologies they spout are not real goals; they are the cynical devices by which these sick men hope to achieve some personal sense of worth and power. Subtle inner lies seduce them into going from bad to worse. Defensive self-deception, arrested insight, evasion of emotional identification with others, degradation of empathy—the mind has many defense mechanisms with which to blind the conscience. A clear example of this can be seen in the way the Nazi leaders defended themselves through continuous self-justification and exculpation when they were brought before the bar at the Nuremberg trials. These murderers were aggrieved and hurt by the accusations brought against them; they were the very picture of injured innocence.

Any form of leadership, if unchecked by controls, may gradually turn into dictatorship. Being a leader, carrying great power and responsibility for other people's lives, is a monumental test for the human psyche. The weak leader is the man who cannot meet it, who simply abdicates his responsibility. The dictator is the man who replaces the existing standards of justice and morality by more and more private prestige, by more and more power, and eventually isolates himself more and more from the rest of humanity. His suspicion grows, his isolation grows, and the vicious circle leading to a paranoid attitude begins to develop.

The dictator is not only a sick man, he is also a cruel opportunist. He sees no value in any other person and feels no gratitude for any help he may have received. He is suspicious and dishonest and believes that his personal ends justify any means he may use to achieve them. Peculiarly enough, every tyrant still searches for some self-justification. Without such a soothing device for his own conscience, he cannot live. His attitude toward other people is manipulative; to him, they are merely tools for the advancement of his own interests. He rejects the conception of doubt, of internal contradictions, of man's inborn ambivalence. He denies the psychological fact that man grows to maturity through groping, through trial and error, through the interplay of contrasting feelings. Because he will not permit himself to grope, to learn through trial and error, the dictator can never become a mature person. But whether he acknowledges them or not, he has internal conflicts, he suffers somewhere from internal confusion. These inner "weaknesses" he tries to repress sternly; if they were to come to the surface, they might interfere with the achievement of his goals. Yet, in the attacks of rage his weakening strength is evident.

It is because the dictator is afraid, albeit unconsciously, of his own internal contradictions, that he is afraid of the same internal contradictions of his fellow men. He must purge and purge, terrorize and terrorize in order to still his own raging inner drives. He must kill every doubter, destroy every person who makes a mistake, imprison everyone who cannot be proved to be utterly single-minded. In Totalitaria, the latent aggression and savagery in man are cultivated by the dictator to such a degree that they can explode into the mass criminal actions shown by Hitler's persecution of minorities. Ultimately, the country shows a real pathology, an utter dominance of destructive and self-destructive tendencies.

The Final Surrender of the Robot Man

What happens to the common man in such a culture? How can we describe the citizen of Totalitaria? Perhaps the simplest answer to this question lies in the statement that he is reduced to the mechanical precision of an insectlike state. He cannot develop any warm friendships, loyalties, or allegiances because they may be too dangerous for him. Today's friend may be, after all, tomorrow's enemy. Living in an atmosphere of constant suspicion—not only of strangers, but even of his own family—he is afraid to express himself lest concentration camp or prison swallow him up. The citizens of Totalitaria do not really converse with one another. When they speak, they whisper, first looking furtively over their shoulders for the inevitable spy. Their inner silence is in sharp contrast to the official verbal bombardment. The citizens of Totalitaria may make noise, and utter polite banalities, or they may repeat slogans to one another, but they say nothing. Existing literature reveals that leading authors, among them H. G. Wells, Huxley, and Orwell, grow more and more concerned about the ghastly future of the robotized man, trained as a machine on a standard of conformity. They translate for us the common fear of a mechanized civilization.

In Totalitaria, the citizen no longer knows the real core of his mind. He no longer feels himself an *I*, an ego, a person. He is only the object of official barrage and mental coercion. Having no personality of his own, he has no individual conscience, no personal morality, no capacity to think clearly and honestly. He learns by rote, he learns thousands of indoctrinated facts and inhales dogma and slogans with every breath he draws. He becomes an obedient pedant, and pedantry makes people into something resembling pots filled with information instead of individuals with free, growing personalities. Becoming wiser and freer implies selective forgetting and changes of mind. This we accept, this we leave behind. Alert adjustment requires a change of patterns, the capacity to be deconditioned, to undo and unlearn in order to become ripe for new patterns. The citizen of Totalitaria has no chance for such learning through unlearning, for growth through individual experience. Official oversimplifications induce the captive audience into acceptance and indoctrination. Mass ecstasy and mass fanaticism are substituted for quiet individual thought and consideration. Hitler taught his people to march and to do battle, and at the end they did not know wherefore they marched and battled. People become herds—indoctrinated and obsessed herds—intoxicated first with enthusiasm and happy expectations, then with terror and panic. The individual personality cannot grow in Totalitaria. The huge mass of citizens is tamed into personal and political somnambulism.

It may be scientifically questionable to compare experiences gained from individual pathological states with social phenomena and to analyze the partial collapse of the ego under totalitarianism by analogy with actual cases of madness. But there is in fact much that is comparable between the strange reactions of the citizens of Totalitaria and their culture as a whole on the one hand and the reactions of the introverted, sick schizophrenic on the other. Even though the problem of schizophrenic behavior in individuals and groups is extremely complicated and cannot be fully handled within the scope of this book, the comparison can be helpful in our search for an understanding of the nature and effects of totalitarianism.

The Common Retreat from Reality

This excursion into the world of pathology is not a description of a merely coincidental resemblance between a disease and a political system. It should serve to point up the fact that totalitarian withdrawal behind official justifications and individual fantasy is something that can occur either in social life or inside the individual mind. And many scholars believe in a relationship between cultural deterioration and schizophrenic withdrawal.

Let us briefly explain the individual schizophrenic's reaction of complete inner automatization and mental withdrawal as a personal failure to adjust to a world experienced as insecure and dangerous. Often rather simple emotional incidents may lead to such schizophrenic retreat—for instance, the intrusion of schedules and habits forced on the mind during infancy or a sly hypersensitivity to our overactive and ototverbose culture. Many a child is forced into schizophrenic withdrawal by an overcompulsive parent. Sometimes lack of external contact may drive a man into a state of utter loneliness and isolation, sometimes his own preference for solitude. A certain tendency to so-called schizophrenic withdrawal has been proved to be inborn. Yet it can be provoked in everybody. Whatever the cause, the schizophrenic patient becomes a desocialized being, lost in loneliness. Conscious and unconscious fantasy life begins to become dominant over alert confrontation of reality. In the end his weird fantasies become more real for the schizophrenic than the actual world. He hides more and more behind his own iron curtain, in the imaginary dreamland and retreat he has built for himself. This is his nirvana, in which all his dream wishes are fulfilled. Inertia and fanaticism alternate. The patient regresses to an infantile, vegetative form of behavior and rejects everything that society has taught him. In his fantasy, he lives in a world which always obeys his commands. He is omnipotent. The world turns around according to his divine inclinations. Reality, requiring as it does, continual and renewed adjustment and verification, becomes a persecutor, attacking his illusion of divine might. Every disturbing intrusion into his delusional world is encountered by the schizophrenic either with tremendous aggression or with the formation of secondary delusion to protect the first delusion, or with a combination of both. The schizophrenic displays tremendous hostility toward the real world and its representatives; reality robs him both of his delusions of omnipotence and his hallucinatory sense of being utterly protected, as he was in the womb.

Clinical experience has shown that the disease of schizophrenia often begins with negativism—a defense against the influence of others, a continual fight against mental intrusion, against what is felt as the rape of the oversensitive mind. Gradually this defensive attitude toward the world becomes a hostile attitude toward everything, not only toward influences from the outside, but also toward thoughts and feelings from the inside. Finally, the victim becomes paralyzed by his own hostility and negativisms. He behaves literally as though he were dead. He sits, unmoving, for hours. He may have to be force-fed, force-dressed. The schizophrenic moves like a puppet on a string, only when someone compels him to. Clinically, we call this catatonia—the death attitude.

The Retreat to Automatization

Introverted schizophrenics prefer the automatic routine life of the asylum to life in the outside world, on the condition that they be allowed to indulge their private fantasies. They surrender utterly to self-defeatism. They never congregate in groups, they seldom talk with one another; even when they do, they never have any real mutual contact. Each one lives in his own retreat.

In the totalitarian myth—think, for instance, of *das Dritte Reich* —in the psychological folklore of our mythical state, the vague fantasy of the technically perfected womb, the ideal nirvana, plays a tremendous role. In a world full of insecurities, a world requiring continual alert adjustment and readjustment, Totalitaria creates the delusion of the omnipotent, miraculous ideal state—a state where, in its final form, every material need will be satisfied. Everything will be regulated, just as it was for the fetus in the womb, the land of bliss and equanimity, just as it is for the schizophrenic in the mental hospital. There is no social struggle, no mental struggle; the world moves like clockwork. There is no real interplay between people, no clash of opinions or beliefs, there is no emotional relationship between these womb-fellows; each exists as a separate number-bearing entity in the same filing system. In Totalitaria, there is no faith in fellow men, no *caritas,* no love, because real relationships between men do not exist, just as they do not exist between schizophrenics. There is only faith in and subjection to the feeding system, and there is in every citizen a tremendous fear of being expelled from that system, a fear of being totally lost, comparable with the schizophrenic's feeling of rejection and fear of reality. In the midst of spiritual loneliness and isolation, there is the fear of still greater loneliness, of more painful isolation. Without protective regulations from the outside, internal hell may break loose. Strong mechanical external order must be used to cover the internal chaos and approaching breakdown.

We have had experience in postwar years with several refugees from the totalitarian world who broke down when they had to cope with a world of freedom where personal initiative was required. The fear of freedom brought them to a state of panic. They no longer had strong enough egos to build and maintain their defenses against the competitive demands of free democratic reality. As in schizophrenia, a maneuverable and individual ego cannot exist in Totalitaria. In schizophrenia the ego shrinks as a result of withdrawal, in Totalitaria, as a result of constant merging in mass feelings. If such a shrunken ego should grow up, with its own critical attitude, its needs for verification of facts and for understanding, it would then be beaten down as being treacherous and nonconforming.

Totalitaria requires of its citizens complete subjection to and identification with the leader. It is this leader-dominance that makes people nearly ego-less, as they are in schizophrenia. This again may result in loss of control of hostile and destructive drives. Psychologists have seen this time and time again in what we can call the concentration-camp psyche. When the victims first came to the camp—dedicated to their gradual extermination—most of them displayed a complete loss of self, an utter depersonalization, combined with apathy and loss of awareness. The same observations have been made among our P.O.W.'s in Korea. Some concentration-camp victims got better immediately after their return to a normal society; in others, this schizophrenic reaction of lost ego remained and, as we mentioned above, sometimes developed into a real psychosis.

The Womb State

Totalitarianism is man's escape from the fearful realities of life into the virtual womb of the leader. The individual's actions are directed from this womb—from the inner sanctum. The mystic center is in control of everything; man need no longer assume responsibility for his own life. The order and logic of the prenatal world reign. There is peace and silence, the peace of utter submission. The members of the womb state do not really communicate; between them there is silence, the silence of possible betrayal, not the mature silence of reticence and reservedness. Totalitaria increases the gap between the things one shows and communicates and the things one secretly dreams and thinks deep within oneself. It develops the artificial split-mindedness of political silence. Whatever little remains of individual feeling and opinion is kept carefully enclosed. In the schizophrenic world of Totalitaria, there is no free mutual exchange, no conversation, no exclamation, no release from emotional tension. It is a world of silent conspirators. Indeed, the atmosphere of suspicion is the big attacker of mental freedom because it makes people cling together, conspiring against mysterious enemies—first from outside, then among themselves.

In Totalitaria each citizen is continually watched. The mythical state molds the individual's conscience. He has hardly any of his own. His neighbors watch him, his postman, his children, and they all represent the punishing state, just as he himself must represent the state and watch others. Not betraying them is a crime.

The need to find conspiracies, to discover persecutors and criminals is another schizophrenic manifestation. It is psychologically related to an infantile need for a feeling of omnipotence. Megalomaniac feelings grow better in an atmosphere of mysterious secrecy.

Secrecy and conspiracy increase the delusion of power. That is why so many people like to pry into other people's lives and to play the spy.

This feeling of conspiracy also lies behind the pathological struggle with imaginary persecutors, a struggle we find both in mentally ill individuals and in our mythical Totalitaria. "It is there!" "It is chasing us!" All the inner fears of losing the nirvanic womb-illusion become rampant. Mysterious ghosts and vultures chase people out of nirvana and paradise.

In these fantasies, the patriarch, the dictator, the idol, becomes both the universal danger and the omnipotent savior at the same time. Not even the citizens of Totalitaria really love this cruel giant. Suspicion against the breast that feeds and the hand that guides and forbids is often found in the phantasy of schizophrenic children, who experience the nourisher as the enemy, the dominating ogre, bribing the growing mind into submission.

The deep hate the sick individual feels toward the parental figure cannot be expressed directly, and so it is displaced onto the self or onto scapegoats. Scapegoatism is also part of the totalitarian strategy. As we pointed out before, the scapegoat temporarily absorbs all the individual's inner fury and rage. Kulaks, Negroes, Jews, Communists, capitalists, profiteers and warmongers—any or all of them can play that role. Perhaps the greatest dangers, to the totalitarian mind, is the use of intellect and awareness and the "egghead's" demand for free, verifying thinking. Aberration and perversion are chosen by the citizens of Totalitaria, as they are by the inhabitants of madhouses, over tiring, intellectual control.

In the center of the totalitarian fears and fantasies stands the man-eating god and idol. He is unconquerable. He uses man's great gift of adjustment to bring him to slavery. Every man's inner core of feelings and thoughts has to belong to the leader.

Is the citizen of Totalitaria consciously aware of this? Probably not. Modern psychology has taught us how strongly the mental mechanism of denial of reality works. The eye bypasses external occurrences when the mind does not want them to happen. Secondary justifications and fantasies are formed to support and explain these denials. In Totalitaria we find the same despising of reality facts as we do in schizophrenia. How else are we to explain the fact that Hitler was still moving his armies on paper after they were already defeated?

Totalitarian strategy covers inner chaos and conflict by the strict order of the police state. So does the compulsive schizophrenic patient, by his inner routine and schedules. These routines and schedules are a defense against painful occurrences in external reality. This internal robotization may lead to denial of internal realities and internal needs as well. The citizen of Totalitaria, repressing and rejecting his inner need for freedom, may even experience slavery as liberation. He may go even one step further—yearn for an escape from life itself, a delusion that he could become omnipotent through utter destruction. The S. S. soldiers called this the magic action of the *Blutkitt,* the tie of bloody crime binding them together and preparing them for Valhalla. With this magic unification, they could die with courage and equanimity. Anarchic despair and need for greatness alternated in them as they do in the psychotic patient. In the same way, the citizens of Totalitaria search for a "heroic" place in history even though the price be doom and annihilation.

Many soldiers—tired by the rigidities of normal life—look back at violent moments of their war experiences, despite the hunger and terror, as the monumental culminating experiences of their lives. There, in the *Bruderbund* of fighters, they felt happy for the first and only times in their lives (Dicks).

This all sounds like a bitter comedy, but the fantasy of schizophrenics has taught us how the mind can retreat into delusion when there is a fear of daily existence. Under these circumstances, fantasy begins to prevail over reality, and soon assumes a validity which reality never had. The totalitarian mind is like the schizophrenic mind; it has a contempt for reality. Think for a moment of Lysenko's theory and its denial of the influence of heredity. The totalitarian mind does not observe and verify its impressions of reality; it dictates to reality how it shall behave, it compels reality to conform to its fantasies.

The comparison between totalitarianism and psychosis is not incidental. Delusional thinking inevitably creeps into every form of tyranny and despotism. Unconscious backward forces come into action. Evil powers from the archaic past return. An automatic compulsion to go on to self-destruction develops, to justify one mistake with a new one; to enlarge and expand the vicious pathological circle becomes the dominating end of life. The frightened man, burdened by a culture he does not understand, retreats into the brute's fantasy of limitless power in order to cover up the vacuum inside himself. This fantasy starts with the leaders and is later taken over by the masses they oppress.

What else can man do when he is caught in that tremendous machine called Totalitaria? Thinking—and the brain itself—has become superfluous, that is, only reserved for the elite. Man has to renounce his uniqueness, his individual personality, and must surrender to the equalizing and homogenizing patterns of so-called integration and standardization. This arouses in him that great inner emptiness of the savage child, the emptiness of the robot that unwittingly yearns for the great destruction.

🔖

CHAPTER SEVEN

The Intrusion by
Totalitarian Thinking

🔖

In order to investigate the social forces at work undermining the free individual development of man's mind, we have to look at manifold aspects of political life. As a clinician and polypragmatist, I don't want to bind myself to one political state or current, but want to describe what can be experienced in social life everywhere. Where human thinking and human habits are in the process of being remolded, they are under the influence of tremendous politi-cal upheaval. In one country this may happen overnight, in others more slowly. The psychologists' task is to observe and describe the impact of these processes on the human mind.

When once a nation is under the yoke of totalitarianism, when once its people have succumbed to the oversimplifications and blandishments of the would-be dictator, how does the leader maintain his power? What techniques does he use to make his countrymen docile followers of his bloody regime?

Because man's mature self resists totalitarianism, the dictator must work and scheme constantly to keep his subjects in line and to immobilize their need for individual development, rebellion, and healthy growth. As we examine his techniques, we will come to a better understanding of totalitarianism and of the interaction between the dictator's methods and the personalities of his subjects. We need this understanding desperately, for we have to recognize

125

that the forces in Totalitaria that make humorless robots out of living men can also develop, albeit unwittingly, in the so-called free, democratic societies.

The Strategy of Terror

The weapon of terror has been used by tyrants from time immemorial to make a meek instrument of man. In Totalitaria, the use of this weapon is refined to a science which can wipe out all opposition and dissent. The leaders of Totalitaria rule by intimidation; they prefer loyalty through fear to loyalty through faith. Fear and terror freeze the mind and will; they may create a general psychic paralysis. In the panic caused by totalitarian terror, men feel separated from one another as by an impassable vacuum, and each man becomes a lonely, frightened soul. Even panicky hovering together could be suspected of being conspiracy against the state. Separated from any real emotional contact with his fellow men by his own inner isolation, the citizen of Totalitaria becomes increasingly unable to fight against its dehumanizing influences.

Totalitaria is constantly on the alert for social sinners, the critics of the system, and accusation of dissent is equivalent to conviction in the public eye. Insinuation, calumny, and denunciation are staples of the totalitarian strategy. The entire nation is dedicated to the proposition that every man is a potential enemy of the regime. No one is excluded from the terror. Any man may be subjected to it no matter how high his rank.

The secret police create awe and panic inside the country, while the army serves to create awe and panic outside. Just the thought of an outbreak of terror—of even a possible future terror—makes men unwilling to express their opinions and expose themselves. Both the citizens of Totalitaria and those of her neighbors are affected by this general fear. A clear example of how this fear paralysis operates in reality may be seen in the fact that as far back as 1948 western Europeans, who felt the shadow of anticipated totalitarian occupation, thought it safer to criticize and attack their American friends than to find fault with a totalitarian enemy who might sweep in suddenly and without warning.

In Totalitaria, jails and concentration camps by the score are built in order to provoke fear and awe among the population. They may be called "punishment" or "correction" camps, but this is only a cheap justification for the truth. In these centers of fear, nobody is really corrected; he is, as it were, expelled from humanity, wasted, killed—but not too quickly, lest the terrorizing influence be diminished. The truth of the matter is that these jails are built not for real criminals, but rather for their terrorizing effect on the bystanders, the citizens of Totalitaria. Jails represent a permanent menace, a continual threat. They put an almost insupportable strain on the empathy and imagination of those citizens who are, temporarily at least, on the outside of the barbed wire. In addition to the fear of undergoing the same cruel treatment, the fear of abasement, humiliation, and death, the very concept of the concentration camp rouses every man's deep-seated fear of being himself expelled from the community, of being alone, a wanderer in the desert, unloved and unwanted.

There exist several milder forms of mass terror, for instance, *the strategy of no political rest*. In Totalitaria man is always caught by some form of official planning. He is always conscious of control and surveillance, of spying, leering powers lying in wait to chase him and to punish him. Even leisure time and holidays are occupied by some official program, some facts to be learned, some political meeting, some parade. Quiet and solitude no longer exist. There is no time for meditation, for pondering, for reminiscing. The mind is caught in a web of official thinking and planning. Even the delights of self-chosen silence are forbidden. Every citizen of Totalitaria must join in the singing and the slogan shouting. And he becomes so caught in the constant activity that he loses the capacity to realize what is happening to him.

The emphasis on more production by individuals, factories, and agricultural enterprises also can become a weapon of increased control and terror. The Stakhanovite movement in Russia, urging a constant increase in production norms, became a threat for many. The workers had to increase the pace of their labor and production, or they would be severely punished. The emphasis on pace and speed makes man more and more a soulless cog in the totalitarian wheel.

Terror can almost never stop itself; it thrives on compliance and grows in a vacuum. Terror as a tool means a gradual transfer into terror as a goal—but terror is actually a self-defeating strategy. Man will ultimately revolt even under an absolute dictatorship. When men have been reduced to puppethood by Totalitaria, they will finally have become immune to all threats. The magic spell of terror will finally lose its force. First the citizens of Totalitaria will become dulled to the terror and will no longer consider even death a danger. Then a few will initiate the final revolt, for Totalitaria's government by fear and terror fosters internal rebellion, in the few who cannot be broken down. Even in *gleichgeschaltet* Nazi Germany a resistance movement was active.

The Purging Rituals

Cleaning out the higher echelons of government is an old historic habit. The struggle between fathers and sons, between the older and the younger generation, became ritualized far back in prehistoric times. Frazer's classic, *The Golden Bough,* has told us a great deal about this. The ancient priest of the heathens acquired his high post by killing his predecessor. Later in history, the newly proclaimed king offered criminals instead as sacrifices to the gods on the day of his anointment.

In Totalitaria, the killing and purging ritual is part of the mechanism of government, and it serves not only a symbolic but also a very real function for the dictator. He must eliminate all those he has bypassed and double-crossed in his ruthless climb to power, lest their resentments and frustrated rage break out, endangering his position or even his life.

The purge reflects another characteristic of life in Totalitaria. It dramatizes the fiction that the party is always on the alert to keep itself pure and clean. Psychiatry has demonstrated that the cleanliness compulsion in neurotic individuals is actually a displaced defense against their own inner rage and hostility. It plays the same sort of role in communities, and when it is elevated to the level of an officially sanctioned ritual, it reduces the citizenry to infancy. It makes the inhabitants of Totalitaria feel like babies—still struggling to learn their first toilet training habits, still listening to their parent's reiterated commands to be clean, be clean, be clean, be good, be good, be good, be loyal, be loyal, be loyal. The constant repetition of these commands reinforces each citizen's sense of guilt, of childishness, and of shame.

The totalitarian purge is always accompanied by an elaborate confession ceremonial, in which the accused publicly repents his sins, much as did the witches of the Middle Ages (Lea). This is the general formula: "I confess my doubts. Thanks to the criticism of the comrades, I have been able to purify my thinking. I bow in humility to the opinion of my comrades and the Party and am thankful for the opportunity to correct my errors. You enabled me to repudiate my deviational questions. I acknowledge my debt to the selfless leader and the government of the people."

This stategy of public expression of shame has two effects: it serves, like the purging rituals themselves, to provoke feelings of childish submissiveness among the people, and, at the same time, it offers each citizen a defense against his own deep-seated psychological problems and feelings of guilt and unworthiness. Somewhere deep inside him, the citizen of Totalitaria knows that he has abdicated his maturity and his responsibility; public purgings relieve his sense of shame. "It is the others, who are guilty and dirty, not I," he thinks. "It is they who are constantly plotting and conniving." But the very things of which he suspects others are also true of himself. He is afraid others will betray him because he cannot be sure in his own mind that he will not betray them. Thus his inner tensions increase, and the purge provides a periodic blood offering to his own fear and to the god of threat.

The very fact that this ritual of coercive confession and purge must be repeated again and again indicates that man develops an inner mental defense against it and that the more it is used, the less effective it becomes as a means of arousing guilt and terror. Just as the citizen of Totalitaria becomes hardened or dulled to the terror of constant official intrusion into his private life, so he becomes almost immune to the cries of treason and sabotage.

In the same way, as the purge becomes less effective as a taming tool, the tyrant uses it more frequently to soothe his own fears. History provides us with many examples of revolutions which eventually drowned in a bloody reign of terror and purge. Some of the most devoted heroes and leaders of the French Revolution met their death on the guillotine of the republic they helped to create.

Wild Accusation and Black Magic

Wild accusation and black magic, like all the other taming tools of Totalitaria, are nothing new, but in primitive civilizations and in prehistoric times the craft of black magic was rather simple. The shaman had merely to destroy or mutilate a small statuette of the accused criminal, to point or thrust a special stick at the man himself, or to curse and berate him with furious words and gestures in order to bring his victim to collapse and death. In his blind acceptance of the magic ritual, the victim was possessed by fear, and often he gave himself up to the spell and just died (Malinowski).

This magic slaying of the foe has plural psychological implications. The victim of the magic spell was often looked upon as the representative of the tribal god, the internalized authority and father. He must be killed because his very existence aroused guilt and remorse among his people. His death may silence the inner voices in every man which warn against impending downfall. Sometimes the victim comes from a different tribe than that of his accusers. In this situation, the stranger is an easier scapegoat, and punishing him serves to still the clash of ambivalent feelings in the members of the killing tribe. Hate for an outsider checks and deflects the hate and aggression each man feels toward his own group and toward himself. The more fear there is in a society, the more guilt each individual member of the society feels, the more need there is for internal scapegoats and external enemies. *Internal confusion looks for discharge in outside wars.*

In Totalitaria, the air is full of gossip, calumny, and rumor. Any accusation, even if it is false, has a greater influence on the citizenry than subsequent vindication. Bills of particulars, made out of whole cloth are manufactured against innocents, especially against former leaders who have been able to develop some personal esteem and loyalty among their friends and followers. Trumped-up charges made against us always revive unconscious feelings of guilt and induce us to tremble. In our analysis of the psychological forces that lead prisoners of war and other political victims to confession and betrayal, we saw how strongly the sense of hidden guilt and doubt in each man impels him under strain to surrender to the demands and ideologies of the enemy. This same mechanism is at work constantly among the citizens of Totalitaria. Accusations against others remind him of his own inner rebellions and hostilities, which he does not dare to bring out into the open, and so the accused, even when he is innocent, becomes the scapegoat for his private sense of guilt. Cowardice makes the other citizens of our mythical country turn away from the victim lest they be accused themselves.

The very fact that character assassination is possible reveals the frailty and sensitivity of human sympathy and empathy. Even in free, democratic societies, political campaigns are often conducted in an atmosphere of extravagant accusation and even wilder counteraccusation. The moment the strategy of wild accusation, with all its disagreeable noises of vituperation and calumny, begins, we forget the strategic intention behind the words and find ourselves influenced by the shouting and name calling. "Maybe," we say to ourselves, "there is something in this story." This, of course, is just what the slanderer wants. In the minds of the politicians the illusion still persists that the end justifies the means. But campaigns of slander produce paradoxical results because the very fact that an unfounded accusation has been made weakens the moral sense of both listener and accuser.

Spy Mania

In Totalitaria this vicious circle of vituperation reaches its fullest flowering. Drowned in a reign of suspicion, the citizen of Totalitaria suffers from a terrible delusion of persecution—"spyonoia," the spy mania. He is continually on the alert, watching his fellow men. His good neighbor may at any moment become a saboteur or a traitor. The citizen of Totalitaria hardly ever looks for confusion or flaws in his own soul, but projects them onto scapegoats—until he himself finally becomes the victim of someone else's spyonoia. Every citizen is constantly trying to search out everyone else's innermost thoughts. Because one's own hidden thoughts are projected on one's neighbors, thinking in itself becomes the enemy. This great fear of the inner thoughts of our fellow men is related to a general process of paranoiac re-evaluation of the world as a result of fear and totalitarian thinking. In the denial of human loyalty and in the constant delusion of treason and sabotage are expressed the whole infantile mythology of Totalitaria and its repudiation of mature human relationships.

Through interrogation, character assassination, humiliation, mental terror, and demoralization—such as happens in individual and collective brainwashing—man can be so utterly demoralized that he accepts any political system. He is nothing any more; why should he oppose matters? In Totalitaria there is no open policy, no free discussion, no honest difference of opinion; there is only intrigue and denunciation, with their frightening action on the masses.

The strategy of wild accusation is used not only against Totalitaria's citizenry, but also against the rest of the world. Totalitaria needs the images of outside enemies—imaginary cruel monsters who spread plague and disease—to justify its own internal troubles. The remnants of the individual citizen's conscience are calmed and held in check by a paranoiac attack on the rest of the world. "The enemy is poisoning our food, throwing beetles and bacteria into our crops." This myth of an imaginary world conspiracy aims at bringing the fearful citizens of Totalitaria into a concerted defense against nonexistent dangers. It conceals, at the same time, internal failures leading to diminishing crops and lack of food. Projecting blame onto others reinforces each citizen's sense of participation in the totalitarian community and stills the nagging internal voice demanding that he act as a self-responsible individual. The myth of external plotting also increases the individual citizen's feeling of dependence and immaturity. Now only his dictatorial leader can protect him from the evil world outside—a world which is described to him as a vast zoo, inhabited by atomic dragons and hydrogen monsters.

The Strategy of Criminalization

As we said before, the citizen of Totalitaria may be able to fulfill some of his irrational, instinctual needs in return for his submission to totalitarian slavery. Hitler Germany taught us the accepted pattern. The citizen (and party member) is encouraged to betray his friends and parents, something the angry, frustrated baby in him has often wanted to do. He may live out in action his deeply repressed aggressions and desires for revenge. He no longer has to suppress or reject some of his own primitive impulses. The system assumes the full burden of his guilt and hands him a ready-made list of thousands of justifications and exculpations for the release of his sadistic impulses. Flowery catchwords, such as "historical necessity," help the individual to rationalize immorality and evil into morality and good. We see here the great corruption of civilized standards.

In his strategy of criminalization, the totalitarian dictator destroys the conscience of his followers, just as he has destroyed his own. Think of the highly learned and polished Nazi doctors who started their professional life with the Hippocratic oath, promising to be the helping healer of man, but who later in cold blood inflicted the most horrible tortures on their concentration-camp victims (Mitscherlich). They slaughtered innocents by the thousands in order to discover the statistical limits of human endurance. They infected other thousands as guinea pigs because the *Fuhrer* wanted it so. They had lost their personal standards and ethics completely and justified all their crimes through the *Fuhrer's* will. Political catchwords encouraged them to yield their consciences completely to the dictator. The process of systematic criminalization requires a *deculturation* of the people. As one of Hitler's gangmen said, "When I hear the word 'civilization,' I prepare my gun." This is done to consistently arouse the instinct of cruelty. People are told not to believe in intellect and objective truth, but to listen only to the subjective dictates of the Moloch State, to Hitler, to Mussolini, to Stalin.

Criminalization is conditioning people to rebellion against civilized frustrations. Show them blood and bloody scapegoats, and a thousand years of acculturation fall away from them. This implies imbuing the people with hysteria, arousing the masses, homogenizing the emotions. All this tends to awaken the brute Neanderthal psyche in man. Justify crime with the glamorous doctrine of race superiority, and then you make sure the people will follow you.

Hitler knew very well what he was doing when he turned the

German concentration camps over to the unleashed lusts of his storm troopers. "Let them kill and murder," was the device. "Once they have gone so far with me, they must go on to the end." The strategy of criminalization is not only directed toward crushing the victims of the totalitarian regime, but also toward giving the elite hangmen—the governing gang—that poisonous feeling of power that drags them farther and farther away from every human feeling; their victims become people without human identity, merely speaking masks and ego-less robots. The strategy of criminalization is the systematic organization of the lower passions in man, in particular in those the dictator must trust as his direct helpers.

Under the pressure of totalitarian thinking, nearly every citizen identifies with the ruling gang, and many must prove their loyalty by murder and killing, or at least expressing their approval of murder and killing. The boredom of Totalitaria's automatic patterns of living leads the deluded citizens to welcome the adventure of war and crime and self-destruction. Each new act of torture and crime makes new bonds of fidelity and unscrupulous obedience, especially within the leading gang. In the end, driven by crime and guilt, the ruling members have to stick it out together because the downfall of the system would bring about the downfall of the entire gang, both leaders and followers. The same thing holds true in the criminal world. Once a man has taken the first step and rejected the laws of society and joined the criminal gang, he is at war with the outside world and its moral evaluations. From that point on, the gang can blackmail him and subdue him.

In Totalitaria, the vicious circle of criminalization of the citizenry, in which the means become ends in themselves, grows into a cynical conspiracy covered with the cynical flag of decent idealism. The country's leaders use such simple words as "the universal campaign of peace," and the citizens rejoice and take pride in these words. Only a few among them know what deceptive deeds lie behind the flowery phrases.

These perversions are also incorporated into a great nationalistic myth—the Third Reich, the New Empire, the People's Republic—and the citizen's desire to do something heroic becomes identified with doing something violent and criminal. Blood becomes a magic fluid, and shedding someone else's blood becomes a virtuous and life-giving deed.

Unlimited killing, as it is practiced in totalitarian systems, is related to deep, unconscious fears. The weak and emotionally sick in any society kill out of fear, in order to borrow, in a magic way, their dead victims' strength and happiness—as well as, of course, their material possessions. The killing of millions in the Nazi gas ovens was part of this ancient mythology of murder. Perhaps the members of the master race thought that slaughtering the Jews would ensure that the Germans would endure pain for as many centuries as had their victims! It is part of an old primitive myth that through killing one fortifies and prolongs one's own life. Let us not forget that forces of reason and understanding in man are rather weak. It is difficult to control the fire of explosive drives, once they are lighted.

Totalitarianism must kill, slaughter, make war. Totalitaria preaches hatred, and the totalitarian mouthpiece is a lonely, deluded, tough "superman," calling for hatred and injustice and arousing intensified fanaticism unhampered by any moral feeling or remorse. His battle cry reinforces the dictator's hold on his subjects, because each citizen, in and through his guilty deeds, learns to hate his victim, whose very suffering arouses even more the criminal's deeply buried sense of guilt.

Verbocracy and Semantic Fog—Talking the People into Submission

After the First World War, we became more conscious of our attitude toward words. This attitude was gradually changing. Our trust in official catchwords and clichés and in idealistic labels had diminished. We became more and more aware of the fact that the important questions were what groups and powers stood behind the words, and what their secret intentions were. But in our easygoing way we often forget to ask this question, and we are all more or less susceptible to noisy, oft-repeated words.

The formulation of big propagandistic lies and fraudulent catchwords has a very well-defined purpose in Totalitaria, and words themselves have acquired a special function in the service of power, which we may call verbocracy. The Big Lie and the phoney slogan at first confuse and then dull the hearers, making them willing to accept every suggested myth of happiness. The task of the totalitarian propagandist is to build special pictures in the minds of the citizenry so that finally they will no longer see and hear with their own eyes and ears but will look at the world through the fog of official catchwords and will develop the automatic responses appropriate to totalitarian mythology.

The multiform use of words in *double talk* serves as an attack on our logic, that is, an attack on our understanding of what monolithic dictatorship really is. Hear, hear the nonsense: "Peace is war and war is peace! Democracy is tyranny and freedom is slavery. Ignorance is strength! Virtue is vice and truth is a lie." So says the Ministry of Truth in George. Orwell's grim novel, *1984*. And we saw this nightmare fantasy come true when our soldiers who had spent long years in North Korean prison camps returned home talking of totalitarian China with the deceiving cliché of "the people's democracy." Pavlovian conditioning to special words forces people into an *automatic thinking* that is tied to those words. The words we use influence our behavior in daily life; they determine the thoughts we have.

In Totalitaria, facts are replaced by fantasy and distortion. People are taught systematically and intentionally to lie (Winokur). History is reconstructed, new myths are built up whose purpose is twofold: to strengthen and flatter the totalitarian leader, and to confuse the luckless citizens of the country. The whole vocabulary is a dictated set of slowly hypnotizing slogans. In the semantic fog that permeates the atmosphere, words lose their direct communicative function. They become merely commanding signs, triggering off reactions of fear and terror. They are battle cries and Pavlovian signals, and no longer represent free thinking. *The word, once considered a first token of free human creation, is transformed into a mechanical tool*. In Totalitaria, words may have a seductive action, soothing or charming their hearers, but they are not allowed to have intrinsic meaning. They are conditioners, emotional triggers, serving to imprint the desired reaction patterns on their hearers.

Man's mental laziness, his resistance to the hard labor of think-.ing, makes it relatively easy for Totalitaria's dictator to bring his subjects into acceptance of the Big Lie. At first the citizen may say to himself, "All this is just nonsense—pure double talk," but in the very act of trying to shrug it off, he has become subject to the power of the inherent suggestion. That is the trick of double talk; once a man neglects to analyze and verify it, he becomes lost in it and can no longer see the difference between rationale and rationalization. In the end, he can no longer believe anything, and he retreats into sullen dullness. Once the citizen of Totalitaria has accepted the "logic" of his leaders, he is no longer open to discussion or argument. Alas, in our Western world, we often meet this evasion of semantic clarity. Let us not forget that the battle for words is part of the ideological cold war in our world.

Something has crept into our mechanized system of communication that has made our modes of thinking deteriorate. People too casually acquire ideas and concepts. They no longer struggle for a clear understanding. The popularized picture replaces the battle of the pros and cons of concepts. Instead of aiming at true understanding, people listen to thoughtless repetition, which gives them *the delusion of understanding.*

Communication has an even more infantile, magic character for the citizen of Totalitaria. Words no longer represent intelligible meanings or ideas. They bind the citizen of Totalitaria to utter dependence on his commander, much as the infant is bound to the word pictures of his parents.

Logocide

Byfield points out in his pamphlet on logocide that words are commonly used as instruments of social revolution. Politicians seeking power must coin new labels and new words with emotional appeal, "while allowing the same old practices and institutions to continue as before . . . The trick is to replace a disagreeable image though the substance remains the same. The totalitarians consequently have to fabric a hate language in order to stir up the mass emotions. We all have experienced how the word *peace* doesn't mean peace any more, it has become a propagandistic device to *appease* the masses and to disguise aggression."

The *verbocracy* in totalitarian thinking and the official verbosity of demagogues serve to disturb and suffocate the free minds of citizens. We can say that verbocracy turns them into what psychology calls symbol agnostics, people capable only of imitation, incapable of the inquisitive sense of objectivity and perspective that leads to questioning and understanding and to the formation of individual ideas and ideals. In other words, the individual citizen becomes a parrot, repeating ready-made slogans and propaganda catchwords without understanding what they really mean, or what forces stand behind them.

This parrotism may give the citizen of Totalitaria a certain infantile emotional pleasure, however. *Heil, heil!—Duce, Duce!—* these rhythmic chants afford him the same kind of sound-enjoyment children achieve through babbling, shrieking, and yelling.

The abuse of the word and the enshrinement of propaganda are more obvious in Totalitaria than in any other part of the world. But this evil exists all over. We can find all too many examples of it in actual conversation. Many speakers use verbal showing off to cover an emptiness of thought, to stir up emotions and to create admiration and adoration of what is essentially empty and valueless. Loud-mouthed phoniness threatens to become the ideal of our time.

The semantic fog in Totalitaria is thickened by the regimentation of information. The citizens of our mythical country have no access to sources of facts and opinions. They are not free to verify what they hear or read. They are the victims of their leader's "labelomania"—their judgments are determined by the official labels everything and everybody bears.

Labelomania

The urge to attach too much meaning to the label of an object or institution and to look only casually at its intrinsic value is characteristic of our times and seems to be growing. I call this condition labelomania; it is the exaggerated respect for the scientific-sounding name—the label, the school, the degree, the diploma —with a surprising disregard for underlying value. All about us we see people chasing after fixed formulas, credits, marks, ranks, and labels because they believe that if one is to have prestige or recognition these distinguishing marks are necessary. In order to obtain acceptance, people are prepared to undergo most impractical and stylized training and conditioning—not to mention expense—in special schools and institutions which promote certain labels, diplomas, and sophisticated façades.

Not long ago a psychiatric colleague worked in a clinic where a different terminology was used, and the ideas of his former teachers, because they were expressed in terms other than those of the clinic, were criticized and even vilified. My colleague was a good practical therapist; yet he came to need psychotherapy himself, to counteract the utter confusion resulting from daily contacts with aggressive adepts of a different terminology, just as much as some of our soldiers released from the Korean prison camps.

There is something essentially unpleasant in the need to express and judge all opinions and evaluations in accepted clichés and labels. It implies a devaluation of the work or of the idea involved, and it denies the subtle human differences between people and the phenomena their words describe. In Totalitaria, man is so anxiety-ridden, so fearful of any deviation from the prescribed opinions and ways of thinking that he only allows himself to express himself in the terms his dictators provide. To the citizen of Totalitaria, the acknowledged label becomes more important than the eternal variation that is life.

As words lose their communicative function, they acquire more and more of a frightening, regulatory, and conditioning function. Official words must be believed and must be obeyed. Dissension and disagreement become both a physical and an emotional luxury. Vituperation, and the power that lies behind it, is the only sanctioned logic. Facts contrary to the official line are distorted and suppressed; any form of mental compromise is treason. In Totalitaria, there is no search for truth, only the enforced acceptance of the totalitarian dogmas and clichés. The most frightening thing of all is that parallel to the increase in our means of communication, our mutual understanding has decreased. A Babel-like confusion has taken hold of political and nonpolitical minds as a result of semantic disorder and too much verbal noise.

The Apostatic Crime in Totalitaria

Totalitaria makes the thinking man a criminal, for in our mythical country the citizen can be punished as much for wrong

thinking as for wrongdoing. Because the watchful eyes of the
secret police are everywhere, the critic of the regime is driven to
conspiratorial methods if he wants to have even a safe conversation
with those he wants to trust. What we used to call the "Nazi
gesture" was a careful looking around before starting to talk to a
friend.

The criminal in Totalitaria can be an accidental scapegoat used
for release of official hostility, and there is often need for a scapegoat.
From one day to the next, a citizen can become a hero or a villain,
depending on strategic party needs.

Nearly all of the mature ideals of mankind are crimes in Totalitaria. Freedom and independence, compromise and objectivity—
all of these are treasonable. In Totalitaria there is a new crime,
the apostatic crime, which may be described as the obstinate refusal to admit imputed guilt. On the other hand, the hero in
Totalitaria is the converted sinner, the breast-beating, recanting
traitor, the self-denouncing criminal, the informer, and the stool
pigeon.

The ordinary, law-abiding citizen of Totalitaria, far from being
a hero, is potentially guilty of hundreds of crimes. He is a criminal
if he is stubborn in defense of his own point of view. He is a
criminal if he refuses to become confused. He is a criminal if he
does not loudly and vigorously participate in all official acts; reserve, silence, and ideological withdrawal are treasonable. He is a
criminal if he doesn't *look* happy, for then he is guilty of what the
Nazis called physiognomic insubordination. He can be a criminal
by association or disassociation, by scapegoatism or by projection,
by intention or by anticipation. He is a criminal if he refuses to
become an informer. He can be tried and found guilty by every
conceivable *ism*—cosmopolitanism, provincialism; deviationalism,
mechanism; imperialism, nationalism; pacifism, militarism; ob-
jectivism, subjectivism; chauvinism, equalitarianism; practicalism,
idealism. He is guilty every time he *is* something.

The only safe conduct pass for the citizen of Totalitaria lies in
the complete abdication of his mental integrity.

CHAPTER EIGHT

Trial by Trial

For the Special Marine Corps Court of Inquiry in Washington that had to judge one of the cases of brainwashing, I was asked, as an expert witness, if I could explain why some of the American officers yielded rather easily to mental pressure exerted by the enemy.

It was in the days when Congressional investigations in our country were in full swing. In all honesty I had to answer that sometimes coercive suggestions underlying such investigations could exert conforming pressure on susceptible minds. People are conditioned by numerous psychological processes in our daily political atmosphere.

Though we have been forewarned of what totalitarian techniques may do to the mind, there is reason to be alarmed by the possible disruption of values brought about 'by some of our own troubles.

The totalitarian dictator succeeded in transforming his apparatus of "justice" into an instrument of threat and domination. Where once a balanced feeling of justice had been recognized as the noblest ideal of civilized man, this ideal was now scoffed at by cynics—like Hitler and Goebbels—and called a synthetic emotion useful only to impress or appease people. Thus, in the hands of totalitarian inquisitors and judges justice has become a farce, a piece of propaganda to soothe the people's conscience. Investigative power is misused—to arouse prejudices and animosities in those by-standers who have become too confused to distinguish between right and wrong.

The totalitarian has taught us that the courts and the judiciary can be used as tools of thought control. That is why we have to study how our own institutions, intentionally or unobtrusively, may be used to distort our concepts of democratic freedom.

The Downfall of Justice

To a psychologist, perhaps the most interesting aspect of the Moscow purge trials between 1936 and 1938 was the deep sense of moral shock felt by people all over the world, whose trust in the judicial process was shaken to its foundations by these perversions of justice. Discussions about the trials always concerned themselves less with the question of guilt or innocence of the accused than with the horrifying travesty of justice the trials presented. Somewhere deep in the soul of men lies the conviction that a judge is, by definition, a righteous, impartial man, that an appeal to the courts is the road to truth, that the law stands above corruption, degradation, and perversion. Of course, we recognize that judges are human beings like ourselves, that they can make mistakes, as the rest of us do, and we are even willing to accept temporary injustice because we believe that there will be eventual vindication and that the rule of law and justice will remain triumphant. The moment the judicial process becomes a farce, a show to intimidate the people, something in man's soul is profoundly affected. When justice is no longer blind, but has her eye on the main chance, we become frightened and alarmed. To whom shall a man turn if he cannot find justice in the courts?

During the course of psychotherapy, one of my patients was called to jury duty. The experience disturbed him deeply, for apparently the prosecutor in this case was more interested in getting a conviction than in finding out the truth. Although the jury had the last word, and, by its verdict, condemned the prosecutor's strategy, our juror was greatly upset. "What happens," he asked me, "in other cases? Suppose the jurors cannot see through the lawyer's sophisms? Suppose they are taken in by his constant suggestion and insistence?"

Indeed, any trial can be used as a weapon of intimidation; it can, in a subtle way, intimidate the jurors, the witnesses, the entire public. In Totalitaria, some higher courts exist only to carry out this function of intimidation; their purpose is to prove to their own citizens and to the world at large that there is a punishing and threatening force controlling the government and that this force can use the judiciary for its own purposes.

An apparently objective official investigation may become a weapon of political control simply through the suggestions that inevitably accompany it. The man who is under investigation is almost automatically stigmatized and blamed because our suspicions are thrust on him. The very fact that he is under scrutiny makes him suspect. Thus, even the so-called "democratic power to investigate" may become the power to destroy. We must beware of this danger! Already the approving or disapproving way of interrogation changes man's thinking about facts.

Any judicial action, whether legal or investigative, which receives widespread publicity, exerts some mental pressure on the entire public. It is not only the participants in the action who have a stake in its eventual outcome, the citizens as a whole may well become emotionally involved in the proceedings. Any official investigation can be either a mere show of power or an act of truth. As show of power, by a totalitarian government or by an unscrupulous demagogue, it can have frightening consequences. The German Reichstag fire case, the Moscow purge trials, and the court actions against our P.O.W.'s in China are prime examples of "legal" action which served to consolidate the political power of ruthless men and had for their object confusion of a helpless citizenry. An additional intention was to shock the public opinion of the world.

If we look at legal inquiry from the point of view of each of its participants, we will see even more clearly the dangers we must guard against.

The Demagogue as Prosecutor and Hypnotist

Recent happenings in our own country indicate clearly that the methods used to satisfy a quest for power show a universal pattern. The ancient magic masks used to frighten the people may have been replaced by an overconfident show of physical strength by a "hero" artificially shaped as an object of admiration and identification for infantile minds, but the loud noises of propaganda are still with us, magnified a thousandfold by the radio and television, and serving to intimidate and hypnotize our less alert contemporaries. A world-wide audience, watching and listening to the demagogue playing all his different roles—the righteous accuser, the martyred victim, the voice of conscience—is temporarily thrown into a semifrightened, trancelike state of exhausted inattentiveness through the monotonous repetition of threats, accusations, and clichés.

The demagogue, like the totalitarian dictator, knows well how to lay a mental spell on the people, how to create a kind of mass suggestion and mass hypnosis. There is no intrinsic difference between individual and mass hypnosis. In hypnosis—the most intensified form of suggestion—the individual becomes temporarily automatized, both physically and mentally. Such a clinical state of utter mental submission can be brought about quite easily in children and in primitive people, but it can be created in civilized adults too. Some of the American P.O.W.'s in Korean prison camps were reduced to precisely this condition.

The more the individual feels himself to be part of the group, the more easily can he become the victim of mass suggestion. This is why primitive communities, which have a high degree of social integration and identification, are so sensitive to suggestions. Sorcerers and magicians can often keep an entire tribe under their spell.

Most crowds are rather easy to influence and hypnotize because common longings and yearnings increase the suggestibility of each member of the group. Each person has a tendency to identify with the rest of the group and with the leader as well, and this makes it easy for the leader to hold the people in his grip. As Hitler said in *Mein Kampf,* the leader can count on increasing submissiveness from the masses.

Sudden fright, fear, and terror were the old-fashioned methods used to induce hypnosis, and they are still used by dictators and demagogues. Threats, unexpected accusations, even long speeches and boredom may overwhelm the mind and reduce it to a hypnotic state.

Another easy technique is to work with specially suggestive words, repeating them monotonously. Arouse self-pity! Tell the people that they have been "betrayed" and that their leaders have deserted them. From time to time, the demagogue has to add a few jokes. People like to laugh. They also like to be horrified, and the macabre, especially, attracts them. Tell them gory tales and let them huddle together in sensational tension. They will probably develop an enormous awe for the man who frightens them and will be willing to give him the chance to lead them out of their emotional terror. In the yearning to be freed from one fear, they may be willing to surrender completely to another.

Radio and television have enhanced the hypnotizing power of sounds, images, and words. Most Americans remember very clearly that frightening day in 1938 when Orson Welles's broadcast of the invasion from Mars sent hundreds of people scurrying for shelter, running from their homes like panicky animals trying to escape a forest fire. The Welles broadcast is one of the clearest examples of the enormous hypnosuggestive power of the various means of mass communication, and the tremendous impact that authoritatively broadcast nonsense can have on intelligent, normal people.

It is not only the suggestive power of these media that gives them their hypnotizing effect. Our technical means of communication make of the people one huge participating mass. Even when I am alone with my radio, I am technically united with the huge mass of other listeners. I see them in my mind, I unconsciously identify with them, and while I am listening I am one with them. Yet I have no direct emotional contact with them. It is partly for this reason that radio and television tend to take away active affectionate relationships between men and to destroy the capacity for personal thought, evaluation, and reflection. They catch the mind directly, giving people no time for calm, dialectical conversation with their own minds, with their friends, or with their books. The voices from the ether don't permit the freedom-arousing mutuality of free conversation and discussion, and thus provoke greater passive acceptance—as in hypnosis.

Many people are hypnophiles, anxious to daydream and daysleep throughout their lives; these people easily fall prey to mass suggestion. The lengthy oration or the boring sermon either weakens the listeners and makes them more ripe for the mass spell, or makes them more resentful and rebellious. Long speeches are a staple of totalitarian indoctrination because finally the boredom breaks through our defenses. We give in. Hitler used this technique of mass hypnosis through monotony to enormous advantage. He spoke endlessly and included long, dull recitals of statistics in his speeches.

The din of constant verbal intimidation of the public is a recognized tool of totalitarian strategy. The demagogue uses this suggestive technique, too, as well as the more tricky maneuver of attacking opponents who are usually considered to be beyond suspicion. This maneuver is often combined with a renewed appeal to self-pity. "Fourteen years of disgrace and shame," was the slogan Hitler used to slander the very creative period between the Armistice in 1918 and the year he seized the helm. "Twenty years of treason," a slogan used in our country not too long ago, sounds suspiciously like it, and is all too familiar to anyone who watched Hitler's rise and fall.

The stab-in-the-back myth reduces everyone who is taken in by it to the level of suspicious childhood. This inflammatory oratory aims toward arousing chaotic and aggressive responses in others. The demagogue doesn't mind temporary verbal attacks on himself—even slander can delight him—because these attacks keep him in the headlines and in the public eye and may help increase people's fear of him. Better to be hated and feared than forgotten! The demagogue grows fat on prolonged and confused discussion of his behavior; it serves to paralyze the people's minds and to obscure completely the real issues behind his red herrings. If this continues long enough, people become fed up, they give in, they want to sleep, they are willing to let the big "hero" take over. And the sequel can be totalitarianism. As a matter of fact, Nazism and Fascism both gambled on the fear of Communism as a means of seizing power for themselves.

What we have recently experienced in this country, unplanned though it doubtless is, is frighteningly similar to the first phase of the deliberate totalitarian attack on the mind by slogans and suspicions. Violent, raucous noise provokes violent emotional reactions and destroys mental control. When the demagogue starts to rant and rave, his outbursts tend to be interpreted by the general public as proof of his sincerity and dedication. But for the most part such declarations are proof of just the opposite and are merely part of the demagogue's power-seeking strategy.

There is in existence a totalitarian "Document on Terror" which discusses in detail the use of well-planned, repeated successive *waves of terror* to bring the people into submission. Each wave of terrorizing cold war creates its effect more easily—after a breathing spell—than the one that preceded it because people are still disturbed by their previous experience. Morale becomes lower and lower, and the psychological effect of each new propaganda campaign becomes stronger; it reaches a public already softened up. Every dissenter becomes more and more frightened that he may be found out. Gradually people are no longer willing to participate in any sort of political discussion or to express their opinions. Inwardly they have already surrendered to the terrorizing dictatorial forces.

We must learn to treat the demagogue and aspirant dictator in our midst just as we should treat our external enemies in a cold war —with the weapon of ridicule. The demagogue himself is almost incapable of humor of any sort, and if we treat him with humor, he will begin to collapse. Humor is, after all, related to a sense of perspective. If we can see how things should be, we can see how askew they can get, and we can recognize distortion when we are confronted with it. Put the demagogue's statements in perspective, and you will see how utterly distorted they are. How can we possibly take them seriously or answer them seriously? We have important business to attend to—matters of life and death both for ourselves as individuals and for our nation as a whole. The demagogue relies for his effectiveness on the fact that people will take seriously the fantastic accusations he makes; will discuss the phony issues he raises as if they had reality, or will be thrown into such a state of panic by his accusations and charges that they will simply abdicate their right to think and verify for themselves.

The fact is that the demagogue is not appealing to what is rational and mature in man; he is appealing to what is most irrational and most immature. To attempt to answer his ravings with logic is to attempt the impossible. First of all, by so doing we accept his battling premises, and we find ourselves trapped in an argument on terms he has chosen. It is always easier to defeat an enemy on your own ground, and by choosing your own terms. In addition, the demagogue either is, or pretends to be, incapable of the kind of logic that makes discussion and clarification possible. He is a master at changing the subject. It is worse than criminal for us to get ourselves involved in endless, pointless, and inevitably vituperative arguments with men who are less concerned with truth, social good, and real problems than they are with gaining unlimited attention and power for themselves.

In their defense against psychological attacks on their freedom, the people need humor and good sense first. Consistent approval or silent acceptance of any terror-provoking strategy will result only in the downfall of our democratic system. Confusion undermines confidence. In a country like ours, where it is up to the voting public to discern the truth, a universal knowledge of the methods used by the demagogue to deceive or to lull the public is absolutely necessary.

The Trial as an Instrument of Intimidation

Man's suggestibility can be a severe liability to him and to his democratic freedom in still another important respect. Even when there is no deliberate attempt to manipulate public opinion, the uncontrolled discussion of legal actions, such as political or criminal trials, in newspaper headlines and in partisan columns helps to create a collective emotional atmosphere. This makes it difficult for those directly involved to maintain their much-needed objectivity and to render a verdict according to facts rather than suggestions and subjective experiences.

In addition, any judicial process which receives widespread publicity exerts mental pressure on the public at large. Thus, not only the participants but the entire citizenry can become emotionally involved in the proceedings. Any trial can be either an act of power or an act of truth. An apparently objective examination may become a weapon of control simply by the action of the suggestions that inevitably accompany it. As an act of power by a totalitarian government, the trial can have frightening consequences. The

Moscow purge trials and the German Reichstag fire case are prime examples.

We do not, of course, have such horrifying travesties on justice in this country, but our tendency to turn legal actions into a field day for the newspapers, the radio, and television weakens our capacity to arrive at justice and truth. It would be better if we postponed discussion of the merits of any legal case until after the verdict was in.

As we have already seen, any man can be harassed into a confession. The cruel process of menticide is not the only way to arrive at this goal; a man can be held guilty merely by accusation, especially when he is too weak to oppose the impact of collective ire and public opinion.

In circumstances of abnormal fear and prejudice, men feel the need for a scapegoat more strongly than at other times. Consequently, people can be easily duped by false accusations which satisfy their need to have someone to blame. Victims of lynch mobs in our own country have been thus sacrificed to mass passion and so have some so-called traitors and collaborators. In public opinion, the trial itself becomes the verdict of "guilty."

The Congressional Investigation

Let me first state that I firmly believe that the right of the Congress to investigate and to propose legislation on the basis of such investigation is one of the most important of our democratic safeguards. But like any other human institution, the Congressional right to investigate can be abused and misused. The power to investigate may become the power to destroy—not only the man under attack, but also the mental integrity of those who, in one way or another, are witnesses to the investigation. In a subtle way, the current wave of Congressional investigations may have a coercive effect on our citizenry. Some dictatorial personalities are obsessed with a morbid need to investigate, and Congressional investigations are made to order for them. Everybody who does not agree with them, who does not bow low and submit, is suspect, and is subjected to a flow of vilification and vituperation. The tendency on the part of the public is to disbelieve everything that the demagogue's opponents say and to swallow uncritically the statements made by those who either surrender to his browbeating or go along with it because they believe in the aims he pretends to stand for.

Psychologically, it is important to understand that the simple fact of being interviewed and investigated has a coercive influence. As soon as a man is under cross-examination, he may become paralyzed by the procedure and find himself confessing to deeds he never did. In a country where the urge to investigate spreads, suspicion and insecurity grow. Everybody becomes infected with the feelings of the omnipotence of the inquisitor. Wire tapping, for instance, has the same power; it is grasping the secrets of others.

In psychological circles a good deal of attention is now being given to the impact of interviews and interrogations on people. The psychological interviewer himself must be aware of the various interpersonal processes involved in this kind of communication; if he is not, he will not be able to find out where the truth lies. Instead he will get answers which are implicit in his own questions, answers which may have little relation to the real truth. This does not happen only in cases where both the interviewer and the man he is interviewing show bad faith. It can happen despite their best intentions. For everybody brings to an interview the sum total of all his earlier interpersonal relationships. In the initial verbal "trial and error," during what we could call the smelling-out period, each party mobilizes himself to find out what the other party expects and where his weaknesses are and, at the same time, tries to hide his own weaknesses and emphasize his own strengths. The man in the street who is suddenly interviewed tends to give the answer he thinks his questioner expects.

Every conversation, every verbal relationship repeats, at least to some degree, the pattern of the early verbal relationships between the child and its parents. To a man or woman under investigation, the interrogator becomes the parent, good or bad, an object of suspicion or of submission. Since the interrogator himself is often unaware of this unconscious process, the result can be a confusing battle of unconscious or half-conscious tendencies, in which the spoken words are often merely a cover for suspicion-laden conversation between deeper layers of both personalities.

All people who are systematically interrogated, whether in a court, during a Congressional inquiry, or even when applying for a job or having a medical examination, feel themselves exposed. This very fact in itself provokes peculiar defensive mental attitudes. These attitudes may be useful and protective, but at times they may be harmful to the individual. When a man is looking for a job, for example, he may become overeager, and in his zeal to "make a good impression" to "put his best foot forward," he may make a bad impression and arouse suspicion. For it is not only what we say but the way we say it that can indicate our honesty and poise. Nervous sounds; gestures, pauses, moments of silence or stuttering may give us away. Aggressive zeal may seduce us into saying too much. Inhibition may prevent us from saying enough.

The defendant in a court action or in an inquiry is defensive not only about the accusations leveled against him or the questions he has to answer, he is even more defensive about his own un-conscious guilt and about his doubts about his own capabilities. Many of my colleagues in medicine and psychiatry who have been called as expert witnesses in legal actions have told me that the very moment they were under cross-examination, they felt them-selves on trial and nearly convicted. Cross-examination seemed to them often less a way of getting at the truth than a form of emo-tional coercion, which did a great disservice to both the facts and the truth. This is the reason that every kind of investigative power can so easily become a coercive power. Making witnesses and de-fendants suffer from acute stage fright can be a nasty weapon of totalitarianism.

Because psychologists and psychiatrists appreciate these facts, there is now a strong tendency in these circles to use what we might call a passive technique in interviewing. When the inter-viewer's questions are not directed toward any specific answer, the man being questioned will be encouraged to answer on his own initiative, out of his own desire to communicate. The neutral ques-tion "What did you do afterwards?" provokes a freer and more honest response than the question "Did you go home after that?"

The Witness and His Subjective Testimony

We have seen in recent years a long parade of recanting Communists, who have testified freely and openly about their pasts. Currently, we have still another kind of parade: the recanting recanters. How are we to know the truth from falsehood in all this morass of conflicting testimony? How are we to prevent ourselves from becoming confused by the contradictory testimony of men and women whose words can influence the course of our nation's actions? How are we to learn to evaluate what they say? Psychologically, how reliable is their testimony, whether friendly or unfriendly?

In general, we can say that those who are most vituperative in their statements are usually the least reliable. Many of them are men and women who in the past adopted a totalitarian ideology out of their own deep sense of inner insecurity. Later there came the moment when they felt that their chosen ideology had failed them. Though it had held their minds relentlessly imprisoned for a long time, at that point they were able to throw off the system completely. This they did through a process of inner rearrangement of old observations and convictions. However, what they shed was merely a particular set of rigid ideological rules. Most of them did not shed, along with these rules, their hidden hatreds and early insecurity. They may have given up the political ideology which offered them defenses and justifications, but they retained their resentments.

It is extremely common to find such people seeking immediate sanctuary in some other strictly organized institution. Because they now see things in a different light, old facts and concepts acquire a different significance. Yet, all the while, the ever-present urge toward self-justification and self-exculpation, which operates in all men and which in these cases motivated the former allegiance to Communism, is at work. Now they must prove their guiltlessness and their loyalty to their newly adopted ideas. Their emotions, now in new garb, are still directed toward the goal of self-justification.

In the eyes of the convert, the fresh outlook—this new arrangement of inner demands and of ways of satisfying them—is just as logical and rational as were his former set of expectations and satisfactions. Now he rediscovers several experiences long since past. His former friends become his enemies; some of them are seen as conspirators, whether they were or not. He himself is unable to distinguish between truth and fantasy, between fact and subjective demand. Consequently, a complete distortion of perceptions and memories may take place. He may misquote his own memories, and this process is for the most part one of which the convert himself is not aware. I remember vividly one example of such behavior during the Second World War. A former Nazi became a courageous member of the anti-Nazi underground. He sought to rectify his past behavior not only by fighting the Nazis, but also by spreading all kinds of anxiety-provoking rumors about his former friends. By making them appear more cruel, he thought he could show himself more loyal.

Similarly, the denials and misstatements that may be made by the convert before the courts or the Congressional committees are often not so much conscious falsehoods as they are products of the new inner arrangements. Every accusation about the convert's past may be twisted by him into a new tool for use in the process of self-justification. Only a few such men have the moral courage to admit that they have made real mistakes in the past. The distance between a white lie and selective forgetting and repressing is often very short. I discovered this for myself while carrying on investigations of resistance members who had been in Nazi hands. I found that it was almost impossible to obtain objective information from them about what they had revealed to the enemy after torture. Reporting upon their enforced betrayal, they immediately colored their stories by white lies and secondary distortions. Depending on their guilt feelings, they either accused themselves too much or found no flaw at all in their behavior.

The Right to Be Silent

Out of the action of Congressional investigating committees has recently come a serious legal attack on the right to be silent when the giving of information clashes with the conscience of the one on the stand. This attack can become a serious invasion of human privacy and reserve. Undermining the value of the personality and of private conscience is as dangerous to the preservation of democracy as is the threat of totalitarian aggression.

We have to realize that it is often difficult for witnesses to make a choice between contempt of Congress and contempt of human qualities. Administrators may conceivably discover a few alleged "traitors" by compelling witnesses to betray their former friends, but at the same time they compel people to betray friendships. Friendship is one of our most precious human possessions. Any government or agency that, under the guise of "contempt of Congress," can force confessions and information can also force the betrayal of former loyalties. Is this not comparable with what the coercive totalitarians do? And at what cost? We obtain a pseudo-purge resulting from weakness of character and anxiety in the victim. In addition we violate one of democracy's basic tenets—respect for the strength of man's character. We have always believed that it is better to let ten guilty men go free than to hang one innocent—in direct opposition to the totalitarian concept that it is better to hang ten innocent men than to let one guilty man go free. We may punish the guilty with this strategy of compelling a man to speak when his conscience urges him to be silent, but just as surely we break down the innocent by destroying their conscience. Supreme Court Justices Douglas and Black in their dissenting opinion about the constitutionality of the Immunity Act of 1954* emphasize the right to be silent as a Constitutional right given by the Fifth Amendment—a safeguard of personal conscience and personal dignity and freedom of expression as well. It is beyond the power of Congress to compel anyone to confess his crimes even when immunity is assured.

The individual's need *not* to betray his former allegiances—even when he has made a mistake in political judgment at an age of less understanding—is morally just as important as the need to help the state locate subversives. Let us not forget that betrayal of the community is rooted in self-betrayal.† By forcing a man to betray his inner feelings and himself, we actually make it easier for him to betray the larger community at some future date. If the law

* *The New York Times,* March 27, 1956.
† See Chapter Fourteen.

forces people to betray their inner moral feelings of friendship, even if these feelings are based on juvenile loyalties, then that very law undermines the integrity of the person, and coercion and menticide begin. The conscience of the individual plays an enormous role in the choice between loyal opposition and passive conformity. The law has to protect the individual also against the violation of his personal moral standards; otherwise, human conscience will lose in the battle between individual conscience and legal power. Moral evaluation starts with the individual and not with the state.

Mental Blackmail

The concept of brainwashing has already led to some legal implications, and these have led to new facets of imagined crime. Because the reports about Communist brainwashing of the prisoners of war in Korea and China were published widely in newspapers, they aroused anxieties among lay people. As mentioned in Chapter Three, several schizophrenics and borderline patients seized upon this rather new concept of brainwashing, using it as an explanation for a peculiar kind of delusion that beset them—the delusion of being influenced. Some of these persons had, as it were, the feeling that their minds had been laid open, as if from the outside, through radio waves or some other mystic communication, thoughts were being directed.

During recent years, I received several letters from such patients complaining about *their feelings of continual brainwashing*. The new concept of political mental coercion fitted into their system of delusions. Several lawyers consulted me for information about clients who wanted to sue their imaginary brainwashers.

The same concept, used above to account for pathological suspicions, could be used maliciously to accuse and sue anybody who professionally gave advice to people or tried to influence them. At this very moment (fall, 1955) several court procedures are going on wherein the defendants are being sued for the crime of brainwashing by a third party. They are accused of having advised, in their professional capacity, somebody to do something against the plaintiff's interests. The shyster lawyer is now able to attack subtle human relationships and turn them into a corrupt matter. This is the age-old evil of using empathy not for sympathy but for antipathy and attack. In so doing, the accuser may misuse a man's hesitation to bring these human relationships into the open; the accuser also makes use of the strange situation in the United States that even the innocent winner of a court procedure has to pay the cost of his legal help. Practically, this means that in a difficult judicial question, he has to pay at least thirty thousand dollars before he can reach the Supreme Court—if it is a Supreme Court case —and appeal to the highest form of justice in our country.

Because of this new angle, which has developed during the past few years, of the brainwashing situation, the psychiatric profession has been made more vulnerable to unreasonable attack. In one case, a third party felt hurt by a psychological treatment that made the patient more independent in an unpleasant commercial situation in which he had formerly been rather submissive. In another case, the doctor was sued because he was able to free his patient from a submissive love affair and an ambiguous promise of marriage. In a third case, the patient during treatment changed from a commercial agency that had treated him badly. In all those cases, the disappointed party could bring suit on the basis of so-called brainwashing, and malicious influence. In several cases of this form of blackmail, an expensive settlement was made out of court because the court procedure would have become far more costly.

The practicing psychiatrist who is attacked in this way experiences not only financial pressure imposed on him by the dissatisfied party and a malicious lawyer, but in several states the court does not even recognize his professional oath of secrecy. The Hippocratic oath says:

> Whatever, in connection with my professional practice, or not in connection with it, I may see or hear in the lives of men which ought not to be spoken abroad, I will not divulge, as reckoning that all such should be kept secret.

Some courts hold that only physical investigation and treatment are valid as medical treatment not to be divulged; personal conversation—the quintessence of psychiatric treatment—is not looked upon as a medical action. Hiding behind professional secrecy is regarded as contempt of court. An additional difficulty is that this accusation of malpractice by a third party—not by the patient himself—is not covered by the usual malpractice insurance.

The importance of such perfidious attack on psychological relationships—however rare the number of cases may be at this moment —is that it opens the road for many other forms of mental blackmail. It means that subtle personal relationships can be attacked and prosecuted in court, merely because a third party feels excluded or neglected or financially damaged. I cannot sue my broker because he gave me wrong financial advice, but I can sue a psychological counselor for malpractice because he "brainwashed" my client.

What new possibilities for mental blackmail and sly accusation are open! Gradually we can make punishable wrong intention and anticipation, nonconformist advice and guidance, and, in the end, simple honest human influence and originality—things that are already considered criminal in totalitarian countries.

The word "blackmail" was originally used in the border warfare between England and Scotland. Blackmail was the agreement made by freebooters not to plunder or molest the farmer—in exchange for money or cattle. The word comes from the Middle English *maille* meaning speech or rent or tax.

The French equivalent *chantage* brings us even nearer to the concept of mental coercion. It means forcing the other fellow "to sing," to confess things against his will by means of threatening physical punishment or threatening to reveal a secret. It is, in the last analysis, mental coercion.

We may call mental blackmail the growing tendency to overstep human reserve and dignity. It is the tendency to misuse the intimate knowledge of what is going on in the crevices of the soul, to injure and embarrass one's fellow man. Mental blackmail starts wherever the presumption of guilt takes the place of the presumption of innocence. The hunting up of dirt and sensation in order to embarrass a victim we see very often carried on by the yellow press. It is not only playing up indecency, but at the same time it undermines human judgment and opinion. And by its sensationalism it precludes and prejudices justice in the courts.

What the weak baby accomplishes with its tears and pouting can be done by the whining, querulous accuser with his fantasies about malicious influence and brainwashing. The suicidal patient may exert the same kind of pressure.

I am convinced that in the future the Supreme Court has to make rules which will control these new forms of indictment; yet the core of the problem is the growing suspicion within man in our era of transition. We blackmail men's minds with too many security measures, with secret files; we blackmail with gossip, with subtle pressures within political pressure groups, with lobbies within lobbies, and even by withholding our friendship.

The Judge and the Jury

What about the people who are called upon to sift truth from falsehood, to arrive at just and impartial verdicts? The judge and the jury are themselves influenced and affected by the external facets and inner needs that lie behind the behavior of the other principals in the case. Yet they are supposed to rise above their background, their personal needs and desires and to render a verdict strictly on the evidence, unswayed by any prejudice or subjective desires. And let us bear in mind that it is not only those officially connected with a case who make a decision about it, it is everyone who knows about it. You and I, the public, are judge and jury too.

Judge and jury face the difficult task of finding and asking on the basis of the facts alone, and yet even in them, under the influence of strong group emotions, an emotional rearrangement of remembered facts may take place.

Judges and jurors are affected by the collective emotional atmosphere surrounding controversial issues, and it is difficult for them to maintain their much-needed objectivity. The average juror already submits to the popular emotional demand before the trial is started, as several trials about racial persecution proved.

Lately two authorities on law attacked the system of *trial by jury,* one because of its delaying action on the process of justice (Peck) and the other because he considered it an outmoded means of

administering justice (Newman). Trial by jury is a relic of the
thirteenth century intended to replace the magic trial by ordeal—
the gods and coincidence decided the guilt—and to replace the trial
by battle—physical skill and power decided which of two parties
was guilty. The trial by a *jury of peers,* by all those who knew the
accused and the circumstances of the alleged crime, served its purpose in rather simple organized communities for a long time. But
in our complicated society, where people know less about each
other and where a thousandfold communications intrude the mind,
things have changed. "The average juror is swayed by the emotion
and prejudice of his heredity and background training." (Newman)
Our juries are not always able to follow the intricacies of pros and
cons, of interpretation of facts. In addition, many a trial lawyer
knows how to fascinate a jury, how to catch their minds and
influence their judgment. Beyond this, the selection of jurors delays
more and more the process of justice.

As a simple example of how individual, personal, and social conditioning can affect a juror's current reactions, let us look at the
inner confusion usually caused by the word "traitor." Here we have
an emotionally loaded trigger-word. If somebody is accused of being
a traitor or a subversive, on the basis of undeniable facts, any
attempt at a scientific, psychological explanation of this person's
behavior is already considered a treacherous intellectualism. The
consensus is that the traitor should be punished; he belongs to the
scum of society, better let him die. Even the lawyer who defends
him before the court may be accused of collaboration in treason.

All of us know many other trigger words which immediately
provoke confusion in our objective perception and judgment because they touch unsolved, unconscious feelings. Words like "Communist" and "homosexual," for instance, can become confusing
trigger words which bring a reservoir of dark feelings into action.
Demagogues like to use such words in order to stir up mass feelings, which they cannot control but which they believe are very
suitable for the strategy of the moment. This can become, however,
like playing with dynamite. Any one of us may be swayed by
allusive clichés such as "Where there's smoke, there's fire" or
"Once a thief, always a thief." I once saw this most interestingly

in a hot debate where someone had once been scolded for being a "dirty monogamist." As soon as the accusation was made, public opinion turned against him.

Even a judge can be swayed by his own emotional difficulties, especially by slanted testimony of witnesses who may be attempting to mislead. In Great Britain the courts are more aware of the effect of a prejudicial attitude on the part of jurors. There the trial process is extensively protected, mostly through prevention of pretrial discussion and deliberation, regardless of the unpopularity of the accused.

Televised Interrogation

An open official interrogation affects those who watch it—and the fact that they are affected may influence its outcome. Various crime hearings in this country, for instance, were brought before the people by means of television. Citizens sitting comfortably at home far from the scene could see how defense lawyers maneuvered facts or instructed their clients (among whom were well-known crime bosses) so that they would appear in a favorable light. Even though their actions may have been transparent tricks with the appearance of a fixed wrestling match, the result was that some of the not-so-jovial-looking victims of the criminals were made ridiculous, while the criminals, calm, assured, self-possessed, seemed more admirable. The victims often couldn't stand being in the limelight; it made them feel ill at ease and embarrassed. The criminals, on the other hand, either denied every accusation in tones of righteous indignation or made confessions which degenerated into hysterical quests for pity. The magic effect of all the anonymous onlookers—because the witness or defendant imagined their approval or disapproval—influenced the outcome of the hearings. All of us who watched them brought our own subjective expectations to bear on these hearings.

Television makes a mass trial of such a hearing, and unwittingly not justice but the variable feelings of the public become part of the courtroom atmosphere. Every piece of evidence in such a hearing is colored by rumor and emotion, and the shocked onlookers are left with feelings of suspicion and deep misgivings that the hearing has not really gotten down to the condemning facts.

The Quest for Detachment

Man's feeling for justice has very subtle implications. As soon as *Justitia* flirts with powerful friends or becomes completely submissive, people feel insecure and their anxiety increases. But man's feeling for justice needs more than mere security for its satisfaction and gratification. The sense of justice is an inner attitude aiming at the realization of ideal rules of law that can inspire the community and raise it to a higher moral level. It requires not merely that minimum of decent behavior that is enforced by law, but more than that a maximum of personal initiative and mutual fair play. It asks for personal and social justice, for mutual limitation of demands in the service of the mutuality of relations between men, and between men and their government. Any ideal feeling of justice requires sacrifice and implies self-limitation. Emotionalism is its enemy. This ideal of justice is not only valid for individuals but should also rule communities and countries. Only in such an atmosphere of free mutual sacrifice of power on behalf of growing justice can democracy grow.

Can people learn to see objectively and in a· manner detached from their personal feelings? Yes, they can. Preconceived ways of seeing and witnessing can be changed. Many people realize the damage men do to themselves and others when they submit to collective passion and prejudice. These people then learn through astute investigation and observation how to be less prejudiced, how to see events with constant readaptation of mind and eye and with a search for reality.

Prisoners in concentration camps or P.O.W. camps are so constantly bombarded with rumors and suggestions, their observations are so distorted by their necessary self-defenses, that they are hardly able to give an objective report regarding the actions of their fellows. The mass attitude of the day directs their opinions. The fellow who has become a scapegoat, whose function it is to alleviate for his fellow prisoners their common anger, will never be able to neutralize all later reports about him, simply because the number of so-called objective witnesses is against him. It is very difficult to separate the rumors from the facts and to neutralize ingrown mental toenails. There is in man an instinctual need to take sides with the majority, to conform to the opinion of the strong. This need is rooted in a biological urge for safety. That is why a strong feeling of participation grew among soldiers in a P.O.W. camp. The result was complete unconscious falsification of what happened. The individual observation got lost in the strong impact of mass opinion.

In the future age of psychology, when insight into man's behavior is more generally understood and applied, we will be more aware of the importance of dependable witnesses. Every report and every piece of testimony pro or con will be examined and weighed in the light of its psychological and historical background. The citizen of the future will laugh as he looks back at the time once lost during trials because obvious facts on one side were not brought out to challenge equally obvious facts on the opposing side. These future citizens will understand that we only revealed our mutual hostilities and feelings of fear and insecurity by our behavior, feelings which moved us compulsively and subtly to make subjective rearrangements of our memories and impressions. He will point out that objective thinking was in its infancy in those days.

CHAPTER NINE

Fear as a Tool of Terror

The Fear of Living

In our era the fear aroused by human relationships is so strong that inertia and mental death often seem more attractive than mental alertness and life. Classical psychology often spoke of the fear of death and the great unknown as the cause of many anxieties, but modern psychological studies have shown us that the fear of living is a much greater, deeper, and more frightening one.

Living often seems beyond our power. Stepping out of a relatively safe childish dependence into freedom and responsibility is both hazardous and dangerous. Living demands activity and spontaneity, trial and error, sleeping and reawakening, competition and cooperation, adaptation and reorientation. Living involves manifold relationships, each of which has thousands of implications and complications. Living takes us away from the dream of being protected and demands that we expose our weaknesses and strengths daily to our fellow men, with all their hostilities as well as their affections. It requires us to build up useful defenses and then to replace them with others because we have to change our goals and our relationships. It expects us to be lonely in order to cooperate in freedom. It asks us to submit and to conquer, to adjust and to rebel. It robs us of our childhood slumber of satisfaction, and of the magic, omnipotent fantasies of our infancy. Living requires mutuality of giving and taking. Above all, to live is to love. And many people are afraid to take the responsibility of loving, of having an emotional investment in their fellow beings. They want only to *be* loved and to be protected; they are afraid of being hurt and rejected.

We can see this clearly in the fact that so many people embrace so fervently all the limitations and frustrations of life that are offered them—the neurotic limitations of the usual prejudices or the totalitarian limitations imposed by power politics. In his book *Escape from Freedom,* Erich Fromm describes clearly how the pressures of freedom, when they are not balanced by responsibility and understanding, can drive men into the totalitarian frame of mind and into surrender of their hard-won liberties. Such surrender is nothing less than a slow mental death.

Totalitarian leaders, whether of the right or of the left, know better than anyone else how to make use of this fear of living. They thrive on chaos and bewilderment. During unrest in international politics, they are most at ease. The strategy of fear is one of their most valuable tactics. The growing complications of our civilization and its administration make the impact of power politics felt more than ever before. When the totalitarians add to their tactics all the clever tricks that we have already discussed— Pavlovian conditioning, repeated suggestion, deconditioning through boredom and physical degradation—they can win their battle for the control of man's mind.

In the earlier chapters of this book we described in some detail the techniques by which man could be turned into a robot in the service of totalitarianism and some of the tendencies that operate, even in the free countries, to rob man of his mental integrity. It is important for us to realize that emphasis on conformity and the fear of spontaneous living can have an effect almost as devastating as the totalitarian's deliberate assault on the mind. Conformity and the fear of living rob the free way of life of its greatest asset in the struggle against totalitarianism.

Our human strength lies in our diversity and independence of thought, in our acceptance of nonconformity, in our willingness to discuss and to evaluate various conflicting points of view. In denying the diversities of life and the complexity and individuality of the human mind, in preaching rigid dogmas and self-righteousness, we begin gradually to adopt the totalitarian attitude we deplore. Delusion has never been the exclusive property of any one country, class, or group, and the totalitarian delusion, which in itself promotes menticide, can invade us from many fronts, from the right as well as the left, from the rich or from the underprivileged, from the conservatives and from the rebels.

Fear and intimidation have not only been the result but also the tools of mental coercion. Although there is as yet no unified theory of fear and anxiety, and we therefore do not know precisely why and how the development of these feelings leads to such dire consequences, it is important for us to understand what useful tools fear and panic are, and to see, through description, what these overwhelming emotions are able to do to people.

Most people think of fear reactions as hysterical expressions of desperation. But, as this chapter should make clear, fear and panic also have their paradoxical expressions in indifference and apathy, reactions which, just because they are less commonly recognized as fear-created, can be much more dangerous to the individual than a good hysterical cry. It is the hidden, silent fears that have such an impact on our social and political behavior.

Fear and panic are reactions not only to overt danger and threat, they are also reactions to the slow, seeping intrusion of disquieting propaganda and the constant wave of suggestion to which we are all exposed. Fear is at work all around us, and often it throws its shadows where we least expect to find them. We may be acting out of fear without even knowing it; we may consider that our behavior is perfectly normal and rational when, in fact, psychology tells us that creeping fear may already have begun to work on us.

Fear and catastrophe fortify the need to identify with a strong leader. They lead to herding together of people, who shy away from wanting to be individual cells any longer; they prefer to be part of a huge mystic social organization that protects against threat and distress, in oneness with the leader. This protection-seeking instinctual reaction is also directed against dissent and individualism, against the individual ego. We see in this a regression toward a more primitive state of mass participation. True, this process of ego-shrinking is the negative side of the back-to-mass reaction. Yet it stimulates a recognition of greater need for cooperation and mutual help. During the last war and the generally experienced emergencies many people became for the first time aware of the affective ties they had with their neighbors. At the same time, anxiety can inspire suspicion and the need for seeking scapegoats. It is the paradox of fear that it propagates warm feelings of immature ties and cold suspicion at the same time.

Although there is throughout the world a conscious trend toward overcoming fear and feelings of insecurity, there is also a less conscious countercurrent provoking new fears and anxieties and insecurities. Whether he is aware of it or not, modern man lives in an atmosphere of fear—fear of war, fear of the H-bomb, fear of totalitarianism, fear of nonconformism, fear of dissent. Fear has already begun to influence our behavior by the time we are aware of it. Once fear has penetrated the mind and stimulated fantasy, it begins to direct our actions, whether we want it to or not. We cannot eliminate all the thousands of stresses and fear-provoking situations in the modern world, but we can learn to recognize and understand some of the most common forms of fear reactions. In this way we can find a partial release from the tensions they create and can learn how to cope with them more effectively.

Our Fantasies About Danger

I remember vividly one sunny afternoon during the Second World War while I was still in Holland. I was playing tennis with some friends. We were all enjoying the satisfying exertion of our sport, but our enjoyment was somewhat marred by the players on the next court. They spoke the language of the hated occupier, and although attired in the same white sports clothes as we, they were obviously Nazi officers who were temporarily forgetting their delusion of conquering the world and were trying to relax like normal human beings. Suddenly we all heard the drone of planes and the sound of antiaircraft off in the distance. Then a group of low-flying Spitfires, our friends from England, came zooming by. My friends and I stopped playing, waved our rackets in greeting, and watched the planes maneuvering. Our neighbors reacted quite differently. They became panicky; one of them flung his racket from him and ran off, the others threw themselves, face down, into a ditch bordering the court. Objectively, we were all faced with the same danger of strafing from the English planes, but for the Germans these were enemy planes, while for us they were friends.

I'm sure it isn't necessary for me to add that after this occurrence my fellow Dutch citizens were forbidden to play tennis on that court.

When, a year later, I had arrived by good chance in London, I found that every time German planes came over during the night, I had that same suspicious feeling the German officers on the tennis court must have had. It seemed as though every bullet and every bomb was meant for me. So great is the role of fantasy in fear that an enemy bomb may have a different meaning for us than a friendly bomb.

Fear may be defined very simply as an inner reaction to danger. This definition is deceptively simple, for as soon as we offer it, we are faced with a new problem: What shall we define as danger? Bombs, fires, earthquakes, and epidemics are easily recognizable as dangers. So are physical torture, direct totalitarian attack, and sudden economic collapse. But there are many subtle emotional dangers, too, arousing fearful fantasies and anticipations often combined with inner visions of doom and disaster. As our examples will show, these dangers are faced differently by different people. It is our personal attitude toward life and toward mankind that determines whether we consider a situation a welcome challenge or an unconquerable danger. Some people enjoy strict control and mechanical conditioning of their lives. For them, totalitarianism and thought control are not danger; they bring a kind of eternal day-sleep without responsibility. To these people, freedom is a danger, while dependence is a pleasurable safety. Others loathe any intrusion into their personal freedom and integrity and are continually on the alert to defend themselves against any external pressure—real or fancied.

Paradoxical Fear

Even when people are well prepared and trained to meet an anticipated disaster, such as imprisonment and brainwashing, the actual impact of the danger may provoke all kinds of defensive behavior. Overtraining may even weaken the person because the long anticipation allows all kinds of hidden fantasies to run rampant. In a minority of persons this may be expressed in such pathological fear reactions as complete nervous breakdown or utter paralysis. Every person shows a different mental threshold of resistance to danger, and this threshold may change day by day, depending on our physical and mental fortitude. As a rule, inexperienced troops do not immediately show pathological fear in combat; such behavior takes some time to develop. Paradoxically enough, fear reactions and moments of weakness often develop after the real danger has passed. When the tension of battle or the daily stress of life in the prison camp is over, and there is no longer any need to hide one's fears and to control one's behavior, many people let go completely and give free vent to all their anxieties.

In Dover, England, in 1944, the population suffered a kind of collective nervous breakdown when after the tension of four years of continual shelling by the Germans they heard only silence. The shelling suddenly stopped completely after the Allied troops swept victoriously across the Belgian coast. At that moment, many of the people of Dover broke down. It was as if the unexpected silence had brought them into a state of shock.

This paradoxical fear reaction after danger has passed is important for us to understand. The totalitarian strategists know that during a period of temporary quiet and relaxation of tension, people lose their alertness and thus can be more easily caught in the totalitarian mental grip. In their strategy of terror they consciously make use of the psychological action of the breathing spell. As soon as we let go and drop the defenses we have built up against danger, we can be brought to swallow any strong suggestions. The totalitarians also, in their "Document on Terror," call the technique of taking advantage of such relief the "strategy of fractionalized fear." In a quiet period between acute tensions, they can easily condition their victims' minds. Hitler used the Munich period of appeasement in precisely this way. During this time, his propaganda barrage was doubly effective.

Whether the reaction to fear and danger is immediate or delayed, most people show, under stress, behavior that can be said to fall into one of the following patterns:

1. *Regression*—loss of learned behavior.
2. *Camouflage and disguise*—the so-called "feign or faint" reactions.
3. *The explosive panic*—defense through "fight or flight."
4. *Our psychosomatic conditioning*—the body takes over.

Regression

Although most people are more or less acquainted with the concept of regression, of setting the cultural clock back, they are surprised, nevertheless, to see staid men and women lose their acquired habits of civilization in times of catastrophe and panic.

I once treated an engineer who had been the victim of an earthquake in a foreign country. After the earthquake, he behaved completely like a baby. All kinds of treatments were tried, but none were successful; we were never able to change his childish behavior. He never found his way back to normal, adequate behavior. From that fateful day, he remained barricaded in his cave of escape. It was as if with one blow he had forgotten everything he had ever learned. He was no longer a grown man, a professional scientist. He was an infant. He babbled like an infant, he had to be fed like an infant. Another earthquake victim of whom I know, a professor of mathematics, was found in his garden after the quake was over, half-naked and playing with his child's toys. He completely rejected any recognition of the real emergency situation in which he found himself and regressed to a period of infantile irresponsibility.

Such regressive behavior as a form of defense is encountered everywhere in the animal kingdom. When an organism is in danger, it drops its complexity and retreats to a simpler form of existence. When circumstances of living become too dangerous, some easily exposed multicellular organisms turn into well-protected, simple monocellular beings. This regressive process, called encystication may, for instance, take place when the organism is exposed to abnormal temperatures or abnormal dryness.

Man is subject to the same biological rule of defense. When life is too complex for him, he often turns the clock of civilization back and becomes primitive again. A sudden disintegration and breakdown of functions may occur. This form of regressive behavior is common in children. When they are frightened, they often revert to baby talk or to bed-wetting. In the bombed areas during the Second World War, many girls in their late teens started to play with their dolls again. Even seemingly mature, hypersophisticated men and women may display thousands of symptoms of this return to infantilism when fear attacks them. Their symptoms are not always as dramatic as the examples above; nevertheless, they are symptoms of fear. When grown people begin to stutter and to lose their daily decorum, when they take to carrying around special protective charms, when they invent stories about their magic invulnerability, when they boast more, eat more cake and candy, whistle more, talk more, cry more, and lose their formal stiff and staid·behavior, they are acting out of fear.

During the Second World War, in the prison camps and the air-raid shelters, people really got to know each other, as do children in the playpen who have the simple intuitive gift of knowing whom they can trust. In our age of anxiety, we feel possessed by the same frightening shadows that once haunted the Stone-Age man, and we may react to them by acting more like our simpler ancestors.

Camouflage and Disguise

A different pattern is that of camouflage and disguise—playing hide-and-seek with fate. This useful protective trickery is often seen in lower animals who temporarily acquire the form or color of their environment. It is just like military camouflage. Everybody is acquainted with the color changes of the chameleon, and there are many other animals which are able to change their skin or body form in times of danger. Yet many people are not aware that human skin, too, shows rudimentary attempts at camouflage. The phenomenon of goose flesh resembles the reaction of a frightened, bristling cat; sudden graying of the hair or discoloration of the skin, which is known technically as fear melanosis, changes our outer color.

During the Second World War, I went with a first-aid team to Rotterdam after the city had been heavily bombed. As we looked at the people, our first impression was that they were all wearing masks. Their skin was wrinkled and showed a typical camouflage reaction. They were all still badly frightened. It was as if they were in hiding from the tremendous hell of fire that had been thrown down on them.

There is a psychological parallel to these physical reactions; it is called the "feign or faint" pattern. Actual psychology looks at both reactions, feigning and fainting, as a passive retreat from reality. This reaction is comparable to shell-shock or battle neurosis, the study of which is one of the most absorbing chapters of medicine. Soldier and civilian alike can go into a state of mental paralysis. In such a state the victim becomes apathetic; he is unable to talk or to move. No dangerous reality exists for him anymore. He looks dead; only his frightened, burning eyes seem alive. This death attitude or cataleptic reaction often has a completely terrifying effect on bystanders. There is nothing so contagious as fainting in any crowded place.

It is of the utmost importance to realize how passive, paralyzed, indifferent, and submissive people can become under circumstances which should demand the utmost activity. The totalitarians are making use of man's passive reaction to terror when they put their prisoners into huge concentration camps with only a few guards; they are gambling that the reaction of passivity will keep the victim from rebelling or trying to escape. Like the bird which stands stock-still when the snake approaches, man may surrender passively to what he dreads and fears in order to get rid of the tension of anticipation. The thief who surrenders to the police because he cannot stand the tension and insecurity of not knowing when he will be found out is an obvious example.

A psychological camouflage reaction lies behind emotional shock and silent panic—the mental paralysis that overcomes some people when they can no longer cope with the circumstances in which they find themselves. Passive surrender to what he fears is one of man's most common reactions to sudden danger; it is not limited to pathological personalities. It occurs much more frequently than wild and overt panic, and displays itself in numerous subtle behavior mechanisms. People may escape into complaints about physical disease. They may take refuge in "very important" pseudo-tasks and hobbies. They may deny real danger in a seemingly self-securing complacency. They become obstinate and disobedient; nothing can activate them. They are not interested in politics, they say. Some will try to sell to themselves and others the paralyzing theory of hopelessness and the inevitability of doom. But don't talk about the nuclear bomb! Others will throw themselves into the oblivion of excessive drinking or hide themselves in long, pointless conferences.

Every man has his own psychological Maginot line—a mental fortress that he believes inviolable. We used to call this the ostrich policy—and the ostrich policy is one of the most dangerous strategies in the world. Beware the totalitarian who preaches peace; his intention may be to push the world into passive surrender to that which it fears.

The cult of passivity and so-called relaxation is one of the most dangerous developments of our times. Essentially, it too may represent a camouflage pattern, the double wish not to see the dangers and challenges of life and not to be seen. We cannot escape all the tensions that surround us; they are part of life, and we have to learn to cope with them adequately and to use our leisure time for more creative and gratifying activities. Silent, lonely relaxation—with alcohol, sweets, the television screen, or a murder mystery—may soothe the mind into a passivity that may gradually make it vulnerable to the seductive ideology of some feared enemy. Denying the danger of totalitarianism through passivity, may gradually surrender to its blandishments those who were initially afraid of it.

Explosive Panics

Most people are far more familiar with the explosive motor reactions we call panic and stampede than they are with the other fear reactions. This is what we call mass hysteria, the *chacun pour soi* reaction. The baby has its temper tantrums, and older people have their uncontrolled fury and "fight or flight" reactions. Although we usually think of the word "panic" as describing such phenomena as the hysterical stampede out of a burning theater or the flight of whole populations in terror, there are many subtle steps that lead from the first symptoms of unrest we all feel when something is threatening, to the great outbursts of crying and running and fighting we see in severe panics. Man shows many forms of panicky, frenzied behavior—epileptic fits (as in trench or war epilepsy), fury, rage, self-destruction, criminal aggression, running amok, deserting from the army, rioting, uncontrolled impulsiveness, breakneck speed in driving. A soldier in a state of panic may behave like an angry child. He may attack his friends or shoot at the members of his own troop. In panic, civilians may begin to cry, shout, walk aimlessly about wringing their hands. Or they may shout and scold or cry for help. The panicky person spreads panic; every time he shouts, he incites others to run. Panic is never a queston of crude strength or failing energy, but rather of lack of inner structure, of a failing capacity to organize. The panicky leader hesitates to use the powers entrusted to him.

The child with temper tantrums lies deep within all of us. The more mysterious and unaccountable the danger, the more primitive our reactions may be.

Riots, furious mass movement, and outbreaks of criminality serve to increase fear and panic, and thus can be used to deepen man's sense of insecurity and further his passive surrender to the totalitarian environment. Any terroristic regime compels its victims to repress their reactions of rebellion and anger. The more these reactions are repressed, the more the victims develop tremendous inner rage, which must bide its time and wait until it is permitted some socially sanctioned form of explosion. War is often such a universal panic, a mass discharge of accumulated internal rage. Here, too, the inner fears of mankind are discharged in mass destruction.

The Body Takes Over

The great group of psychosomatic reactions, although they are no mystery, are more difficult to explain. Let us look at an example which may make this phenomenon more clear. In my home town in Holland, after a few bombardments during the Second World War, an epidemic of bladder disease broke out—at least that was the first explanation. People suffered from the need to urinate so often that their sleep was disturbed; almost no one had a full night's rest. For a short time, there was a boom in the practice of urologists. Then psychiatrists were able to explain that this urge to urinate was one of the first reactions to fear. The victims had only to think back to their childhood and to recall their bodily reactions before taking examinations at school to see what was happening. Increased urination may be described as one of the tension-reducing devices of the body.

The body may react to danger and panic with a variety of physical symptoms. Perspiration, frequent urination, heart palpitations, diarrhea, high blood pressure are only a few. We know that many of these reactions are related to the body's mobilization of specific defenses against threatening dangers. The specific ways in which bodily diseases related to fear and anxiety develop are conditioned largely by the individual's personal life history, especially his development during childhood. The infant whose early tensions and yearnings were drowned in milk and pablum will grow up into an adult who tries to fill his mouth again as soon as something threatening occurs. Overeating has become for him a fear-allaying device. In the process of rearing the child, the parent unwittingly train certain of the child's organs to react to the tensions of life.

Because man has many bodily organs, he can show a tremendous variety in his physical and emotional responses to threats, both from without and within. Psychosomatic medicine distinguishes between different character types in terms of the different organs which respond to outside stress or danger. There is the ulcer type, the asthma type, the colitis type, the heart failure type. Each of these types shows a different reaction to the same battle—the battle against fear. Feelings of social tension may be expressed in various organic diseases. In acute fright, however, certain organs of the body more commonly react than others. As we saw in our earlier example, the need for frequent urination is a nearly universal reaction to fright. The "upset stomach" is another almost universal fear reaction.

During the Second World War, a medical team looked in vain for the bug causing an unknown intestinal disease among American soldiers who were preparing to land on one of the enemy islands in the Pacific. The doctors and biologists searched and searched; they found nothing. The mysterious disease vanished, as suddenly as it had appeared, after the invasion began and the soldiers were able to discharge in action the tension of waiting for the invasion. These men were not strange or abnormal in any way. Even when one consciously accepts the challenge of danger and is prepared to face it, counterforces in the body may defeat the mental effort. The mind wants to be brave, but the body escapes into disease. Consistency of child-rearing, emotional security at home, and lifelong conditioning to acceptance of the various challenges of life—all these are the factors that determine how we will react when we are put to the test.

In their treatment of panicky soldiers during the last war, psychiatrists gave some of their time to an explanation of these various danger reactions. As the victims began to understand their reactions and saw how common they were, they took the first and most important step toward cure. No longer were they so afraid of their fears; no longer were they in such dread of cowardice. It was important for them to know that what had reduced them to the level of helpless childhood was part of a universal pattern of defensive behavior. As they understood this, they became less afraid and ashamed of their own private fears. They knew that their bodies were reacting like many others, and they became able once more to accept their duties quietly and with better control. Stamina and resourcefulness depend as much on self-knowledge as they do on the help and support we get from others.

In times of stress and calamity, people begin to probe for the vulnerable spots and weaknesses in both their friends and their enemies. This testing goes on constantly during a hot war, but it happens during a cold war as well. The cold war exerts a continual pressure on human imagination and mental fortitude and is the cause of many peculiar escape reactions or bodily reactions.

Whenever fear and danger confront him, man has to make a choice: Shall he indulge in unchecked fury? Shall he concentrate upon self-protection? Or shall he accept his responsibilities? The fear reactions we have described show how the primordial impulse to self-protection (misguided though it may be) can break through all our civilized defenses. Only training and conscious preparation for danger, both inner and outer, can give a man strength to hold these reactions in check. This training starts within the nucleus of the family and is supported by the example of a peaceful, free community. These are the first teachers in the constant battle between inner fear and outer danger.

Those who are in danger of being brainwashed can be helped simply by making them familiar with the facts. Foreknowledge has a partial protective function, and this belongs to the best security we can give to them. It takes away the weakening influence of anxious and mysterious anticipation. With this aid, their mental vulnerability is then furthered by innate inner strength, by the example of good rearing, and by the challenge and opportunity their society gives to them.

PART THREE

UNOBTRUSIVE COERCION

IN THE COURSE OF OUR INVESTIGATIONS CONCERN-
ING THOUGHT CONTROL, MENTICIDE, AND BRAIN-
WASHING, IT HAS BECOME CLEARER THAT MORE
ATTENTION MUST BE GIVEN TO THE MEANS BY
WHICH INNER PREPAREDNESS FOR MENTAL SUB-
MISSION IS BROUGHT ABOUT. UNOBTRUSIVELY,
PERSONAL DEVELOPMENT AND VARIOUS CULTURAL
INFLUENCES CAN MAKE MAN MORE VULNERABLE
TO SUGGESTION AND IDEOLOGICAL ATTACK. IN PART
THREE I CALL TO THE READER'S ATTENTION THE
CREEPING INTRUSION INTO OUR MINDS BY TECH-
NOLOGY AND BUREAUCRACY, AND HOW SPECIAL
FORMS OF PREJUDICE AND MASS DELUSION CAN
TAKE POSSESSION OF OUR MINDS BEFORE WE ARE
AWARE OF IT. THE FINAL CHAPTER, AN INQUIRY
ON TREASON AND LOYALTY AGAIN CALLS TO OUR
ATTENTION THE TREMENDOUS INFLUENCE OF MASS
THINKING ON OUR PERSONAL CONCEPTS OF
LOYALTY.

CHAPTER TEN

The Child Is Father to the Man

The time has come to ask ourselves if it is possible that there is something in our own growth and development that may make us more vulnerable to mental intrusion and ultimate brainwashing. Are there, for instance, special coercive needs in us? What is communicated and taught to the child that may keep him a spiritual prisoner of his environment?

These are important questions and would require a thorough philosophic and pedagogic investigation. Nevertheless, for practical purposes, we may limit our attention to two different spheres of development: the influence of parents and the influence of certain social habits. The latter has already been investigated in the second part of this book. Indeed, I must repeat that in my experience all those who are educated under rules of too strict obedience and conformity break down more easily under pressure. During World War II when the so-called *tough* S.S. officers were interrogated after they had become prisoners, they readily surrendered their military secrets. Having lived for years under totalitarian command, they were just as obedient to the new commanding voices. Sometimes we only had to imitate the shouting voices of their masters and they would exchange their former boss for the new one. For them every command had become the automatic trigger for new conforming obedience.

In dealing with members of the Communist Party in this country, we had a comparable experience: the members were politically submissive and changed their obstructive party-strategy to an opposite set of tactics the moment Moscow ordered them to do so.

How Some Totalitarians May Develop

Increasing attention has been given to the various psychological motivations leading to political extremism and a totalitarian mentality in men and women who have been brought up in a democratic atmosphere; but who have voluntarily chosen to associate themselves with some totalitarian ideology. Psychologists who have come into contact with the totalitarian attitude and have studied those who are easily influenced by it agree, by and large, that in the free, democratic countries the option for totalitarianism is nearly always determined by an inner personality factor—frustration, if you will. It is usually neither poverty nor social idealism that makes a man a totalitarian, but mostly internal factors such as extreme submissiveness and masochism on the one hand or a lust for power on the other. Unsolved sibling rivalry plays a role too; I have treated several Nazi collaborators whose political behavior was motivated to some extent by the fact that they were older sons and could not stand the competition with their younger brothers. All these factors help to explain why the totalitarians everywhere can use their propaganda of violence to exploit resentment, hatred, racialism, and political fury. They know that they have only to play on these immature feelings of deprivation and dissatisfaction to bring people under a spell.

In my own experience, I have been amazed to see how unrealistic are the bases for political option in general. Only rarely have I found a person who has chosen any particular political party— democratic or totalitarian—through study and comparison of principles. Too often man's choice of his political affiliations is determined by apathy, by family tradition, by hope for financial gain, or by other irrelevant factors. It is this lack of rational motivation that can make men more susceptible to totalitarian blandishments, even in a democratic community. I remember very clearly, for example, a Dutch physician with whom I went to medical school. He fell in love with the daughter of a Communist and eventually married her. At first he was disturbed by the conflict between his principles and his adoration, but gradually his principles gave in and he started to justify the party line. Later on I met him from time to time. He was an excellent doctor and a jovial fellow, and he took our half-serious quips about his politics in good part. But the moment we began a really serious discussion, he crouched in his official defensive corner and became a different man—sour, mechanical, handing out ready-made arguments. During the war I met him frequently in the course of our common underground work. He had been completely dazed by Stalin's pact with the Nazis, but the moment Russia was invaded and became an ally, he started his aggressive robotism again. Not only was he a staunch fighter against the Nazis, but he insisted that his was the only way to fight. He lost his life on a dangerous mission for the underground, and I always had the feeling that it was in a way welcome to his latent suicidal feelings.

In other Nazis and Communists, both, I have seen dramatic examples of how personal resentments, outside the suffering of real injustice, can lead a man to the side of the rebels. Some of these people were the type who simply submitted passively to a movement stronger than themselves—men and women whose ideology was a reflection of whichever side had caught them first; others were motivated by the need to vent their own personal anger and resentment in some direction and used political action to satisfy this need.

But if we are to come to any real understanding of the internal factors that lead a man to adopt a totalitarian ideology, we must dig a little deeper than this and must give our attention to some basic roots of this problem.

The Molding Nursery

One of the important things we have learned from modern psychology is that the roots of many of our adult attitudes and problems lie far back in the seeming quiet of the nursery and childhood years. The infant's life may appear to be placid and uneventful, but from the moment he is born he hears thousands of rumblings both from inside his own mind and from the world outside. In his mother's womb he knew neither warmth nor cold;

now his skin transmits these sensations to him. As he lay protected in his mother's body, he did not have to breathe, eat, or excrete; now he must do all these things himself. He needs help in doing them, he needs protection, and for this protection and help he must rely on those grown-up giants, Mother and Father. He is utterly and completely dependent, unable by himself to find adequate responses to his needs. There he is, with his pitifully limited means of adaptation, with his minimum of innate patterns of action. Warmth, food, and love, things which he needs to sustain his life, come to him when he does the "right" thing—and the right thing is the learned, civilized thing, not the instinctual, primitive thing. The giants, his parents, make demands on him—they begin to mold him according to their own habits, and the infant must submit to all these external demands in order to get what he wants and needs. He must follow the hundreds of subtle, incomprehensible educational rules in order to be paid back with the affection and protection on which he is so dependent. All of this transforms him into a more or less conforming being. His parents' morality is, as it were, sucked in and becomes an ever-present force inside him. He is imprinted with all kinds of habits which serve to condition him into the particular form of adaptation his parents and his society think good for him. The forms his adult behavior will take are foreshadowed by the forms his parents' behavior take. The patient mother imprints patience on her child; the anxious, compulsive mother imprints tensions on hers.

The child who is brought up in a loving environment will develop inner pictures of love and affection and will be better able to accept all the restrictions his parents impose on his freedom, all the rules they lay down. He will accept timetables, toilet training, parental confusion, without too much inner protest even when his needs run contrary to these social demands. He may want to be fed at a time when, according to his schedule, he should not be hungry. He may want to sleep when his parents want him to be awake. Society demands of him that he learn to postpone his own gratifications, and he will react to this demand in a manner contingent on his own sense of security in his parents' affection. Having to wait for food, not being allowed to suck any more, having to control his need to excrete—all of these require the child to make new and difficult adaptations. His urge for immediate and unconditional satisfaction of his needs has to be transformed into something much more complicated—a whole pattern of learned responses.

It is not important for us to describe here the different ways in which these early cultural obligations are met by the child. But it is important to understand that the cradle and the nursery change and recondition the innate natural responses of the unsocial, primitive child to mold him into an adult, who may be left from his childhood a legacy of frustrations stemming from this molding process. Individual problems are caused by individual patterns of child-rearing; these very patterns are themselves to some degree the product of the cultural traditions in which they are rooted and the mores of the community into which the child is born. To the degree that our society imposes on children frustrations and restrictions for which they are neither biologically nor emotionally ready, to that degree our culture paves the way for adult behavior problems and for neurotic attitudes of submission or aggression, which may find expression in allegiance to some totalitarian group.

Conditioning a child into a servile and submissive attitude, for example, may start when parents rigidly imprint automatic rules of conduct on the infant. They may make a time maniac out of him or a cleaning automaton. They may compel him to speak too early or to be silent when his voice itches to burst out of his throat or to sleep when his body is throbbing with the energy of wakefulness. Such parents impose on their child a constant feeling of guilt—he feels disturbed and unhappy every time he does not comply with their demands. And at the same time they force him to love them even when they are disagreeable. They may compel him to apologize for behavior which seems to him to be perfectly acceptable; they may demand that he confess to crimes which do not exist as crimes for him at his age. Some techniques of brainwashing can be seen at the cradle; the parents may cross-examine him, tie him to their apron strings, or keep him constantly under their eyes. With their solicitous attention they never leave him alone to enjoy feeling of being secure with himself. The helpless child in such an environment becomes emotionally insecure; in exchange for more borrowed security, he becomes more conforming and submissive, although this conforming behavior covers up tremendous inner protest and hostility.

When parents do not permit a child to express his instinctual needs openly and directly, they force him to look for other ways to express them. If during his early training—which may start on the day of his birth—the infant encounters endless restrictions to the direct expression of his needs, he will try to communicate these needs in indirect ways—through tension, restlessness, and crying. Instead of being able to use natural outlets for his instinctual drives, the child is permitted and conditioned to act only through suppression and control of the drive. In his struggle to bring the drive under control in order to please his parents, the child's natural means of expression may become inverted. Instead of expression, he acquires repression. This is where the roots of such adult behavior as abject submissiveness and the urge for conformity lie. The groundwork for this masochistic pattern of giving in is formed in infancy. Submission and confession are the only strategies possible for the child in a world that is too overpowering for him to handle. Inner rebellion, hostility, and hatred must be expressed in a paradoxical way. The child's rigid silence is proof that he wants to cry and yell. He may reproach and attack the hostile world indirectly, through magic gestures, clownish behavior, or even epileptic fits. Compelled to suppress his instinctual needs and his means of achieving their gratification, he may conceal their existence even from himself. Surface conformity becomes his only means of communication, and when this happens words and gestures acquire a concealing function. He never says what he means, and gradually he doesn't even know what he means.

The carry-overs into adult life of this kind of child-rearing are obvious. Trained into conformity, the child may well grow up into an adult who welcomes with relief the authoritarian demands of a totalitarian leader. It is the welcome repetition of an old pattern that can be followed without investment of new emotional energy. Trained previously to divert his aggression to scapegoats, he may now displace his hidden resentments against his parents' rules and regulations toward society as a whole. Or he may find release for them in the wild explosion of pent-up aggression which is exemplified by the lynch mob or by Hitler's storm troopers.

Other forms of parental behavior also have their effect on the child. If the child is trained precociously in habits that would otherwise develop spontaneously at a later age, he may show all kinds of distortions in his natural behavior. The example of the effect of precocious toilet training is common, but there are many other parental commands that can have the same effect on the child. The way the child is clothed or the parents' constant demand that he always be quiet, asleep, and motionless are equally valid examples. When any command is too strictly applied before the child is able to cope with it, it exerts an enormous frustrating influence. What was enforced on the child by some outside power becomes an inner, automatic rule, a compulsion. Let us return to the toilet training example for a moment, though it is only one single part of the whole pattern of training. The child who is trained to control his need to excrete at too early an age learns to keep himself clean and constipated under all circumstances. His body learns how to control itself automatically, but somewhere inside him the child feels contempt for those who have forced him into this behavior. He may grow up to be a chronically hostile adult, ripe for the appeal of some hostile ideology. In less severe cases, the conflict between outside prohibitions and the inner need to let go may create a continuing pattern of inner insecurity. Or it may lead to constant querulous resentment, which can be easily utilized by any would-be dictator.

What we have to emphasize is this: the earliest web of communication between parents and child takes place on what psychology calls a pre-verbal and unconscious level. There is contact without words. The mother transfers her moods directly to the child; he senses and catches her feelings. The child also transfers his moods to her; she feels his pains and joys almost as soon as he does. This sensitivity of the infant makes him react with great intensity—he is profoundly aware of his parents' feelings. Such negative parental factors as anxiety, insecurity, infantilism, mutual disharmony, neurotic love, poverty, the struggle for existence, and compulsive tyranny have an enormous effect on the child. Not long ago I treated an infant who refused any offer of handling or feeding by its mother. The infant "knew" that the mother had a deep-seated hostility against it; it felt her aversion and rejection.

But the infant accepted food and affection from everyone else. The interplay between parental attitudes and child development starts at birth.

Perhaps one of the clearest examples of a distorted growing-up may be seen in one case I treated during the Second World War when I was asked to do a psychological study of an alleged collaborator with the Nazis. This man, who was in England when I saw him, said that he had left Holland, which was then occupied, because he no longer agreed with the German conquerors. When he arrived in England he was, as a matter of careful routine, put in a home for people under investigation as suspected spies. From here, he was very soon taken to a mental institution because of his strange behavior. He was not actually psychotic, but he did have great difficulty in relating to other people. When I went to interview him, it became apparent to me that he was completely confused. He babbled so much that it was almost impossible to understand him. I asked him about his childhood. It was not easy for him to speak about it, but he finally told me something of his background. He was an only child. His mother had been the dominant member of the family, actively working in scientific research. His father, a weak, nebulous figure, had seldom been at home; in his job as the manager of a large firm, he had traveled a great deal. On the rare occasions when the father was at home, the patient remembered long silences between his parents, his father only occasionally protesting against his mother's constant stream of directives. Sometimes the boy joined with his mother in criticizing his father's detachment and lack of interest, sometimes he turned to his father for love and help against his mother's smothering behavior. But he was mostly lost and alone at home. In his late teens, the boy developed some homosexual attachments, in which he played the passive, submissive role. But he only came alive mentally after one of his friends made him attend a fascist rally. The show of strength and aggression excited the boy enormously and even aroused sexual sensations in him. He joined the fascist group, to the great dismay of his parents, but he was never very active in party work because the party did not provide him with the guidance and love for which he yearned.

After the Nazi invasion and occupation, the party demanded that he be more active as a collaborator with the Germans. Now his conscience bothered him, and he became ill and developed all kinds of stomach ailments which were, to a psychiatrist, obviously emotional in origin. He was not, however, strong enough to withdraw from the party completely. He felt caught between two opposing dangers—the party and treason. The childhood struggle began all over again; he felt himself unsafe with either father or mother. So he decided to flee the country because he had a vague feeling that this would help him get away from his conflicts.

Once in England, in the asylum, he felt completely contented. He simply did not understand the serious nature of the accusations that had been made against him. When I spoke to him about world affairs and his political activity, he fell into silence. He did not remember any of the details of his political behavior. It was as if he had lived in a dream since the moment he ran away from Holland. It is entirely possible that the enemy had used him as a tool, but at the time I saw him he was only a near-psychotic, fear-ridden young man. He remained in the institution for the duration of the war.

One thing stands out clearly in this case (aside from its complexity as a pathological phenomenon) and that is the young man's continual search for male authority. This search for spiritual backbone is very common among people who develop totalitarian attachments.

The Father Cuts the Cord

Psychological studies have shown us over and over again that the child's attitude toward the parental authority, with all its subtle internal complications, plays a primary role in determining how he will handle his hostilities—whether he will learn to cope with them or whether he will direct them toward destructive aims. As we said earlier, parents and family form almost the whole environment of the child during the first years of its life. They condition the foundations of his future character. And in the family it is the influence of the father that determines whether the child will stick to its strong natural ties with its mother, to its dependency needs and its needs for protection, or will step out of this maternal realm and will form new ties with new people. The father is the first one who cuts into the essentially biological relation between mother and child. He is what the psychoanalyst calls the first transference figure, the first new prototype to whom the child can transfer its expectations of gratification, its feelings of relatedness, of satisfaction, of fear. This first new trial relationship with the father giant may become the conditioning prototype for every subsequent social relationship.

The child's initial relationship with its mother is purely biological and symbiotic. The womb is replaced by the crib. The mother is the know-all and do-all. Psychoanalysis describes the child's relationship with its mother as one of oral dependency because the helpless infant is completely dependent on the food, care, and warmth the mother provides. The little human being's dependency need lasts longer than that of the other animals. It is this fact that makes man gregarious, dependent on cooperation with others.

The father brings a third person, who has no part in this relationship of biological dependency, into the life of the child. When he cuts into the child's relationship with its mother, he is cutting the psychological umbilical cord just as the doctor cuts the physical one when the infant is delivered. First, he gives the child the opportunity to transfer feelings and expectations to him; later, he brings the child more actively outside the maternal realm and teaches him more and more about social relationships. The specific role of the father as a transference prototype is not so simple as it seems to many fathers. Father is not merely a toy with whom the child can occasionally play. The child needs to identify with this giant who lives with him and with Mother; he wants to become familiar with the giant, he wants the giant to become part of his world. The child wants more than this—he wants to be gratified by Father so that he can love Father as much as he does Mother. But the child will transfer some of its love and emotional investment to Father only if it sees something of Mother in him. Father can do the same things Mother does—he can feed the child, can solace him, can take care of him—and thus the child can maintain a feeling of gratitude and affection toward this third person. This transference of feelings can only take place, however, when the relationship between the parents themselves is tranquil. How can the child identify with and love his parents when they are in constant conflict with each other?

This picture is, of course, something of an oversimplification. There are mothers who behave like cold, distant fathers, and fathers who behave like warm, cuddling mothers. There are grandparents or adoptive parents who can take over. There are many mother or father substitutes. But this is not my point. My point is that in every situation there must be some individual who can become the conditioning prototype for the child's relationships with new beings. This first person is most likely to be the father, and it is he who changes the child's biological dependency into a psychological relationship. When there is no father figure, or if the father is too weak or too busy or is denying and tyrannical toward the child, the result is that the child's relationship with and dependence on the mother remains strong and lasts too long. Consequently, the child's need for social participation and for gregarious ties with others may become to him a consuming need. As an adult he may be willing to join with any social group which promises him support and reassurance. Or his unconscious resentment against the father who did not help him to grow up and become independent may be diverted into a resentment against other symbols of authority, such as society itself. Either way the child may be headed for maladjustment and for difficulties. Either way the child may grow up into an immature adult.

In a study on living by proxy, I described the arrested emotional development that results when the father does not play his proper role or is not present. A child brought up in such an emotionally defective atmosphere searches continually for strong figures who may serve as a proxy for the normal relationships the child would otherwise have had in life. I have treated several cases of homosexuality and other forms of arrested development, both in men and women, which were almost directly attributable to the too strongly tied, symbiotic life with the mother which results from such an environment.

In the building up of man's awareness of an independent self and the establishment of his ability to have easy, relaxed relationships with his fellow men, the father, as the natural chief and protector of the family, plays an important role. He cuts the cord. He may condition the later pattern of dependence and independence. His potential psychological' dominance can become a blessing or a curse, for the child's emotional attitude toward its father becomes the prototype for its attitudes toward future leaders and toward society itself.

We saw this clearly in the case of our "spy" who had never had a strong male guide in his life. Many of the people I investigated, who had chosen to identify themselves with aggressive totalitarian groups, had this problem. For such people, the totalitarian party became both the good father who accepted them and the proxy which gave expression to all their hidden and frustrated hate. The party solves, as it were, their inner problems.

Parental conflict in early childhood, inconsistency, and a threatening, unloving attitude toward the child pave the way for rebellion and submission, and a repetition of this pattern later in life. The wish to break away from the family pattern may lead to rebellion, but the particular form the rebellion takes depends on what political movements can modify and channelize the person's resentment.

This does not mean, of course, that there is not a hard core of totalitarian-minded people, nourished in the cradle by the dogmas of their totalitarian parents, who give themselves to their party tasks because they have never known a different world. According to Almond, these types are found particularly in our Western world among high-echelon extremists. They take in the totalitarian form of socialism with their mother's milk; they are members of an increasing group of hereditary totalitarian conformists. Here, no father rebellion is needed to become an extreme revolutionary.

But the bulk of the totalitarian-minded in the democratic societies are men and women who are attracted to this destructive way of life for inner emotional reasons unknown to themselves. My own experiences with both Communists and Nazis during the Second World War has shown me this truth over and over again. In Holland, as in the other Nazi-occupied countries, the Communists and their sympathizers fought bravely with us in the underground as our temporary companions. Even during that time of national crisis and terror, they were never free from bitter reproach and resentment toward us. They insisted that their ideology was the only correct one and showed, sometimes openly, sometimes covertly, that when the Nazis were defeated, they would renew their struggle against the social order. Let me give just one example to illustrate this point. One of the Communists was a very brave physician (not the same man about whom I spoke earlier). He had killed a Nazi leader, and later he himself died a horrible death. Here was a grown man who had never been able to overcome a certain adolescent self-righteousness and aggressiveness. On the very night when, in deadly peril, he sought refuge in my home, he felt compelled to engage me in a long theoretical political discussion with him, full of bitterness. He disdainfully reproached the other resistance groups because they did not share his political views. His views and ideals, I must say in all justice to him, seemed sincere to me, but he was filled with so much unresolved hostility toward the government of his fatherland that he was ready at all times to overthrow it. The core of his fallacious reasoning I found was the confusion about ends and means in the struggle for social justice. For him, tactics and strategy had become more important than the final aim of peaceful coexistence between men on earth. His violent death—after murdering an S.S. officer—was partly the result of the fact that he pursued tactics beyond the strategic needs of the moment. True, in the end he gave his life for his ideals and for his native land, but up to the end he carried a bitter grudge against all those who were not in complete agreement with everything he thought and felt. It was that personal grudge and hostility which led him to bad planning and his ultimate fate.

Most of us are not clearly and completely aware that alongside our wish to be good, adjusted citizens, we also have hidden wishes to violate our allegiances to the social formation of which we are members. These wishes are not based on reason and intelligence; they are purely emotional. They are founded by the ways we have been brought up, by our relationships with our parents, by our educational system, by our attitudes toward ourselves and toward authority. But all men who adhere rigidly to any set of political convictions, and especially those who have embraced some totalitarian ideology, believe that their attitudes emerge from rational conviction and are the result of normal intellectual development. They insist that those who do not agree with them are committed to a stuffy, outmoded way of thinking. They cannot see their own vengeful and disloyal attitudes as something asocial and abnormal.

To the psychologist, it is eminently clear that these attitudes have their roots not in intellectual conviction but in some deep-seated emotional need. I have often seen cases where this blind, rigid allegiance to a totalitarian ideology was actually a defiant rebellion against a compelling inner need to grow and to change and to become mature. In these people, the selection of a special political party was only a substitute for their need for dependency. Ideologic stubbornness is often tragic because it may cover up basic neurotic reactions that may lead to self-destruction. One of my patients was a young woman whose ultra-left beliefs were a defense against her hidden incestuous feelings toward a reactionary father. It took protracted therapy to bring her to an understanding of the real nature of her difficulty and to get her to see that there was nothing shameful or disgusting about the infantile love and resentment she was trying to conceal through her political behavior.

The need for authority, when it is not understood, and the confused resistance to authority are the roots from which the totalitarian attitude may grow. Whenever the father-leader fails, he sets up a pattern of future trouble with authority. Instead of a mature relationship with his fellow men, the child becomes an adult who is forced to choose the tyrannical totalitarian tie to keep his inner tensions in check.

Whenever there is parental conflict, the child grows into an adult burdened with conflicts who may be eager to accept the simple solutions totalitarianism offers. Whenever there is parental compulsion, which gives the child no chance to develop its own attitudes and evaluations, the child grows up into a conforming adult, whose entire life may be spent in a search for outside authority, for someone to tell him what to do.

CHAPTER ELEVEN

Mental Contagion and Mass Delusion

During disturbed times such as these, the thoughts of everyone follow the diplomatic play going on at the various political conferences. It would be worth while to investigate whether it is possible for leaders of nations to arrive at a common understanding as a result of mutual exchange of words, ideas, and the negotiating of treaties. Yet, the various cultures in the world and the different ideologies not only speak different languages, but even their ways of thinking are different. Unobtrusively, our personal past and our cultural environment creep into our thinking habits. Our feelings and thoughts are conditioned and coerced by various social influences.

It is already possible to bring to the surface some of the illusions and prejudices people have about one another. We may say that the special environments in which people develop and the habits they build up foster subtle illusions and delusions in persons, of which they are, for the most part, unaware. Through research in the field, anthropology and psychology have been able to compare different ideologies in people by observing the growth of the wholesome and the unwholesome—in the child, in groups, in tribes, and, lastly, in nations. The findings call to our attention the difficult art of argument in situations where there is scarcely any common ground of communication and understanding.

In a study on mental coercion we have to trace some of these mass psychological influences which condition our attitude in life.

The Affirmation of My Own Errors

The lie I tell ten times gradually becomes a half truth to me. And as I continue to tell my half-truth to others, it becomes my cherished delusion.

We rediscover this phenomenon every day in that huge laboratory of human relations we call psychological counseling and psychotherapy. Let us look at just one simple example, the case of a perfectly healthy child who decides one day that she doesn't want to go to school because schoolwork seems so very difficult. So she tells her mother that she has a headache, and mother agrees to let her stay at home. Thus the girl avoids the schoolwork she dreads and gets the additional gratification of her mother's solicitous and tender nursing.

The next time our little girl wants to stay home it is easier to pretend she has a headache—and the third time it is easier still. Gradually the girl herself begins to believe in her recurrent illness. Her conscience bothered her the first time she lied, but by now her initial lie has become an ingenuous truth to her. By the time our heroine becomes a grown woman she will have to consult with a doctor about her constantly recurring headaches. Doctor and patient will have to spend many hours untangling the web of half-lies, innuendos, and self-pitying complaints until the patient rediscovers that her headaches all began on that one day she didn't want to go to school.

Delusional headaches afflict the world itself. Political demagoguery is, to some extent, a problem in our country. The particular form this demagoguery takes is only a passing phase, and when our current dragons and inner phantoms have been laid to rest, the eternal demagogue may arise anew. He will accuse others of conspiracy in order to prove his own importance. He will try to intimidate those who are neither so iron-fisted nor so hotheaded as he, and temporarily he will drag some people into the web of his delusions. Perhaps he will wear a mantle of martyrdom to arouse the tears of the weak-hearted. With his emotionalism and suspicion, he will shatter the trust of citizens in one another. His delusions of grandeur will infect those insecure souls who hope that some of his dictatorial glamour will rub off on them.

Unfortunately the problem of delusion has been studied almost exclusively in terms of its pathological manifestations. The psychiatrist who has encountered delusions of grandeur in his patients has in the past lacked the philosophical and sociological background necessary to enable him to form comparisons between his patients' delusional systems and mass delusion in the world. In dealing with patients suffering from megalomania or persecution mania, he has tended to rely too much on hypotheses which explain pathological delusions as the product of anatomical changes in the individual brain; he has not given enough attention to the question of whether or not these phenomena are in any way related to an abnormal way of thinking in a physically normal person.

Since the growth of anthropology and the social sciences in the last decades, new light has been thrown on the subject of mass feelings and mass delusion. Obviously these are not phenomena which a pathologist can examine under a microscope. They demand a knowledge of history and social psychology and of all the studies which concern interhuman relations and man's collective thinking.

To arrive at a clinical stage of study of this subject, it is necessary to divest oneself of various fixed philosophical ideas which have dominated scientific thought since Aristotle. There is, for example, the doctrine of the identity of all thinking processes and the possible universality of human understanding. This is essentially founded on the belief that all human beings think in the same way. But against this hypothesis is the observable truth that philosophers themselves have the utmost difficulty in reaching mutual understanding. This may be largely due to the fact that different men have different methods and standards of thinking. For centuries, science has adopted the Aristotelian dictum that most thought is carried on according to the established rules of logic, which apply in the same way as the laws of nature. It was the philosopher Francis Bacon who first pointed out, in his theory of idols, that although the laws of logic and clear thinking certainly exist, men may or may not make use of them; depending on the emotional circumstances, "thoughts are often the theatrical curtains to conceal personal passions and reactions." In this statement the philosopher who lived during Shakespeare's time might almost be attacking the seeming logic of modern demagoguery. Since the Renaissance, therefore, it has been acknowledged that human feelings and personal inclinations mold and direct thought, and this point of view rather early found its most moving expression in the works of Spinoza and Pascal.

When we come into contact with the phenomena of collective passion and mass delusion, it is impossible to keep modern psychology out of the picture whether we look at it philosophically or politically. For, when examining this problem, we are immediately confronted with the question, Do these disquieting phenomena in group life, which lead to so much mutual misunderstanding, arise from the fact that the group is in a particular, immature, and adolescent phase of psychological and political development?

It will be illuminating and may help us answer the question if we study briefly the history of the growth of consciousness and awareness in the individual mind as it passes through successive stages from infancy to maturity, since we can, in fact, find a parallel between such stages of growth in the individual and the human group.

Stages of Thinking and Delusion*

The psyche is constantly confronted with and communicating with the outside world, and at every phase of an individual's development that world and its events are experienced differently. Although different scientists have drawn different conclusions about the various phases and their implications, the very recognition of change and growth of personal outlook is one of the most important scientific findings in psychology and is agreed on by all psychologists. Let me briefly explain here the developmental approach to human psychology. It is not the only one, but it will serve to illustrate the tremendous impact of immature and delusional thinking on our final opinions.

Developmental psychology—as studied in children and primi-

* Here I follow in part the classification of S. Ferenczi and that of my own book on delusion.

tives—posits at the origin of thinking, in both the individual and the race, a hallucinatory stage of the mind, in which there is no experience of difference between the inside and the outside world; the mental separation and distantiation between the self and the world has not yet taken place. The psyche is felt to be omnipotent —all that is experienced inside the self is attributed to the universe as well and is imagined to be part of that universe. According to developmental psychology, the infant experiences the world in this way, and in certain types of insanity the adult will revert to this hallucinatory stage. Yet, even mature man does not succeed completely in separating internal fantasy from outside reality, and often he thinks that his private and subjective moods are caused by some external actuality.

In the next stage, that of animistic thinking, there is still a partial sense of oneness between the ego and the world. The individual's inner experience, his fears, his feelings, are projected onto seeming causative agents in the outside world. The outside world is a continual demonic threat to him. The child who bumps against the table projects onto that table a hostile living power, and hits back. The primitive tribesman, hunted by beasts of prey, attributes to the animal he feared a divine power, that of a hostile god. The entire outside world may in fact be peopled with the fears of men. In times of panic and fear, we all may populate our neighborhood with nonexistent traitors or fifth columnists. Our animistic thinking is continually busy accusing others of what actually occurs inside our own minds. Nowadays there are no devils and ghosts in trees and in wild animals; they have made their homes in the various scapegoats created by dictators and demagogues.

The third stage is that of magical thinking in which there is still a sense of intimate connection between man and his outside world. However, man places himself more in opposition to the world than in union with it. He wants to negotiate with the mysterious powers around him. Magic is in fact the simplest strategy of man. He has discovered that he can manipulate the world with signs and gestures or sometimes with real actions or changes. He erects totem poles and sacrificial blocks; he makes talismans and strange medicines. He uses words as powerful signs to change the world. He develops a ritual to satisfy his need for coming to terms with the outside world.

Which of us has not felt a sudden desire to count cobblestones or is not the jealous possessor of an amulet or some other secret token whose power would be lost if its existence were known to others?

Immature as they are, these tokens serve to build up happiness and a good life. We all still live in the world of magic and are caught in the delusion of happy manipulation of nature. The modern tribe drives around in mechanized cars and becomes a megalomaniac sorcerer of the wheel. Millions of victims are brought to the altar of the god Speed because of our hidden delusion that frenzied rapidity prolongs life. The engine and the gadget have replaced the more mysterious amulet of earlier days. Knowledge is still in the service of power instead of in the service of understanding.

In the last phase of mental development, man makes a complete separation between himself and the outside world. He not only lives with things and tries to manipulate them, but he also lives in opposition to them. In this phase of mature reality confrontation, man becomes an observer of his own life. He recognizes the abyss of his own being. He sees his body and mind as separate from the world. With hands, ears, eyes, and his controlling mind, he confronts reality. He steps back from the world and observes it. He is, in fact, the only animal that walks erect, straightforwardly facing the world. He is the only animal that uses his hands and his senses as verifying instruments. Gradually his own mind-body becomes an instrument whose drives he may accept or reject. Only man is able to see his drives and instincts as either dangerous or useful. Man not only knows an externally imposed fear, but he knows an inner fear, fear of losing the inner controls he has acquired at so high a price. With arms and hands man reaches out— not only toward the outside which he once hoped to conquer with magic gestures as a baby does, but also he knowingly reaches out toward an inside world. Mature man lives between an inner and an outer world.

There is something tragic about this laborious process of becoming conscious of a separate inner and outer reality. In becoming mature, man awakens from a sweet primitive dream in which he was part of an individual whole, part of a nirvanic world of equanimity. The sense of lost unity with the universe lingers on, and in moments of mass tension, or in times of crisis, he reaches toward that ancient experience of impersonal, irresponsible bliss.

Utter passivity or self-destruction, artificial ecstasy obtained by means of drugs, the suicidal wish for eternal sleep—all are devices by which man hopes to fulfill that eternal yearning.

At what stage in connection with these developments of human experience may we speak of delusion? When the member of a primitive tribe placates the mysterious and hostile world by prayer to his totem animal, we do not call this delusion; but if a man who has attained to a more advanced stage of thinking relapses into such a primitive habit of thought, then it is possible to call this falling back (retrogression) a delusion.

The Loss of Verifiable Reality

Delusion we may thus tentatively define as the loss of an independent, verifiable reality, with a consequent relapse into a more primitive stage of awareness. Just as the young woman we spoke about earlier began to believe in and suffer from her headaches, so the man who sells his private fantasy first as a rumor and then as a factual truth gradually loses his awareness that his initial statements were in fact deceits, and his delusion becomes a kind of permanent petrification of his original primitive wishful thinking.

There are several factors which promote deluded thinking. Retrogression and primitivization may occur as a result of physical disease, particularly diseases of the brain, and it is with this type of delusions that psychiatrists deal. Many brain diseases put out of operation the brain cortex, the organ which developed last in the evolutionary process and which makes us aware and controls our thinking. When this disturbance of function happens, genetically older types of brain functioning have to take over.

Most of the causes of delusions are not purely organic, however. The same effect of regression may be produced by hypnosis and mass hypnosis, which, by dislocating the higher forms of alert consciousness, reduce the subject to the primitive stage of collective participation and of oneness experience.

If awareness and reality confrontation become rigid and automatic, if man does not look for alert and repeated verifications of what he finds in the world, he may develop delusions—ideas not adapted to the reality situation. Apparently the human being requires constant confrontation and verification with various aspects of reality if he is to remain alive and alert. When experience is petrified into dogma, the dogma itself stands in the way of new verification and of new truth. The delusion of a nation that calls itself the "chosen" country makes it harder for that nation to collaborate with other nations.

How deeply involved the process of thought control is with the general formation of ideas in our time can be shown by the following experience. After the First World War, I made the acquaintance of a German philosopher dedicated to the idealistic philosophy of his country. Germany went through a creative phase, new ideas arose of fraternity and world peace. Germany, the defeated country, would show its spiritual power. During our vacations we walked together through the sunny mountains of Ticino and devoted our philosophical conversation to the eternal yearnings of mankind for harmony and friendship. We became friends and wrote to each other about our mutual work, till the shadow of totalitarianism came over his country. At first he was skeptical and even critical about Nazism. Our correspondence diminished, and when he gradually became *gleichgeschaltet* and a member of the party, the final mental cleavage followed. I never heard about him any more.

So many philosophers surrender their theoretical thinking under the impact of powerful mass emotions. The reason lies not only in anxiety and submissiveness. It is a much deeper emotional process. People want to speak the language of their country and fatherland. In order to breathe, they have to identify with the ideological clichés of their surroundings. Spiritually they cannot stand alone. Stefan Zweig wrote during the First World War that this inner process of speaking along with the chauvinistic voices around him was experienced by him as a deep inner conflict. *"Ich hatte den Willen nicht mehr gerecht zu sein* (I did not have the will any more to be just to the others)."

Mass Delusion

It is interesting to note that the phenomenon of institutionalized mass delusion has so far received little scientific treatment, although the term is bandied about wherever the problems of political propaganda are discussed. But science has shied away from scrutinizing the collective mental aberration we call mass delusion when it is connected with present-day affairs; it is the historical examples, such as witchcraft and certain forms of mass hysteria, that have been examined in great detail.

In our era of warring ideologies, in a time of battle for man's mind, this question demands attention. What is mass delusion? How does it arise? What can we do to combat it?

The fact that I have made an analogy between the totalitarian frame of mind and the disease of mental withdrawal known as schizophrenia indicates that I consider the totalitarian ideology delusional and the totalitarian frame of mind a pathological distortion that may occur in anyone. When we tentatively define delusion as the loss of an independent, verifiable reality, with a consequent relapse into a more primitive state of awareness, we can see how the phenomenon of totalitarianism itself can be considered delusional.

For it is delusional (unadapted to reality) to think of man as an obedient machine. It is delusional to deny his dynamic nature and to try to arrest all his thinking and acting at the infantile stage of submission to authority. It is delusional to believe that there is any one simple answer to the many problems with which life confronts us, and it is delusional to believe that man is so rigid, so unyielding in his structure that he has no ambivalences, no doubts, no conflicts, no warring drives within him.

Where thinking is isolated without free exchange with other minds and can no longer expand, delusion may follow. Whenever ideas are compartmentalized, behind and between curtains, the process of continual alert confrontation of facts and reality is hampered. The system freezes, becomes rigid, and dies of delusion.

Examples of this can be found in very small communities cut off from the world. On fishing vessels which have been at sea a long time, contagious religious mania coupled with ritual murder has been known to break out. In small village communities there are instances of collective delusion, often under the influence of one obsessed person. The same thing happens in the more gigantic totalitarian communities, cut off from contact with the rest of the world. Is this not what happened in Hitler Germany, where free verification and self-correction were forbidden? Indeed, we can show that historically this is the case with every secluded civilization. If there is not interchange with other people, the civilization degenerates, becomes the victim of its own delusions, and dies.

We can phrase the concept of delusion in a different way. It is a more primitive, distorted form of thinking found in groups or individuals, looked at only from their limited viewpoint. Delusional thinking doesn't know the concept of delusional thinking. The fakir lying on his bed of nails would be called a deluded man if he exhibited his devotion on Fifth Avenue, but among his own people his behavior is considered saintly and eminently sane. A member of a primitive tribe will not see in the ceremony of devil exorcism or a revival meeting an instance of mass delusion. But a man who has passed through this stage of mental development to a level of greater perspective and awareness will recognize that delusional notions lie behind such ceremonies.

Whether or not we are able to detect delusion when it appears depends entirely on circumstances, upon the state of civilization in which we live, upon the groups and the social class to which we belong. For delusion and retrogression are terms which imply a special social and intellectual level of awareness. That is why it is so difficult to detect the delusions and primitive rituals in our own midst. Our present-day civilization is full of mass delusions, prejudices, and collective errors which can be recognized easily if viewed from above, but which cannot be detected if they are seen from within. While the delusion of witchcraft has been banished, we have never freed ourselves from the delusion of cultural or racial inferiority and superiority. Medieval mass obsessions such as tarantism and St. Vitus's dance are little known now among Western nations; in their place we have mass meetings with shouting crowds expressing in delusional ecstasy their affiliation to some political delusion. Instead of the dance fury, we have the raving frenzy of the motor, or the passive peeping contagion of the television screen.

As we saw in the chapter on Totalitaria, mass delusion can be induced. It is simply a question of organizing and manipulating collective feelings in the proper way. If one can isolate the mass, allow no free thinking, no free exchange, no outside corrective, and can hypnotize the group daily with noises, with press and radio and television, with fear and pseudo-enthusiasms, any delusion can be instilled. People will begin to accept the most primitive and inappropriate acts. Outside occurrences are usually the triggers that unleash hidden hysterical and delusional complexes in people. Collective madness justifies the repressed personal madness in each individual. That is why it is so easy to sloganize people into the mass hysteria of war. The outside enemy who is attacked by vituperative slogans is merely the scapegoat and substitute for all the anger and anxiety that lives inside the harassed people.

Delusions, carefully implanted, are difficult to correct. Reasoning no longer has value; for the lower, more animal type of thinking becomes deaf to any thought on a higher level. If one reasons with a totalitarian who has been impregnated with official clichés, he will sooner or later withdraw into his fortress of collective totalitarian thinking. The mass delusion that gives him his feelings of belonging, of greatness, of omnipotence, is dearer to him than his personal awareness and understanding.

The lonely prisoner in a totalitarian prison camp is the more easily compelled to surrender gradually to the collective thinking of his guardians when part of his own infantile thinking has been conditioned to give in to strong suggestive power. He has to communicate with his guardians lest he be delivered to his own private delusions. Only a few remain their true selves in that heroic battle.

The situation of our prisoners of war in Korea, who lived there for months and years, cannot be studied without taking into account the atmosphere of mass delusion. In a sphere filled with rumors without an opportunity to verify the facts, the mind is ever on the alert, but its observations are distorted. The process of mass brainwashing, with continual propaganda, made it very difficult for the individual to observe his comrades objectively. In such surroundings, it is easy to make an innocent scapegoat for all the suffering of the group—and facts can easily be hallucinated in such an atmosphere of mass contagion.

In one of the prison camps, I had to make a report about a man who was exorcized and even attacked by the others because of his brute homosexual behavior. During the investigation, no fact, no victim, could be reported. Rumors there were plenty, expressing hatred toward a lonely, sarcastic, unsocial being, who had aroused the latent homosexual feelings of the other campers, thereby attacking their manliness.

No P.O.W. accused of collaboration with the enemy should be convicted without a study having been made of the rumors rampant in his camp.

In totalitarian surroundings, hardly anyone keeps his thinking free of contagion, and nearly everyone becomes, albeit temporarily, the victim of delusion.

The Danger of Mental Contagion

Indeed, there is a continual danger of mental contagion. People are in constant psychic exchange with one another. As a country, we have to ask what dangerous mental pollution may come to us from the other side of the border.

Let me make it crystal clear that I am far from insensitive to the danger of totalitarian subversion and aggression with which we are now faced. My own experiences with the Nazis made it painfully obvious to me that these dangers must not be minimized. As a psychologist, too, I am deeply aware of the contagious nature of totalitarian propaganda and of the fact that free citizens in a free country must be on their guard to protect themselves. But we must learn to fight these dangers in democratic ways; and I am afraid that too often in our fight against them we may take a leaf from the totalitarian book. Let me cite but one example of this.

The Feinberg Law in New York State, enacted in order to protect children against the dissemination of dangerous political propaganda, is partly based on this concept of mental contagion. It aims to protect the schools against the subtle infiltration of subversive ideas. It seems at first sight like a simple solution: you just stop subversion before it can affect the impressionable minds of our children.

But the fact remains that it presents all kinds of psychological difficulties. In our fear of being polluted, we create norms and schemes against which we measure the acceptability of unorthodox ideas, and we forget that the presence of minority ideas, acceptable or not, is one of the ways in which we protect ourselves against the creeping growth of conformist majority thinking in us. U.S. Supreme Court Justice Hugo Black, in his dissenting opinion on the Feinberg Law* made this point:

> This is another of those rapidly multiplying legislative enactments which make it dangerous . . . to think or say anything except what a transient majority happens to approve at the moment.

> Basically these laws rest on the belief that Government should supervise and limit the flow of ideas into the minds of men. The tendency of such governmental policy is to mould people into a common intellectual pattern. Quite a different governmental policy rests on the belief that Government should leave the mind and spirit of man absolutely free.

> Such a governmental policy encourages varied intellectual outlooks in the belief that the best views will prevail. This policy of freedom is in my judgment embodied in the First Amendment and made applicable to the states by the Fourteenth.

> Because of this policy, public officials cannot be constitutionally vested with powers to select the ideas people can think about, censor the public views they can express, or choose the persons or groups people can associate with. Public officials with such powers are not public servants; they are public masters.

We cannot prevent one mental contagion through enforcing another. The only way we can give man the strength to withstand mental infection is through giving him the utmost freedom in the exchange of ideas. People have to learn to ask questions without demanding that they be answered immediately. The free man is the man who learns to live with problems in the hope that they will be solved sometime—either in his own generation or the next. Man's curiosity and inquisitiveness have to be stimulated. We have to fight man's growing fear of thinking for himself, of being original, and of being willing to fight for what he believes in. On the other hand, we also have to learn to resist ideas. Governments may be overthrown not only by physical violence, but also by mental

* *The New York Times,* March 4, 1952.

violence, by suggestive and menticidal penetration of young minds, by rigid conditioning, regimentation, and prohibition of dissent.

The Explanation Delusion

One of the most *coercive* delusions is the *explanation delusion*, the need to explain and interpret everything because the person has a simple ideology in his pocket. Unwittingly the victim of this delusion wraps the magic cloak of omniscience around himself, and this provokes awe and submission in those men who have a strong need for rational explanation of phenomena they do not understand. The quack, for instance, with his gesture of omniscience pushes his victim into a kind of nothingness so that he feels himself become smaller and smaller in relation to the great mysteries of the world. It is this compulsive need to be the wise guy and the magician who knows all the answers that we so often find in the totalitarian world, and nobody, your author included, is completely free from seizing on these premature answers.

It is among the intelligentsia, and especially among those who like to play with thoughts and concepts without really taking part in the cultural endeavors of their epoch, that we often find the glib compulsion to explain everything and to understand nothing. Their retreat into intellectual isolation and ivory-tower philosophy is a source of much hostility and suspicion from those who receive the stones of intellectualism instead of the bread of understanding. The intelligentsia has a special role in our democratic world as teachers of ideas, but every teaching is an emotional relation, a matter of loving your students. It is a moving among them and taking part in their doubts in order to share together the adventure of common exploration of the unknown.

Paradoxically, we may say that we need the experience with the totalitarians if only to discover a reflection of their rigidities in our own democratic system.

The Liberation from Magic Thinking

In our Western civilization, the growth of the mass media of communication has increased the influence of collective pressure on both our prejudices and our unbiased thinking. We live in a world of constant noise which captures our minds even when we are not aware of it.

Already we have in our society the problem of the lonely, unheard voices. I am convinced that there are many wise men among us whose voices and learning would help us to correct that part of our thinking which is delusional. But their wise words are shouted down by an excess of noise from elsewhere. In our society a man can not simply communicate his wisdom and insight any more; in order to be heard, he has to advertise and fortify it with megacyclic power and official labels. An organization must stand behind him and must make sure that he will be rightly timed so that there will be listeners to receive his message. He must have an acknowledged label and official diploma; otherwise his voice is lost.

To correct mass delusion is one of the most difficult tasks of democracy. Democracy pleads for freedom of thought, and this means that it demands the right of all men to test all forms of collective emotion and collective thinking. This testing is possible only if constant personal and collective self-criticism is encouraged. Democracy must face this task of preserving mobility of thought in order to free itself from blind fears and magic. The clash and mutual impact of a variety of opinions which are characteristic of democracy may not directly produce truth, but they prepare the way.

At this very moment the whole world dances around a delusion, around the magic idea that the material and military power behind an argument will bring us nearer to the truth, and nearer to safety. Yet, one push of the button and the atomic missiles may lead us all to mutual suicide.

In a world of warring and contrasting thoughts and delusions, the solution lies in the delineation of frontiers, of awareness of mutual limits. This agreement on what it is we disagree about is the first step to understanding.

CHAPTER TWELVE

Technology Invades Our Minds

It is rather difficult to describe the onslaught on our minds made by the intrusion of technical thinking. This is so because technology has such contrasting influences. The influence can be a blessing, making us more independent of threatening forces of nature; but at the same time the tool and the machine can dominate us. This inner antinomy of technization we *must* master—will we not otherwise be dragged down into the maelstrom of ever-increasing technical development to final atomic catastrophe! The peculiar paradox of technology lies in this: gradually the well-being of the machine (autocar, factory) assumes greater importance and value than the well-being of man and mankind.

The growth of technology, of the manifold mechanical instruments in the services of our fantasies, has thrown mankind back to an infantile dream of unlimited power. There he sits, the little man, in his room with various gadgets around him. Just pushing a button changes the world for him. What might! And what still further power he envisions! Yet what mental danger.

The growth of technology may confuse man's struggle for mental maturity. The practical application of science and tools originally were meant to give man more security against outside physical forces. It safeguarded his inner world; it freed time and energy for meditation, concentration, play, and creative thinking. Gradually the very tools man made took possession of him and pushed him back into serfdom instead of toward liberation. Man became drunk with technical skill; he became a technology addict. Technology calls forth from people, unknown to themselves, an infantile, servile attitude. We have nearly all become slaves of our cars. Technical security paradoxically may increase cowardice. There is almost no challenge any more to face the forces of nature outside us and the forces of instinct within us. Because the very technical world has become for us that magical challenge which nature originally afforded.

It is the very subservience to technology that constitutes an attack on thinking. The child that is confronted from early youth with all modern devices and gadgets of technology—the radio, the motor, the television set, the film—is *unwittingly* conditioned to millions of associations, sounds, pictures, movements, in which he takes no part. He has no need to think about them. They are too directly connected with his senses. Modern technology teaches man to take for granted the world he is looking at; he takes no time to retreat and reflect. Technology lures him on, dropping him into its wheels and movements. No rest, no meditation, no reflection, no conversation—the senses are continually overloaded with stimuli. The child doesn't learn to question his world any more; the screen offers him answers—ready-made. Even his books offer him no human encounter—nobody reads to him; the screen people tell him their story in their way. Technical knowledge forced upon him in this way makes no demand that he think about what he sees and hears. Conversation is becoming a lost art. The machine age rushes on, leaving no time for quiet reading and encounter with the creative arts. We do see a countercurrent, however, in the do-it-yourself movement. Here we probably see a resurgence of the creative spirit and a challenge to the engineer who creates the robot.

In an overtechnical world, body and mind no longer exist. Life becomes only a part of a greater technical and chemical thought process. Mathematical equations intrude into human relations. We learn, for example, through the doctrine of guilt by association, the simple equation that the enemies of our enemies have to be our friends and that the friends of our enemies have to be our enemies—as if only simple addition of positive and negative signs exist by which to evaluate human beings.

The Creeping Coercion by Technology

Radio and television catch the mind directly, leaving children no time for calm, dialectic conversation with their books. The view from the screen doesn't allow for the freedom-arousing mutuality of communication and discussion. Conversation is the lost art. These inventions steal time and steal self-awareness. What technology gives with one hand—easiness and physical security—it takes away with the other. It has taken away affectionate relationships between men. The depersonalized Christmas card with its printed signature, the form letter, the very typewriter are examples of mechanical proxies. Technical intrusion usurps human relationships, as if people no longer had to give one another attention and love any more. The bottle replaces Mother's breast, the nickel in the automat replaces Mother's preparation of sandwiches. The impersonal machine replaces human gesture and mutuality. Children educated in this way prefer to be alone, with fantasies to escape into and gadgets to play with. Mechanization pushes them into mental withdrawal.

Technology suggests and creates the feeling of man's omnipotence on the one hand, but on the other, the smallness of man, his weakness and inferiority compared with the might of machinery. The power of man's creative mind is disguised behind dreams of social machines and world mechanics. Mechanics in political maneuverings are overestimated and go beyond reason. We use intelligence and counterintelligence, trickery and political machines, forgetting the "emotional reasons" which underlie human brilliance and stupidity. There exists a relationship between naive belief in technology only and a naive belief in human intelligence, logic, and innocence that was part of the optimistic liberalist feeling prevalent in the nineteenth century. We see in both beliefs the denial of the irrational depths of the mind.

What is the ultimate result of technical progress? Does it drive people more and more to the fear and despair brought on by a love-empty push-button world? Does it create a megalomaniac happiness won by remote control of other people? Does it deliver people to the unsatisfying emptiness of leisure hours filled with boredom? Is the ultimate result *living by proxy,* experiencing the world only from the movie or television screen, instead of living and laboring and creating one's own?

In cases of television addiction, I observed the following points:

1. The television fascination is a real addiction; that is to say, television can become habit-forming, the influence of which cannot be stopped without active therapeutic interference.

2. It arouses precociously sexual and emotional turmoil, seducing children to peep again and again, though at the same time they are confused about what they see.

3. It continuously provides satisfaction for aggressive fantasies (western scenes, crime scenes) with subsequent guilt feelings—since the child unconsciously tends to identify with the criminal, despite all the heroic avengers.

4. It is a stealer of time.

5. Preoccupation with television prevents active inner creativity—children and adults merely sit and watch the pseudo-world of the screen instead of confronting their own difficulties. If there is a conflict with parents who have no time for their youngsters, the children surrender all the more willingly to the screen. The screen talks to them, plays with them, takes them into a world of magic fantasies. For them, television takes the place of a grownup and is forever patient. This the child translates into love.

As in all mass media, we have to be aware of the hypnotizing, seductive action of any all-penetrating form of communication. People become fascinated even when they do not want to look on. We must keep in mind that every step in personal growth needs isolation, needs inner conversation and deliberation and a reviewing with the self. Television hampers this process and prepares the mind more easily for collectivization and cliché thinking. It persuades onlookers to think in terms of mass values. It intrudes into family life and cuts off the more subtle interfamilial communication.

The world of tomorrow will witness a tremendous battle between technology and psychology. It will be a fight of technology versus nature, of systematic conditioning versus creative spontaneity. The veneration of the machine implies the turning of mechanical knowledge into power, into push-button power. Mechanical instruments of destruction such as the H-bomb have translated the primitive human urge for destruction into large-scale scientific killing. Now, this destructive potential may become an easy tool for any potentate crazy for power. Driven by technology, our own world has become more interdependent, and through our dependence on technical knowledge and devices, we ourselves are in danger of delivering our people to the more brutal totalitarians. This is the actual dilemma of our civilization. The machine that became a tool of human organization and made possible the conquest of nature, has acquired a dictatorial position. It has forced people into automatic responses, into rigid patterns and destructive habits.

The machine has aroused an ever-increasing yearning for speed, for frenzied accomplishments. There exists a psychological relationship between *speedomania* (frenzied swiftness) and ruthlessness. Behind the wheel in a fast car, a driver becomes drunk with power. Here again we see the denial of the concept of natural, steady growth. Ideas and methods need time to mature. The machine forces results prematurely: evolution is turned into revolution of wheels. The machine is the denial that progress has to grow within us before it can be realized outside ourselves. Mechanization takes away the belief in mental struggle, the belief that problem-solving needs time and repeated attempts. Without such beliefs, the platitude will take over, the digest and the hasty memorandum. A mechanized world believes only in condensation of problems and not in a continuous dialectic struggle between man and the questions he construes.

One of the fallacies of modern technique is its direction toward greater *efficiency*. With less energy, more has to be produced. This principle may be right for the machine, but is not true for the human organism. In order to become strong and to remain strong, man has to learn to overcome resistances, to face challenges, and to test himself again and again. Luxury causes mental and physical atrophy.

The devaluation of the individual human brain, replacing it by mechanical computers, also suggests the totalitarian system for which its citizens are compelled to become more and more the servile tools. The inhuman "system" becomes the aim, a system that is the product of technocracy and dehumanization and which may result in organized brutality and the crushing of any personal morality. In a mechanical society a set of values are forcibly imprinted on the unconscious mind, the way Pavlov conditioned his dogs. Our brains then no longer need to serve us or develop the thinking process; machines will do this for us. In technocracy, emphasis is on behavior free of emotions and creativity. We speak of "electric brains," forgetting that actually creative minds are behind these brains and their frailties. For some engineers, minds have become no more than electric lamps in a totalitarian laboratory. Between man and his fellow man there has been interposed a tremendous, cold, paper force, a nameless bureaucracy of rules and tools. Mechanization has brought into being the mysterious "pimp" in human relations, the man in between, the mechanical bureaucrat, who is powerful but impersonal. He has become a new source of magic fear.

In a technocratic world every moral problem gets repressed and is displaced by a technical or statistical evaluation. The problems of sound and speedy mathematics serve to overthrow ethics. If, for instance, one investigates the inner life of the guards of the concentration camps and their inner troubles and tribulations, one understands why those jailers gave so much thought to the technical problem of how to get the murdered corpses of their victims out of the gas chambers as soon as possible. The words "clean" and "practical" and "pure" acquired for them a different dimension than our usual one. They thought in chemical and statistical terms —and stuck to them—in order not to be aware of their deeper moral guilt.

The mind regarded as a computing machine is the result of compulsive rationalization and generalization of the world. This has been so since the time of early Greek thinkers. This concept implies denial or minimization of emotional life and of the value of marginal experiences. In such a philosophy, spontaneity is never understood—nor creativity and historical coincidence, nor the miracles of human communication as revealed by telepathy. Technology based on this concept is cold and without moral standards of living, without faith and "feeling at home" in our own world. It continually stimulates new dissatisfaction and the production of new luxury without knowing why. It stimulates greediness and laziness without emphasizing restraint and the art of living. Indeed, technology as a goal instead of a means gives us the fiction of simple equality instead of the continual pursuit of freedom, diversity, and human dignity. Technology disregards the fact that our scientific view of the world is only a gradual correction of our mythical and prescientific view. Technology, once a product of courageous fantasy and vision, threatens to kill that same vision, without which no human progress is possible. The idol, technology, must become a tool again and not the omnipotent magician per se, who drags us into the abyss.

The industrial development in our Western culture created a new problem, that of making man more distant from the rhythm of nature. First industrial man was tied to factory and engine, and then technological progress increased leisure time, bringing a new question: leisure for what?

The increased growth of time, and time space, and of the sizes of towns, and the reduction of distance through the increased means of transport affected deeply the roots of our feelings of belonging and security. The family—the atom of society—often became disrupted, and sometimes even deteriorated. The raving frenzy of the family car on Sunday replaced the quiet being together of family groups in mutual exchanges of affection and wisdom.

Only when man learns to be mentally independent of technology —that means when he learns to do without—will he also learn not to be overwhelmed and swept away by it. People have to become lonely Robinson Crusoes first, before they can really use and appreciate the advantages of technology.

Our education has to learn to present simple, natural challenges and needs to the child in order to immunize him against the paralyzing and lazy-making tendencies of our technicized epoch.

The Paradox of Technology

Paradoxically enough, technical security may increase cowardice. The technical world we ourselves have created has replaced the very real challenge which nature originally afforded man's imagination, and man is no longer compelled to face the forces of nature outside himself and the forces of instinct within him. Our luxurious habits and complicated civilization have a tendency to appeal more to our mental passivity than to our spiritual alertness. Mentally passive people, without basic morals and philosophy, are easily lured into political adventures which are in conflict with the ethics of a free, democratic society.

The assembly line alienates man from his work, from the product of his own labor. No longer does man produce the things man needs; the machine produces for him. Engineers and scientists tell us that in the near future automation—running factories without human help—will become a reality, and human labor and the human being himself will become almost completely superfluous. How can man have self-esteem when he becomes the most expendable part of his world? The ethical and moral values which are the foundation of the democratic society are based on the view that human life and human welfare are the earth's greatest good. But in a society in which the machine takes over completely, all our traditional values can be destroyed. In venerating the machine, we denigrate ourselves; we begin to believe that might makes right, that the human being has no intrinsic worth, and that life itself is only a part of a greater technical and chemical thought process.

Man's progressive retreat toward a mechanized, push-button world is best illustrated by his love for automobiles and other machines. The moment he can retreat to his car seat and direct the world by remote control, he dreams an old, long-forgotten childhood dream of tremendous omnipotence. Man's servility to his automobile and other machines takes something away from his individuality. We are hypnotized by the idea of remote control. The wheels and the push-buttons give us a false sense of freedom. Yet, at the same time, the creative part of man resists the machine's cold, mechanical intrusion into his inner freedom.

As I drive, every time I pass something beautiful along the road, be it an exhilarating view, a museum, a river, a tall tree, at that very moment a kind of tense conflict is aroused in me. Shall I stop the car and drink in the beauty around me or shall I give in to my machine and keep racing along?

For the psychologist and biologist such behavior raises important questions. How will it end? Will man's tendency to become more and more an immobile technological embryo finally get the better of him and his civilization? The Dutch anatomist Bolk—one of my teachers—long ago described the regressive retardation in growth characteristic of human beings as compared to the rapid development of the higher primates. As a result of the fetalization and anatomical retardation of man, he acquired his erect posture, the use of his grasping and verifying hands, the possibility of speech. This long youth made it possible for him to learn, and to build up his own thought world.

Since the Renaissance and the advent of modern science, the scientist himself has been forced to retreat more and more to his technological womb—his laboratory, his study, his armchair. He has done this for the sake of greater intellectual concentration, but as a result he gradually became more isolated from living people—unobtrusively. Only in the last decades has the scientist begun to come in contact with social problems more and more, partly forced to do so by the growth of social science.

From his magic corner, the scientist has learned how to control the world with his inventions and mental dictates. Increasingly the population has been seduced by the idea of remote control. The arsenal of buttons and gadgets leads us into the magic dream world of omnipotent power. Our technical civilization gives us greater ease, but it is challenge and uneasiness that make for character and strength.

The repeated outlet in work, through which we not only sublimate our aggressions but also refine and recondition our instinctual aims, is grossly endangered by technical automatization. There exists an intimate relation between the rhythm of work and the rhythm of creation. In a world of mere leisure and no work discipline, our unleashed instincts would gain again. It is the alternating rhythm of work and leisure time that refines our enjoyment of leisure.

A conference in New Haven sponsored by the Society for Applied Anthropology on the effects of automation on the workers* was told that the chief complaint of the workers was that increasing mental tension supplanted muscular fatigue. The strain of watching and controlling machines makes man jumpy, he develops gradually the feeling that the machine controls him instead of he

* The New York Times, December 29, 1955.

the machine. Several of my patients looked at machines as something alive, dangerously alive because machines had no love or other feelings for the man who used them.

The dangerous paradox in the boost of living standards is that in promoting ease, it promotes idleness, and laziness. If the mind is not prepared to fill leisure time with new challenges and new endeavors, new initiative and new activities, the mind falls asleep and becomes an automaton. The god Automation devours its own children. It can make highly specialized primitives out of us.

Just as we are gradually replacing human labor by machines, so we are gradually replacing the human brain by mechanical computers, and thus increasing man's sense of unworthiness. We begin to picture the mind itself as a computing machine, as a set of electrochemical impulses and actions. The brain is an organ of the body; its structure and its actions can be studied and examined. But the mind is a very different thing. It is not merely the sum of the physiological processes in the brain; it is the unique, creative aspect of the human personality.

Unless we watch ourselves, unless we become more aware of the serious problems our technology has brought us, our entire society could turn into a kind of superautomatized state. Any breakdown of moral awareness and of the individual's sense of his own worth makes all of us more vulnerable to mental coercion. Nazi Germany gave us the frightful example of the complete breakdown of all moral evaluations. In the S. S. society, racial persecution and murder became a kind of moral rule.

All this may sound extreme. But the fact remains that any influence—overt or concealed, well- or ill-intentioned—which reduces our alertness, our capacity to face reality, our desire to live as active, acting individuals, to assume responsibility and to face up to danger, takes from us some part of our essential human-ness, the quality in us which strives toward freedom and democratic maturity. The enforced mental intervention practiced by the totalitarians is deliberate and politically inspired, but mental intervention is a serious danger even when its purpose is nonpolitical. Any influence which tends to rob man of his free mind can reduce him to robotism. Any influence which destroys the individual can destroy the whole society.

CHAPTER THIRTEEN

Intrusion by the
Administrative Mind

Since social life has become more and more complicated, a new group of mediators between man and his goals has developed. It is no longer the ancient priest who mediates between man and his gods, between man and the powers beyond him, but a group of administrators have, in part, taken over the job of intervening between man and his government. There are today mediators between man and his bosses, between artist and public, between farmer and market, mediators between everything. The administrative mind is born, often dominating man's social behavior and man's manifold contacts, leading him into complicated actions and compulsions far beyond spontaneous behavior.

All these ties, the rigid bureaucratic ones and the useful administrative ones, have their influence on human behavior and often may befog man's free thinking. I have a special reason for developing this theme in a book on the rape of the mind because this problem of mediation between man and his actions and thoughts exists in our form of democracy as well as in the totalitarian countries. Both halves of the world are grappling with the involved problem of how to administer themselves. The mere technique of governing ourselves and our world can become a threat to free human development—and this may be independent of the ideology the administration adheres to. We have not the same freedom to choose the official men who govern us that we have to select our favorite shop or our doctor. As long as the official man is in charge, we are in his bureaucratic power.

The Administrative Mind

Administrators today cannot handle their jobs adequately within the limits of the simple knowledge of people and nations that served governments in former years. If our leaders can not take into account the irrational forces in themselves and in other men and nations, they may easily be swept off into the maelstrom of mass emotions. If they cannot learn to recognize that their private or official conduct often reflects their prejudices and irrationalities, they will not be able to cope with the often unexpected prejudices of others. If they are, for instance, not sensitive to the paradoxical strategy hidden behind the misleading Aesopian language of totalitarians, they will not be able to counter the cold war. Psychological knowledge has become a must in our era of confused human relations.

Do our people in office, for instance, understand fully the provocative totalitarian strategy of slandering and wild accusation, and are they able to handle it adequately? Do they realize that the mere official denial never has as strong an appeal and impact as the initial accusation, and, in fact, usually fits into the accuser's strategy? Apparently they do not, for many still use simple official denial as a defense against the totalitarian strategy of accusation, when, in fact, only repeated exposure and ridicule of the very root of this technique can defeat it.

Do they realize the implications of the strategy of raising sham problems? The totalitarian and the demagogue often use this confusing technique. By launching emotional inquiries and investigations and asking for attention for quasi problems, they seek to divert attention from their real aims.

Do they understand, for instance, what lies behind the technique of exploiting the chivalry and generosity of the public and black-mailing the pity of the world? The strategy of complaining and calling for justice is a well-known mental defense used by neurotic individuals to arouse guilt feelings in others and to cover up their own hidden aggressiveness. The exploitation of pity and the overt declaration of one's own purity and honest innocence is a familiar trick when it is used by individuals, but we are less likely to recognize it when it is used in international politics.

Do our administrators realize that even the romantic ideals of brotherly love and world peace can be used to cover up aggressive designs? After the First World War, we heard many inspiring idealistic catchwords from the defeated central European countries. Their press and their leaders described in great detail, for all the world to know, the "inner purification through suffering" of the defeated peoples. Thus these countries appealed to the conscience and compassion of the whole world. But it was a questionable conversion. Every therapist knows that those who talk a great deal about their inner change and recovery have for the most part not changed at all. The fine phrases are so often contradicted by actions. Politicians must recognize that this can be as true for nations as it is for individuals. Let us not forget that nations don't talk. Official words are made up by representatives with unofficial and mostly unknown inner motivations.

Administrators, diplomats, and politicians form the nerve centers and paths of communication between peoples and nations. The tensions in the diplomatic regions represent the political tensions in the world. But they represent other things, too. The political profession is subject to special kinds of nervous tensions. The moment the administrator arrives at a top level, an inner change may take place. From then on, he can identify with those who formerly led him. The very fact of being in office and being a leader may change a man's mind in many ways. Often he removes himself more and more from human problems and from the people he represents and thinks only in terms of national strategy, official ideology, and the aims of power politics. Or childhood ambitions, long frustrated, are aroused. He may become the victim of his inflated personal ambitions and his individual notion of responsibility, and, as a consequence, lose control of his own personality.

Leading statesmen, burdened by responsibilities, have to become more careful; indeed, they often have to express themselves in noncommittal language. Yet, they are not aware that such language gradually may reform their way of thinking. Finally, they may think they possess a priority on double talk.

Another difficulty is related to a rather general fear of success. Once a high ambition is reached, a long-hidden fear from childhood may awake, a fear related to an early competition with the father and with the siblings. From this time on, the envy and hostility of those bypassed may start to injure the statesman's life.

The danger of assuming any leadership—even of any form of self-assertion—is that it provokes resistance and hostility, retaliation and punishment. The administrator knows himself to be in the public eye; he feels exposed to criticism and political attack. If he didn't have it before, from now on he has to develop a defensive façade in order to court the public and the voters. The result may be that the former meek democrat, the believer in government by the people, suddenly takes on the stature of an authoritarian personality. He is guided by his frustrated infantile fantasy of leadership.

The administrative "brain trusters," with all their inner problems, nevertheless make history for us. Our minds are deeply affected by their minds. At the same time, we—the great public—influence them, and our civilized impulses may direct them to find the good road, just as our primitive drives and influences may urge them on to push us all into catastrophe. The intrusion of the administrative mind becomes even more precarious when the authorities in power follow patterns of procedure not controlled by court and the law. In such cases, prejudice and arbitrariness can easily develop as we have experienced with many of our security regulations. Official secrecy is a token of magic power; the more hush-hush there is in the world, the less democratic control and the greater the fear of treachery.

It should be, technically, quite simple to administer any group or nation—or even the whole world. Mankind certainly knows enough to do this job. We know a great deal about history, sociology, and the science of human relations and government, at least enough *not* to repeat the mistakes from history. We live in a world of technical and economic abundance. But we have not yet learned to apply what we know or to organize the resources of the world. Somewhere something has gone wrong, and things have gotten out of hand. The will of nations and people to understand one another seems to be paralyzed, and mutual fear and suspicion have been built up by the fantasies of mythical ideologies warring against one another. And tomorrow only the tails of the fighting dogs may remain.

During the Second World War, I was sent as an official representative of the Netherlands government to an international meeting on welfare and war relief. Here I became even more aware of the extent to which private passions can mold the way we handle public problems. All of us at the conference had cold, expressionless faces which implied a sharp, unbiased form of thinking, but our unconscious minds were touched by other problems. Welfare is often much more a subject of hate than of love and sympathy. One's pride and prestige can play a much greater role than pity for the poor victim. The displaced persons and the people of the devastated and underdeveloped countries are very much aware of this fact. They do not like the role in which fate has cast them; they have to play the double role of the eternal victim who is not only the victim of politics and war, but also of the often arrogant provider of charity. As a matter of fact, the representative at the receiving end of the deal resented any offer made to his country. Everybody wants to be himself the generous "uncle from America."

The Ailments of Those in Public Office

In the future, as our psychological understanding grows, leading politicians will have to be better educated in the principles of modern psychology. Just as a soldier must know how to handle his physical weapons, so the politician must know how to face and handle the mental strategy of human relationships and diplomacy. He will have to become aware of the pitfalls in all human communication and the frailties of his own mind.

Bodily disease and neurotic development can have all kinds of effects on those in office. Under their influence, some men are drawn into a life of continuous resentment, as if, in their political and official activities, they were fighting out their infantile struggles against devils, anxieties, and inner guilt. Others are purified by their sufferings and become wiser and more humane than they were.

The modern science of psychosomatic medicine makes it clear that constant worrying, continual competition, repressed aggres-

sions, the will to dominate and to govern others, the fear of responsibility, the burden of one's chosen profession are among the many
factors that influence body and mind to form a pattern of bodily
reactions. These reactions may actually hamper our ability to solve
our problems by incapacitating us physically. Becoming a chosen
statesman in our era of increased human competition and increased
dependence on the masses of voters builds up in officeholders qualities that are nearly psychopathic, that can cripple the body or the
mind or both at a time when we need the healthiest and soundest
leaders. The role the latent psychosis or character disorder plays in
many a *leading* personality cannot be emphasized enough. Not long
ago I treated the leader of a huge humanitarian association, who
was accorded much esteem by his fellow citizens, but who was a
sick, psychopathic tyrant in his own family circle. His children
trembled at the sight of him and developed—of course—a cynical
attitude about all idealism and humanitarianism.

I suspect that many times this pathology is influenced by the way
we select our leaders. Public preference is often directed toward
strong, defensive, overcompensated qualities of character which
show up well at public functions. The outer façade is too much
seen; we are not able to judge the inner core.

In 1949, Burnett Hershey wrote an article which posed the question, Is our fate in the hands of sick men? The article was written
after the tragic death of James Forrestal, the American Secretary of
Defense, who committed suicide under the influence of despair and
delusions of persecution. It describes in some detail the psychosomatic afflictions of various statesmen. Hershey quotes General
George C. Marshall's words to the Overseas Press Club: "Stomach
ulcers have a strange effect on the history of our times. In Washington I had to contend with, among other things, the ulcers of
Bedell Smith in Moscow and the ulcers of Bob Lovett and Dean
Acheson in Washington." The author goes on to point out that
Stalin, Sir Stafford Cripps, Warren Austin, and Vishinsky also
suffered from psychosomatic ailments, as does Clement Attlee. All
of us have heard of the repeated fainting spells of the Iranian ex-
Premier, Mossadegh, the man who might, in a spell of semicon-
sciousness, have changed the balance of power in the Middle East.
The much-debated and headlined Senator McCarthy is another

case in point. At the height of his struggle for headlines, he had a stomach condition that required an exploratory operation, bursitis, frequent sinus headaches and signs of exhaustion—and all of these are known as psychosomatic involvements resulting from extreme tension.*

We have, too, many cheering examples of how physical disability and neurotic development can mature and strengthen the personality. Perhaps the brightest example of the relationship between body and profession is the late Franklin D. Roosevelt, whose political career was inconspicuous until he was stricken by poliomyelitis. His years of physical suffering became years of mental ripening. His conquest of pain and disease changed his attitude toward his own problems and also toward the problems of the world. His growth of empathy and humility, his increase in strategic intuition, and his superior knowledge of the balance of forces in his country must be partly attributed to his inner mental growth during his disease.

Roosevelt will always be a guiding example of how the mind is able to overcome the physical limitations of the body, how the mind grows out beyond it when a man is willing to look inside and fight out the conflicts within himself.

The Conference of Unconscious Minds

Let me return for a moment to the wartime conference on welfare I mentioned earlier and tell you something more about it.

The conference chairman did not feel well; every decision was as painful for him as his ulcer. He hemmed and hawed and refused to accept the responsibility the position placed on him. The representative of one of the eastern European countries was an attractive woman but a misanthrope. Every word she spoke was colored by suspicion, and when a representative from one of the Latin countries attempted a mild flirtation with her, she showed her confusion by arguing furiously against every one of his constructive proposals.

We also had a hesitant, old-school, professional politician in our midst. Though he couched his speech in gentle, polite words, he spoke only to destroy every proposal that was not initiated by his

* *Newsweek,* April 12, 1954.

faction. When he had to listen—and this he did not like to do at all—he busied himself constantly with his tie or his eyeglasses, always polishing himself.

In a crowded corner sat an enthusiastic young man who longed to do something important. He wanted to act, he wanted to see something accomplished, and his excitement was regarded by the others with sophisticated disdain. He did not know the rules of conference play.

The sessions were boring. The delegates spoke endlessly and pointlessly. But one day the entire conference was gripped by a kind of uncontrollable fury. Every delegate tried to destroy all his colleagues. Someone had unexpectedly used the word "traitor" to designate a certain guerilla group fighting in Europe, and the smooth discussion was suddenly transformed into a collision of the insurgent passions that had long smoldered behind suave masks.

What agitation was aroused! What rage, what anger! But it was only temporary. It died down; our sophisticated conference spirit reasserted itself, and we settled down to do no work. The chairman made a polite summarizing speech, and we disbanded. The charitable work we planned so carefully is still undone, and many years have passed.

With dogged optimism, political leaders still convene to construct a new peace for the world. We know that many of them will suffer again from ulcers of the stomach, but what do we know of their deeper hidden wishes and resentments?

Although I am afraid that the time is still far away when we shall subject our official representatives and administrators to psychological education and selection, we must become more aware of the many unconscious factors which influence them and us.

Do political leaders try to understand one another and the groups they represent, or are they only measuring the power of their political machines, their words, and their votes? Are they guided by private resentments and ambitions or by the honest wish to serve the community and its ideals?

Are our administrators mentally well equipped to do their tasks? If not, how could psychological insight gradually improve their equipment?

How many of them are conscious of the extent of their private frustrations? Are their destructive impulses rationalized away under the guise of political allegiance? How do illness, disease, and neurosis collide in their deliberations? Watch how, in any debate, polite speeches are interrupted by sudden diatribes.

To what degree do childhood rearing, fixed ideas, or pathological ambitions of administrators influence the destiny of a town or nation?

We recognize that idealistic platitudes may cover inadequate proposals, and we tend to accept this as the well-worn play of political strategy and diplomacy. But far worse than this overt policy of evasion is the hidden political conference and discussion between the unconscious minds and passions of politicians.

How many politicians and their followers are aware of this lurking undercurrent which often wields a stronger influence than overt action? How does the personal element between our administrators obstruct our own mental freedom, and what is the role of the psychopathic element in some of our leaders?

It is important for us to ask these questions. For the development of science has taught us that, even when it is impossible to find immediate satisfactory solutions, posing the right question helps to bring clarity to the future. It prepares the way for a solution.

The Bureaucratic Mind

In a state where terror is used to keep the people in line, the administrative machine may become the exclusive property and tool of the dictator. The development of a kind of bureaucratic absolutism is not limited, however, to totalitarian countries. A mild form of professional absolutism is evident in every country in the mediating class of civil servants who bridge the gap between man and his rulers. Such a bureaucracy may be used to help or to harm the citizens it should serve.

It is important to realize that a peculiar, silent form of battle goes on in all of the countries of the world—under every form of government—a battle between the common man and the government apparatus he himself has created. In many places we can see that this governing tool, which was originally meant to serve and assist man, has gradually obtained more power than it was intended to have.

Is Saint Bureaucratus a devil who takes possession of a man as soon as he is given governmental responsibility? Are administrators infected with a desire to create a sham order, to manipulate others from behind their green steel desks? Governmental techniques are no different from any other psychological strategy; the deadening hold of regimentation can take mental possession of those dedicated to it, if they are not alert. And this is the intrinsic danger of the various agencies that mediate between the common man and his government. It is a tragic aspect of life that man has to place another fallible man between himself and the attainment of his highest ideals.

Which human failings will manifest themselves most readily in the administrative machine? Lust for power, automatism, and mental rigidity—all these breed suspicion and intrigue. Being a high civil servant subjects man to a dangerous temptation, simply because he is a part of the ruling apparatus. He finds himself caught in the strategy complex. The magic of becoming an executive and a strategist provokes long-repressed feelings of omnipotence. A strategist feels like a chess player. He wants to manipulate the world by remote control. Now he can keep others waiting, as he was forced to wait himself in his salad days, and thus he can feel himself superior. He can entrench himself behind his official regulations and responsibilities. At the same time he must continually convince others of his indispensability because he is loath to vacate his seat. As a defense against his relative unimportance, he has to expand his staff, increasing his bureaucratic apparatus. In order to become a V.I.P. one needs a big office. Each new staff member requests new secretaries and new typewriters. Everything begins to get out of hand, but everything must be controlled; new and better files must be installed, new conferences called, and new committees set up. The staff-interaction committee talks for days on end. New supervisors are created to supervise the old supervisors and to keep the whole group in a state of infantile servility. And what was formerly done by one man is now done by an entire staff. Finally, the bureaucratic tension becomes too great and the managerial despotic urge looks for rest in a nervous breakdown.

This creeping totalitarianism of the desk and file goes on nearly everywhere in the world. As soon as civil servants can no longer talk humanely and genially but write down everything in black and white and keep long minutes in overflowing files, the battle for administrative power has begun. Compulsive order, red tape, and regulation become more important than freedom and justice, and in the meantime suspicion between management, employees, and subjects increases.

Written and printed documents and reports have become dangerous objects in the world. After a conversation, even when there are harsh words, inanities are soon forgotten. But on paper these words are perpetuated and can become part of a system of growing suspicion.

Many people become administrators in public affairs out of idealistic feelings of service and avocation. Others try to escape the adventure of life by becoming part of the civil service corps. Such service assures them a settled income, regular promotion, and a sense of job security. It is very alluring, this feeling of security. The smooth automatism and polished rigidity of the red-tape world is very attractive to certain types of men, but it may devitalize others who still believe in challenge and spontaneity.

The burning psychological question is whether man will eventually master his institutions so that these will serve him and not rule him. In totalitarian countries one is not permitted to see the humor of one's own shortcomings. The system, the red tape, and the manifold files become more important than the poor being lost in his chair behind a huge desk, looking much too important for his mental bearings.

The art of being a leading administrator, of being a genuine representative of the people is a difficult one, requiring multiple empathy and identification with other people and their motivations.

Diplomats and politicians still believe in verbal persuasion and argumentative tactics. It is a very old and alluring game, this strategy of political maneuvering with official slogans and catchwords—the subtlety of bypassing the truth in the service of partisanship, of giving faulty emphasis, the skill of dancing around selected arguments to arrive at personal propagandistic aims or party aims. Sooner or later nearly all politicians become infected with the bug. Under the burden of their responsibilities, they give in to the desire to play the game of diplomacy. They start to compromise in their thinking, to bend backwards and to be circumspect, lest their remarks be criticized by the higher echelons. Or they fall back into infantile feelings of magic omnipotence. They want to have their fingers in every pie—to the left and to the right.

All these are dangerous mental streaks of every human being which can develop more easily in politicians and administrators because of the growing impact of modern governmental techniques and their threat to free expression. When a man gets entangled in strategical and political talk, something changes in his attitude. He is no longer straightforward; he doesn't express and communicate what he thinks, but he worries about what others are thinking about him behind their façades. He becomes too prudent and starts to build all kinds of mental defenses and justifications around himself. In short, he learns to assume the strategic attitude. Forget spontaneity, deny enthusiasm; don't demand inner honesty of yourself or others, never reveal yourself, never expose yourself, play the strategist. Be careful and use more buts and howevers. Never commit yourself.

I remember a leader of the opposition who became completely confused and nearly collapsed when, after a long time out of office, his party won an election and he had to assume governmental responsibility. From an aggressive, outspoken critic, he became a hesitating, insinuating neurotic, playing the tactful strategist, having no real initiative.

Some politicians are puppets, spokesmen of their bosses. Some are the cavalier jugglers of words, who transfer human aggressions into slogans. There are also the loudmouthed trumpeters of doom, who resort to the argument of panic. Modern politics is carried out with obsolete rules of conversation, communication, and discussion; and too few politicians are aware of the semantic pitfalls and emotional dishonesties of the word tools they must use to convince others.

Yet mutual understanding can become a basis of political strategy. It is not power politics with verbal deceit and catchwords that is needed but mental probing to find ways in which proposals and suggestions may cut through the resistance of those with different opinions and motivations.

Politicians too often forget that their fight for administrative power may become a form of psychological warfare against the integrity of the minds of those who are compelled to listen. The repetitious mutual calumny, so often used during elections, gradually undermines the democratic system and leads to the urge for authoritarian control. The strategic rumors and suspicions the politicians sow are an attack on human integrity.

When the citizenry no longer has confidence in its leaders, it looks for the man with brute power to be its leader. Where is the politician who is willing to admit that his opponent is at least as capable as he, and perhaps even more capable than he is? In the free admission of equality of ability and of the wisdom of his opponent lies the politician's chance for cooperation. For true cooperation can only be brought about by mutual empathy and sympathy and the understanding of human faults.

In April, 1951, a group of psychologists, psychoanalysts, and social scientists affiliated with the United Nations, the World Federation of Mental Health, UNESCO, and the World Health Organization were guests of the Josiah Macy Jr. Foundation in New York. This was a meeting at which these problems of government, and the impact of governmental systems, were explored and discussed and published later in a report. These experts have become more and more aware of the need for psychological education and selection of government administrators.

Should our administrators be psychoanalyzed? This nearly utopian question does not predicate an immediate rush for psychological training for politicians and administrators, but it does point toward a future period when practical intelligence and sound psychological knowledge will guide man in the various aspects of his life. Education will be more fully permeated with dependable psychological knowledge. Psychology and psychoanalysis are still young sciences, but many of our present-day politicians could already profit by them. Through gain in self-insight, they would become more secure in the strategy of world guidance. They would assume more responsibility—not only for their successes, but also for their failures. And they would take more responsibility, with fewer inner qualms, for the good and welfare of all.

At this very moment our failure to solve the problems of governmental inefficiency and bureaucratic intrusion into human actions may hamper the citizen's mind in its development. Man's need to conform is in constant battle with man's need to go out on his own. The tie-up of our spontaneous freethinking with the unadventurous administrative mind has to be studied and the problem it presents solved by the psychology of the future.

CHAPTER FOURTEEN

The Turncoat in Each of Us

THE CONFUSING INFLUENCE OF THE PROBLEM OF TREASON AND LOYALTY

As soon as "treason" is mentioned, something in man's soul is stirred. Anger and scorn, suspicion and anxiety are aroused, and people want to avoid the subject. The social reaction toward a traitor—even before we are certain that the accusation is deserved—is very spectacular. Former friends of a man accused as a "traitor" retreat and withdraw from this token of evil. In every trial of traitors we feel inwardly, personally accused and guilty.

This is one of the reasons that treason trials make such deep impressions and provoke the most confusing discussions. Dictators can use such trials to cast a spell on the public. In a book on mental coercion and the rape of the mind, an investigation of the problem of treason and loyalty is needed.

The Involuntary Traitor

> Self-betrayal comes out
> of all human pores.
> SIGMUND FREUD

In my home town in Holland there was a little barbershop quite near the government buildings. It was owned by a small man with a gray French beard. Through the years he had served many of the country's most important men. Diplomats and cabinet ministers, proud generals and aggressive leaders of the opposition— they all wanted his service. The little barber was always very courteous and agreeable, eager to please his clients. He danced with prim, servile gestures around them while curling their hair and looking after their mustaches. As he worked, he would ask his distinguished clients polite questions: "What is His Excellency So-and-So going to say about this bill?" "How does the Minister of State feel about that one?" He was not really interested in politics at all, but the little barber knew that his clients were flattered by such questions.

And then one day a puffy, beribboned German general walked in and settled himself in the barber's chair—the Netherlands had been invaded and occupied by the Nazi hordes. Of course, our barber knew this, and he had even managed to hate the invaders for a few days. But he was innately a genteel soul, and he lathered the general's face himself and took care not to soil his uniform. On succeeding days, others of these strangely uniformed men appeared in the shop, and the little barber served them all well. The military men were followed by the Brown Shirts and then the Green Shirts of the Gestapo. The leather of the barber's chair was scuffed by the huge black boots. But the little barber did not complain, and soon the occupiers considered his haircut the most fashionable and best that could be obtained in the entire city.

Our barber was not too conscious of his increasing official importance. He danced attendance on his new clients with as much courtesy as he had showed the diplomats of the old days. He was sorry that his old acquaintances had gradually disappeared. But in the past his work had been seasonal; when parliament was not in session, his shop had been empty. Now his business flourished all the time. The Germans and the collaborators liked the little barbershop, the perfume, the barber's skill. Indeed, our amiable friend was well liked by the uniformed oppressors. They were, after all, thoroughly unused to friendly treatment; the barber's behavior was a welcome change from the contempt with which most of the Dutch people—those stupid, stubborn resisters—regarded them.

One day the barber was invited to buy a membership card in a

newly formed organization of collaborators. Our friend responded
to this request as he would have to any other appeal for charity.
He did not like to give, but he thought of welfare as a special tax
on business, and so he resigned himself to paying as a petty, necessary annoyance. Some of his old acquaintances warned him of the
consequences; he would be accused of collaboration and treason.
But he pacified them by saying, "I am a barber, and I live as a
barber. I have absolutely no interest in politics. I only want to serve
my clients."

When, after the bitter years of struggle and oppression, liberation
came, our friend became officially known as a traitor and a collaborator. When the black-booted, uniformed supermen were thrown
out, their collaborating friends were imprisoned, the barber among
them. After he had served a part of his sentence, a wise and for-
giving judge sent our barber back to his little shop. The first excitement of liberation had passed, and people were becoming more
willing to forgive those who had been collaborators because they
had been weak-hearted.

Our story is by no means finished. The barber came back from
prison a beaten man. He had been in jail for three months; he
still could not understand what had happened to him. He brooded
constantly over his shameful days in jail. An injustice had been
done him. He had served his fellow men as a well-behaved, virtuous citizen should, and he had been treated like a criminal. He
felt self-righteous, abused, insulted, maltreated and misunderstood.
After all, he had only wanted to be kind and helpful. He was a
barber—nothing more.

The barber could not rid himself of his bitterness and resentment.
None of his former friends came to cheer him up or to sympathize
with him. His old clients did not return. His sadness and depression increased daily and in a few months he took his own life. And
so ended the adventures of a little barber who had been completely
unaware of his collaboration and his treachery.

I knew this man. I do not despise him—not at all. I am sure
there were many such pitiful collaborators. I wonder, though, why
the little barber was so unaware. Was it stupidity? Had his apparent kindness always covered up a resentment against his fellow

men? Was he misled by an insidious wave of suggestion stronger than his mental capacity to resist? We will never know.

This tragedy, caused perhaps by unawareness, perhaps by the inability to choose between conflicting loyalties, stimulated me to investigate the problem of the traitor. I had ample opportunity to study this question, both through my experiences with the Dutch underground during the Nazi occupation, and when I was imprisoned in a Vichy detention camp. My first official analysis was made in 1943, when the Dutch government asked me to prepare a psychological report on disloyal Dutch soldiers and citizens being held in detention on the Isle of Man.

I arrived at the prison after a hazardous, stormy journey in a small airplane. The prisoners were a sorry lot. I had anticipated hostility, but I had not expected to find so many weaklings, consumed by bitterness and anger. Some of them were typical of the passive, egotistic, psychopathic personality, whose motto seems to be: "Let the world go to hell! I will never conform." Others seemed to be the victims of an unbearable inner struggle—a conflict between their desire to belong to the stronger group and their resistance to this desire, a resistance which only increased their bitterness and antagonism.

This was a situation which proved to me again that there are certain times when logic and discussion are no help at all. We tried over and over again to convince the semi-collaborators that they should join with us in the fight against the Nazis, but they only retreated further behind their private grudges. They even refused the cigarettes I offered them.

Bad as the trip to the prison had been, the trip back was even worse. The little plane was pushed off course by strong winds. I was depressed and disgusted by my experiences, and when we finally arrived in England, both the pilot and I were sick.

I had many opportunities thereafter to study spies, traitors, and subversives. My last official wartime investigation took me to a prison camp in Surinam, Dutch Guinea, where I made a collective report on all the inhabitants of the prison camp. In many of them, I could discern neurotic and even psychotic traits.

But I have found that perhaps the best understanding of the problem of treason has come to me from my psychiatric work with neurotic patients who have to face a daily struggle with the little betrayals of everyday life, with their own self-betrayal, and with their ambivalent feelings toward those they should love.

The Concept of Treason

Before looking into the subject further, let us make an enquiry into the meaning of the word "treason." It is, after all, used in a confusing variety of senses. The word "treason" has many social and political implications, and the customs, habits, and mores of the group in which it is used affect and color its meaning.

The word itself is derived from the Latin *tradere* or *transdare*, to deliver wrongfully, to betray, to give something across, to give loyalty and secrets away. But from this root, the word has acquired a variety of meanings.

In the first place, it has a purely emotional, individual meaning related to feelings of deprivation and injustice. The infant often experiences all that compels him out of his state of bliss and dependency—which means the very act of growing up—as a betrayal, and sees treason in what he considers rejection by his parents. The person who retains these infantile feelings in his adult life may react to every fancied slight or rejection as to an act of treason or betrayal.

Lack of solidarity with the family or clan—with the in-group—not conforming to its rituals and taboos has often been interpreted by the group as treason, treason through dissent. In this sense, the word implies a primitive moral evaluation; disgust and contempt are associated with it. Treason indicates something deeply emotional, something taboo, something different or strange, like allegiance to an alien ideology, a breach of traditions, or the simple fact of being a foreigner. Rejection of the norms and rules of the community, being one's own judge of morality and ethics, is often considered treasonable.

Utter rejection of the traditions of one's fatherland is an extreme. Often simple nonconformity may be considered treasonable, too. Indeed, in Totalitaria nonconformity and dissent are the most serious crimes against the system, and totalitarian minds have a tendency to look upon even honest mistakes or differences of opinion as deliberate treachery.

Because of its deep emotional content, the very word itself can be used as a political tool with which to manipulate people. In Totalitaria it becomes merely a Pavlovian sign, triggering off reactions of distrust and hatred. After a military defeat or a diplomatic disappointment, or whenever feelings of humiliation and inadequacy run high among the people, it is useful strategy to get them to project their sense of inferiority onto others. The "traitor" is in such a case an easy scapegoat who satifies the collective need to project blame and to relieve unconscious anxiety. In a totalitarian society every citizen is compelled to become a traitor, according to our own Western sense of decency, because it is his duty to betray to the regime every expression of dissension or rebellion. The child has to report his father, the father his child; they are even called traitors in the totalitarian sense as soon as they fail to report.

In the common political interpretation, treason is an act of rebellion, sedition, schism, heresy, conspiracy, or subversion. Its technical-juridical meaning is well known to everybody. Treason is adhering to enemies and giving aid and comfort to them; it is also, in a more modern, modified sense, taking part in an international ideological conspiracy against the fatherland.

To me, as a psychiatrist, its relation to the general problem of self-betrayal is the key to an understanding of the word. The germ of treason arises first in the individual's compromises with his own principles and beliefs. After these initial compromises have been made, it becomes easier to go on and on, to make more and more compromises, until finally the compromiser may become the man who is willing to sell himself and his services to the highest bidder. During the Nazi occupation, we saw this among those who were seduced to do little services for the enemy. The first step led to the second and then to final collaboration. It is because all of us do doubt ourselves from time to time, because we are unsure of what we would do if we were put to the test, and because we may see in ourselves a potential traitor, that the word "treason" has such highly emotional appeal.

But self-doubt is a far cry from actual treason, and the real traitor, in the morbid sense of the word, is not merely a self-doubter. He is a man who believes only in his ultrapersonal rights and who scorns the rights and wishes of the community. He is disloyal even to his own gang. Hitler, for example, was a traitor not only to his own ideas, handling them as changeable tools to help him gain and maintain power, he was repeatedly a traitor to his closest friends and collaborators, many of whom he betrayed and murdered in 1934, during what has been called the night of the long knives. The real traitor is a person with egocentric delusions and the conscious conviction that he alone is right. He is a very different type from an involuntary, pathetic, unaware traitor like our little barber.

The Traitor Who Consciously Takes Option for the Other Side

In my study of political traitors and collaborators, I found that most of them shared two common characteristics: they were easily influenced by minds stronger than their own, and none of them would admit his disloyalty as an act of treason. The traitors I interviewed always volunteered innumerable justifications of their behavior, always surrounded their treachery with a complicated web of sophisms and rationalizations. Actually, they could not tolerate an objective picture of their actions. If they did, they would condemn themselves out of their own mouths. Unconsciously, most of them realized the nature of their crimes and were tormented by guilt feelings. These guilt feelings would have been unbearable if they admitted, even to themselves, the enormity of their deeds.

During the Nazi occupation of the Low Countries, I saw these qualities demonstrated again and again. Many of our native traitors were spineless people, ready to accept almost any new idea or elaborate theory. Their suggestibility was their greatest liability. Most of these would-be Nazis had never possessed strong personalities of their own. They had failed in their ambitions and had been disappointed in life, and they readily transferred their frustrated personal longings to political will-o'-the-wisps. After the German invasion and occupation, these people confronted their defeated countrymen with triumphant I-told-you-so's. They boasted proudly of their wisdom in having bet on the right horse. They gained a tremendous feeling of self-importance, and their newly acquired, blown-up self-assurance, backed by the enemy's armed force, made them hard and contemptuous of their compatriots.

In an effort to justify their own behavior and their greed for power, they tried to convert others to their new way of life. They were possessed by a compulsion to become propagandists for the invader. Turncoats always try to soothe their own bad consciences by persuading others to share their crime.

Of course, they had some real grievances. Everybody does. But these traitors were influenced less by them than by fancied injustices. Through acts of treason, they avenged themselves on society for the private wrongs they had suffered because of their personal failures. Their resentments could be felt in everything they said.

The Nazi strategists were experts in exploiting this sense of dissatisfaction. They seemed to know intuitively whether or not an individual could be ensnared by Nazi propaganda. One case I knew of in Holland concerned the ex-director of a large concern who had been ousted from his position on ethical grounds. Early in the occupation, this man received an invitation to join the Nazi ranks, and in a surprisingly short time he became the leader of an important Nazi business. The Nazis gave him the feeling of having been vindicated.

Among the recruits for the Nazi police force in the occupied territories were turncoats of all sorts and even the inmates of asylums for the criminally insane. The pathological grudge these people had against society was the foil by which the Nazis turned them into traitors. The Germans themselves despised these men, but they were cunning enough to put them to the best possible use.

The Nazis also played a strange game with some authors and artists who had not received enough appreciation. The enemy flattered these men by buying and praising their work. The artists were first told that they could write and create as they pleased, without fear of interference. Gradually, little political services were asked of them, tiny little concessions like a favorable report of a meeting or a favorable reference to a philosophy with which they did not agree.

It is the impact of that first little concession that starts the inner avalanche of self-justification that finally leads to self-betrayal. Following the first compromise and self-justification comes the second; and this one is met with shrewder self-exculpations. After all, the compromiser has had experience in rationalization by now. The repeated concessions turn into submission and voluntary coopera- tion. As I said before, once a man is seduced into a small ideological concession, it is very difficult for him to stop. From now on his imagination produces enough justifications which help him main- tain his self-respect.

The inwardly insecure traitor always feels the urge to identify with the enemy—the hostile invader. He has never "belonged," never had a feeling of identification with his own group, has never felt the rewards of such cohesion, nor has he won the love, sym- pathy, and respect of his fellows. Therefore he wants to join the "others." He may even go so far as to call his former friends trai- tors. Lord Haw-Haw (William Joyce), the British traitor who was executed by his government, considered himself a real "Aryan Ger- man," and in this way justified his fight against England.

In the hectic days immediately following the Nazi invasion of Holland, I myself felt an occasional inner temptation to go over to the enemy, to the stronger party, with its powerful organizations, all ready to support one, to back one up. I even had a dream about visiting Hitler and convincing him in a childish and friendly way of the righteousness of our cause. I did not succumb to this dream temptation, but there were a few who fell for such infantile pic- tures and were unable to withstand their need to submit. The need to conform, to be accepted, to be safe and respectable, is deeply embedded in man. In our analysis of the inner forces that lead men to surrender their mental integrity under the pressure of prison and concentration-camp life, we saw how important a role this mechan- ism plays. Living in a country occupied by the enemy is by no means as horrifying as living in a P.O.W. or concentration camp, but it is, nevertheless, frightening, and in this frightening situation, the need to conform may show itself in surrender to the enemy ideology. Those who resisted this need, even though they felt it, usually became even more fervently anti-Nazi as a consequence of their guilt feelings about this impulse to treachery.

This war experience taught us another truth: traitors can be made by overwhelming collective suggestions. In the ambiguous chaos of shouting ideologies and changing values, the mind becomes sullen and stubborn, and where there is immaturity and lack of inner control, it may become confused in its loyalties and simply surrender to the most powerful group.

The Nazis, with their perverted political methods, tried to supply the weak, the ambitious, the disgruntled, and the frustrated with a ready-made set of bogus ideals to justify surrender to their side. In *Mein Kampf,* Hitler says that when the disappointed are given a sense of importance, they will swallow every suggestion with the utmost docility. He knew that human weakness—even kindness—can be used as a starting point for a systematically nurtured conversion. Hitler knew, too, that unlimited political terror could make a traitor of almost anyone. Spread fear, terror, and hunger, inflict penetrating pain, and finally, as a result of mental coercion and growing confusion, many will succumb and even betray their own families. In many of the concentration camps, the victims themselves were in charge of the gas chamber killings and kept their gruesome jobs until their own turns came. Fear and terror had made will-less slaves out of them.

There is still another human characteristic that can lead to treason and betrayal. There are some people who simply do not know where their loyalties belong. The case of Klaus Fuchs, the man who betrayed atomic secrets to Russia, is a dramatic example of this. Here was a highly intelligent person, an expert on the most difficult theoretical problems, lost in a sea of conflicting loyalties. Because of the Nazi persecution of his Quaker family, he adopted a new fatherland, England. In the meantime, he carried a dream of a mystical universal world which he thought to find in the totalitarian ideology. In the midst of his confusion about world problems, he simply did not know where his loyalty should be.

This was not a case of schizophrenia or a Jekyll-and-Hyde situation, as the newspapers reported, but a case of confusion of loyalties in a hyperintellectual mind. Fuchs did not know emotionally where he belonged.

In other cases people were literally pushed into treason and collaboration because nobody in their environment trusted them. This happened, for instance, in Flanders with the collaborators of the First World War. Several of them were compelled to become collaborators again.

This analysis of the factors that lead men to treason certainly does not imply that every man must remain loyal to the group from which he has originally received his morals and ideals. Better insight and higher ethics may override our childhood loyalties. It is the fate and the need of human beings to go beyond their teachers and to correct, if possible, the traditional rules of their schools. The great philosopher Socrates was accused of being a "traitor" because he "corrupted the minds of the youth of Athens." And yet today we know that Socrates was far from being a corrupter.

Our Treacherous Intellect

Perhaps the most tragic form of unobtrusive treason and self-betrayal is caused by the inertia of the human intellect. We are often betrayed by our own minds. We forget completely what we want to forget. We deny the existence of real problems in order to retreat into wishful thinking. As soon as we do not understand and feel the implications of a problem or an argument, we tend to submit passively to the most powerful side, just as did the overfriendly barber. The ease with which human beings can be corrupted is still one of our most serious psychological and moral problems. Inner confusion can make us submissive to almost any strong suggestion from the outside, no matter how foolish or false.

> *Our doubts are traitors,*
> *And make us lose the good we oft might win*
> *By fearing to attempt.*

There are other more complicated tricks of the intellect which lead to self-betrayal. The feeling of inferiority often arouses in ignorant people a great desire to grasp extremely difficult ideas. Such people like to identify themselves with a quasi-profound system of thought. Hitler and his abstruse writings made temporary pseudo-philosophers and magicians out of the majority of German people. All dictatorial totalitarians buy the services of scholars who can make them such a set of pseudo-philosophic justifications.

Unfortunately, some scholars are easy to buy. In Holland, for example, there was a not too intelligent philosopher who became converted to Nazism after it had shown its overpowering strength. Thereafter he felt free to write on the most abstruse philosophical subjects and to expound the most complicated theories, all for the glorification of his powerful friends from the Third Reich and their myth of conquering the whole world. At the same time, he built a system of inscrutable words around his own deep feelings of guilt; he isolated himself from the world more and more because no words were convincing enough to justify his treason to himself. In the end he lost all contact with reality. Then, of course, the Nazis had no use for him either.

Self-Betrayal

As we have seen, there are various inner motivations which may lead to the crime of disloyalty or treason. Sometimes these motivations operate very subtly, in ways unknown to the subject; sometimes treason is merely a crude selling out to those who pay best. Let us try to arrange and classify some of these motivations, starting with the unconscious ones and ranging toward deliberate treason.

In the first place, an act of self-betrayal may begin as a defense against the feeling of being lost and rejected. In order to win acceptance in a group, the individual may hide and not defend his private beliefs and convictions when attacked. In psychology this may be called—if such passive behavior becomes an unconscious habit—the passive submission to and identification with the stronger person. If you cannot beat the enemy, join him! (A. Freud)

Although the concept of the *inner traitor in us* is not so easy to accept, by studying the contrasting inner drives that lead man, one becomes more convinced of that possibility. The clinical concept of man's inner ambivalence is based on numerous psychological experiences. In studying the deeper motivations of many a traitor, we often see that his treacherous act happened after an inner turmoil threatened to break him down, to make an uncontrolled nervous wreck out of him. It is as if the future mental patient preferred to surrender to an outward enemy rather than to the inward enemies of disease and nervous breakdown. Hess was on the verge of a schizophrenic breakdown when he broke Hitler's rules and flew to England.

Let us consider the British foreign office spies, Donald Maclean and Guy Burgess.* Both showed several symptoms of imminent mental breakdown. It may be known to the reader that both these men left England in May, 1951, in order to go via France to Russia. Both deliberately fled the country. Both had Communist leanings during their student days at Cambridge but later renounced their adolescent affiliations. Both showed abnormal symptoms during their service. Maclean had a breakdown in May, 1950, due to overwork and excessive drinking; Burgess was reprimanded for reckless driving while in service and for neglect of his work. Reading through the report, one is surprised by the amount of mental instability which was tolerated at such a sensitive spot of the government. Both the men had homosexual leanings that can be related to a suppressed hostility for their mothers (and mother country).

Sometimes treason means a one-sided appeal to justice. This is found in the man who demands some sort of private protective justice and who refuses to acknowledge the subtle relationship between rights and duties. Such persons always feel continually deprived and betrayed. They are what Bergler calls the "injustice collectors." In their acts of disloyalty they are seeking to play the role of their own private judges. Many querulous and even paranoiac persons have this kind of character structure.

Then there is the disappointed pseudo-idealist who gradually turns into a cynic, covering his emptiness by many self-justifications and exculpations. Such people betray their intellectual disappointment in all their debunking remarks.

Conflicts between parents may give rise in the child to the need to betray one or both parents, and this need may be transferred in later life to a need to betray the fatherland. I have often found that the unsolved ties of hate and love toward the parents play an important role in forming the turncoat personality. As we saw, this problem often lies at the root of the totalitarian character structure. Although the totalitarian-minded are not by definition overt traitors,

*Text of Britain's "Report on Inquiry," *The New York Times*, September 24, 1955; *Time*, October 3, 1955.

some of these people can easily become traitors to free, democratic ideals—either out of compulsive allegiance to a foreign ideology or out of repetitive nonconformism.

In describing special characteristics of a political group, one has to keep in mind that basic inner contrasts are inherent in all people. The quasi-rational Marxistic interpretation of the world, which satisfies the need for logical clarification and reasonable organization of social life, covers anxiety created by the irrational inner forces so easily detected in the totalitarian-minded. The cult of the "masses" often serves as a defense against loneliness. The belief in progress may be born out of vague despair and insecurity. The fear of deviationism is the fear that the unity of the group will be broken. Suspicion and self-criticism serve to keep, above all, the in-group together.

There are several forms of inner conceit that can turn man into a traitor. The Dutch philosopher of whom I spoke earlier is an example of this, as are any of the verbose ideological apologists for totalitarianism.

Lack of confidence or lack of belief in the guiding traditions and aims of one's own society can also lead to hostility, then to treason. Without such traditional beliefs, suggestibility and receptivity for competing ideologies are increased. The Klaus Fuchs case, which was mentioned earlier, is an example of this.

The personal need to be a pioneer or a martyr, often instilled by the unconscious need to suffer, may lead to a private messianic delusion and cause an attack on the traditional values of the group. Many groups consider such extremism as treacherous behavior.

Another form of self-betrayal may be caused by the inability to grasp the complexity of the real world. Many people have been seduced into unstable behavior and even disloyalty through lack of comprehension of these complexities and through the need to find a single, all-embracing, easy answer to the problems of human life. Who gives them the simple myth to believe in? The Nazis seduced nearly all of Germany into a form of ideological treason in this way!

Treason may also be a paradoxical reaction to a deep-seated neurotic sense of guilt. The neurotic strategy of accumulating more guilt coupled with the consequent development of an inner need for punishment are often the basic causes of criminal action. The treacherous deed is done precisely in order to provoke punishment (Reik).

Treason may also be paid adventure as we find it in international espionage. This kind of life fascinates the immature mind which lives in the world of mystery stories and fairy tales. Bribes with women or money make such treason even more attractive. The enemy gratifies economic and sexual needs, and the traitor is willing to sell his integrity to the highest bidder.

Overt fear and panic can also cause treason. The whole psychology of totalitarian interview and interrogation is based on this principle. People can be frightened and brainwashed into treason.

The Development of Loyalty

From all this we can see that what we call treason takes place more in the emotional than in the intellectual sphere of functioning. In the course of human growth, everybody passes through periods of inner conflict in which he has to turn his love and allegiance from one person to another—from mother to father, from parents to the entire family, from the family to the state, and from the state to mankind. The core of the problem of treason and self-betrayal is found in the difficulties which arise in the repression of former loyalties, as each loyalty is in turn superseded by the next.

Many people experience deep confusion in adolescence when, for the first time, they must leave the safe emotional protection of their homes and create new loyalties and new moral standards for themselves. It is in this period that the critical faculties are developed. In doubting the traditional truths passed on by his parents, each adolescent might be called a traitor; yet he is actually being true to the self he is shaping. During the crisis of adolescence, with its increased feelings of yearning for some unknown happiness, many young people want to "betray" their parental home and their parents' standards. At the same time, they do not want to give up the protection the home offers.

Psychologically, we know, however, that temporary disloyalty is part of normal mental growth. In the process of individual human development, there are stages of progress which lead from initial submission to open rebellion and nonconformity. Every step toward mental maturity and independence involves the growing out of ties with the past. This growth can be effected in different ways, with more or less overt hostility and forsaking of the past, with self-betrayal and passive submission, with renewed submission to pay off feelings of guilt, with sworn conservativism or open rebellion. In this phase of adolescence he is especially vulnerable to totalitarian propaganda.

The youth may retain from the conflict of inner growth a sense of loneliness and guilt. If he puts it to productive use, he may become what we might call a creative revolutionary. The trail blazer, whose own inner forces drive him on to break with tradition, is such a man. Indeed, many of mankind's great moral and spiritual leaders have been of this type. They have been leaders precisely because they broke either with rigid remnants of the past or with the ossified or immoral elements of the present. In my own experience, I have known one such man, a German psychiatrist, whose idealism and moral sense made it impossible for him to go along with the Nazi desecration of human values and who was hanged as a traitor for his part in the abortive German rebellion against Hitler in 1944.

In Praise of Nonconformity

What can be done in general to combat treason, disloyalty, and self-betrayal? In the first place, the child's normal defensive attitude toward authority and his need to break away from it should be watched with favorable vigilance at all times on the part of parents and educators. It is all too easy to force a child into denial of the self. Many times, later disloyalty is a reaction to faulty handling of the problems of childhood. Most traitors are made, not born. Unfortunately, this truth is often forgotten by educators who may, as a result of their own frustrated aggressions, break down by force the feeling of great loyalty toward their own age group that we find among youngsters.

Is it possible to decide whether or not a person is dependable? Only when we have some insight into his hidden motives and drives and into the workings of his unconscious. For complete insight, psychoanalysis is necessary, but the way the unconscious expresses itself in character traits and character defenses can give us some very important indications. A person with excessive dependency needs or a weak ego, a person who is easily suggestible can usually be seduced into disloyalty. So can the boastful, inconsistent man, full of pride and vanity. Material egotism, desire for power, and continual hostility also lead to denial of moral values, among them loyalty.

As is often true in psychology, it is easier to say what character traits the dependable person must not have than to give a positive picture of what he should be like. In general, we can say that the person who is honest with himself and shows a minimum of self-deceit, the man who exhibits a stable structure of character, the person with genuine maturity, is most true to himself, and, as a result, most loyal to others.

Nevertheless, the seeds of treason lie in each of us and may be fortified by environmental influences. In a totalitarian world, for example, everybody is educated in self-denial and self-betrayal; when a person becomes a nonconformist, the label "traitor" will be attached to him. In a world stifled by dogma and tradition, every form of original thinking may be called sedition and treason. In such cases the environmental, social, and political factors, and not the confusing inner processes, determine what is treason. In this chapter, however, I have emphasized the personal factors in producing treason—the influence of family and group prejudices, and the inner instability resulting from complications in the immediate environment. There are so many subtle fantasies of self-betrayal and secret aggression in everyone, and there is so much desire to revenge secret resentments, that any government may make use of these unhealthy neurotic feelings to stir up the country.

The Loyalty Compulsion

Recently Americans have been looking more critically at the concepts of loyalty and subversion. Deeply conscious of the cynical and ruthless nature of the totalitarian attack through subversion, we have begun to let our fear of subversion from within paralyze our democratic freedoms.

We have become so concerned over the specter of a treacherous fifth column in our own land that we have grown both overcautious and oversuspicious.* We require constant reassurance that the intentions of our neighbors and fellow citizens are acceptable and loyal. The danger in this frantic search for security operates both on the political and psychological levels. Politically, in trying to erect invulnerable barriers against the spread of totalitarian ideas, we may find that we have given up those very qualities that distinguish democracy from totalitarianism: freedom and diversity. Psychologically, we may find ourselves the victims of pathological suspicions (which can be clinically termed paranoia), and this suspiciousness may lead us to reject utterly the most valuable qualities we can have as human beings: tolerance and respect for our fellow men.

The political dangers in this situation have been pointed out time and time again by responsible leaders of the American community. As a psychiatrist, I should like to devote my attention to the psychological aspect of this problem and to the dangers to the free mind that are inherent in the current situation. For, as we have already seen, all political behavior is essentially an extension of individual behavior and is rooted in the psychology of the individuals who make up the political group.

Much of our collective suspicion can be attributed to a gigantic multiplication of personal feelings of insecurity. In times of fear and calamity arises the myth of a treacherous aggressor, the myth the totalitarians know so well how to exploit. Our own inner insecurity is displaced and projected onto our neighbors and our environment. We begin to doubt and distrust everyone. We accuse others because we are afraid of ourselves. We feel weak and cover our weakness by growing suspicion and by being continually on the lookout for possible traitors and dissenters.

As we have seen earlier, the whole question of loyalty is a complicated one. In our zeal to create guarantees of trustworthiness, we tend to oversimplify the problem, and thus we may overshoot the mark and become like our totalitarian antagonists, for whom over-

---

* In his well-documented study on *The German Fifth Column*, the Dutch historian Dr. Louis de Jong could prove that Hitler's dreaded network of treason and betrayal was for the greatest part an imaginary ogre created by the panic and fear of the people.

simplification is a stock-in-trade. Asking people for a loyalty oath—asking them to perform that magic ritual through which they forswear all past and future political sin—may have a paradoxical effect. Merely taking an oath does not make a man loyal, although it may later enable a judge to prosecute him for perjury. Our insistence on official expressions of allegiance actually discredits and devalues the basic personal sense of voluntary and self-chosen identification with the community which is the essence of loyalty; it certainly does not either create or insure loyalty. The loyalty oath too easily degenerates into an empty formula, and the man who takes it may forget completely the meaning it is supposed to have. To many it has become simply red tape, another one of those endless, troublesome forms that must be filled out.

The oath compulsion can easily grow into a childish magic strategy, a form of mental blackmail. There are some oriental religions in which devotions are performed through the use of a prayer wheel. When the wheel is set in motion by a flip of the hand, the worshipper has done his job. He need not recite any prayers; he need not think any devout thoughts. The practitioners of these religions no longer have any awareness of the content of their prayers. They are blind subscribers to a ritual whose meaning they have long since forgotten. Signing a loyalty oath can become as empty a gesture as turning the prayer wheel.

True loyalty is not a static thing; as we have already seen, it grows and develops with the personality. It has to be rediscovered and re-experienced every day, since it is, essentially, as a result of an inner battle of contending values that man finds his own particular values and loyalties. When a man is compelled to swear to his loyalty, even though he feels it already deeply within him, the compulsion from outside means that he must lay aside his personal right to weigh values and take counsel with his honest principles. It does not matter whether or not the oath is an expression of his true feelings, the element of enforcement that lies behind it has a psychologically weakening effect on the man who takes it. This may seem strange at first glance, but a simple analogy will make it clear. The man who truly loves his wife, for example, does not need repeatedly to swear to his love; he shows it in his actions. But if she insists on his swearing, her very insistence, implying as it does that she doubts him, may bring questions to her husband's mind—and he begins to grow confused as to what he really thinks.

Both in demanding an oath and in taking it, we perpetuate the ridiculous illusion that enemies can be kept out through this prayer-wheel system. The fact is that deliberate traitors and subversives are the very ones who are not afraid to disguise their motivations and hide their intentions behind prescribed formulations. Nor are they afraid of perjury charges. They feel no hesitation in signing an oath if it is opportune for them to do so. For them, words and oaths are only tools which have no binding moral value. More important than the demand for loyalty should be the demand for integrity, for steadiness of character, for maturity of aims and motivations.

Free man needs loyalty to the self first of all, and this implies the right to be himself. The man who feels that he is nothing, who feels that everyone, himself included, doubts him, who is inwardly weak, may become an easy prey to all kinds of totalitarian political influences. Loyalty hunts and loyalty oaths may provoke disloyalty to one's personal integrity and to personal freedom, since they create suspicion in ourselves and in others. Freedom is kept upright by the very presence of opposition—even at the risk of nonconformism and scattered subversion.

Loyalty comes about as a result of mutual confidence; it cannot be created through compulsion. Any compulsion is, by its very nature, one-sided. *Loyalty has to be deserved and won daily through mutual interaction, and through contact between leaders and citizens.* Because it is based on confidence, loyalty is given spontaneously and of free will. True loyalty cannot be bought or demanded.

In investigating the case of the young American soldiers in Korea who were brainwashed and forgot too easily where their loyalty lay, we usually find in their backgrounds how disloyally one of their parents had behaved toward them. In nearly all the so-called pro-Communist cases we find a disturbed youth. It is important that the community investigate its initial loyalty toward these young men.

In a democratic state we should be prepared to adduce convincing facts in support of our own way of life or to develop new approaches which will reveal the weaknesses of any subversive system.

Prosecution of dissenting ideas, insistence on loyalty according to some prescribed formula—these make it impossible for us to do this and may be the beginning of an unwillingness to argue and persuade. They may even lead to a new form of betrayal, the subtle treason of intellectual detachment, the unwillingness to take responsibility, the treason of doubting relativism which leads to inaction. It may degenerate into a dangerous form of mental laziness which can easily be turned into a life of no commitments or into totalitarian submission. The approaches to truth are multifarious, and it is only where there is a clash of opinion that these approaches can be discovered and the right road to truth be found.

The danger in the loyalty compulsion is, then, that we may conceal mental apathy behind a rigid formula and thus lose sight of the constant need for psychological alertness and the real meaning of loyalty and a free way of life. The mechanical formula of a loyalty oath, because it checks moral alertness and a search for ethical clarification, may be the beginning of the thought control we all fear. True loyalty is a living, dynamic quality.

In the subtle choice between loyalty to people and loyalty to principles (usually a much vaguer feeling) the lawmaker has to leave the individual as free as possible, because the latter type of loyalty is based on the first. Without personal loyalty there is no national loyalty!

There is still another aspect to this problem. We must learn to distinguish between disloyalty in actions and disloyalty in feelings and thought. Subversion of opinion is never a crime. The right to dissent is the keystone of democracy. In a free state we must be willing to correct subversion by our better arguments. Persecuting dissenting ideas is a form of mental laziness. Psychologically speaking, a government cannot concern itself with conscious motivations (and the unconscious motivations which cannot be separated from them) of people because inwardly everybody has contrasting motivations. The quandary that such a government would provide itself is illustrated by the following quotation from the Oppenheimer hearing by the Gray board published in 1954.

We believe that it has been demonstrated that the Government can search its own soul and the soul of an individual whose relationship to his government is in question with full protection of the rights and interests of both. We believe that loyalty and security can be examined within the framework of the traditional and inviolable principles of American justice.

In these beautiful phrases lie hidden all the ominous beginnings of totalitarian thought control. The government that searches the soul of any thinking individual can always find a case against him, because doubt, ambivalence, and groping are traits common to *all* men. We cannot measure anybody's dependability on the basis of his thoughts and feelings as they appear to us. In the first place, we can never know what lies behind a seemingly loyal façade. In the second place, the man whose search for truth leads him to explore many heretical points of view can be the most loyal in his actions. His very exploration may well lead him to the considered judgment that underlies true loyalty. What counts in any man is the consistency and integrity of his behavior, and his courage in taking a stand, not his conformity to official dogma.

And to state that the government can search its own soul is to state absolutely nothing. A government is, after all, merely a collection of individuals. Under the pressure of the loyalty compulsion, of the growing suspicion, these individuals themselves may not search their souls as honestly as they would in less hectic times or if they were acting as private individuals rather than as official representatives of the government. The man caught in official security rules is the prisoner of the anxiety and insecurity rampant in those who want to establish the delusion of certainty and security—a transgression of values!

As soon as the government starts to search the souls of its citizens, it begins to intrude on their rights and interests. It attacks democracy at home and weakens its position abroad. We cannot find the road to peace and fellowship with the rest of the world if we adopt dogmatic, intransigent positions and try to impose our orthodoxy on others. The hallmark of the totalitarian is his insistence that his is the only right way. If we are to maintain our position as the leader of the free world, we must always keep our minds open. Only in that way will we find new ways to peace.

We have seen now that the problem of treachery has to deal with the failure to understand our inner mental processes. Every betrayal is in the first place a self-betrayal, a disloyalty toward one's own standards. When people silence their conscience and compromise for the sake of convenience, at that moment they begin to be disloyal to themselves. Passivity—assumed when our conscience should have forced us to act—is the most common form of self-betrayal. Inwardly a man may be furious because of some injustice he has witnessed, but outwardly he may do nothing about it—this behavior he feels inwardly is treason to the self and is often what makes him so touchy toward other people's flaws. When the pattern of passivity is repeated, the individual continuously piles up more feelings of injustice and grows more and more resentful against society. Evasiveness and skillful dodging of issues of principle—these are among the most dangerous forms of self-betrayal in our time. They are dangerous because they lead unwittingly to the hypocrisy that puts power beyond ethical value.

It is dangerous to let personal grudges and discontent solidify into a permanent resentment against the whole of society. Parents and educators can forestall such difficulties through psychological insight by allowing each individual the freedom to criticize and attack—in a civilized, nondestructive way—the community to which he belongs. By helping to develop in the child the sense that he is responsible for his own views, subversive though they may temporarily appear, parents provide him with the opportunity to overcome his feelings of loneliness and ambivalence and his wish to do violence to those who influence him. Again, loyalty is a relationship—loyalty to family, friends, or country has to be *deserved*.

Loyalty is possible only when mutual mental aggression and hostility are allowed and tolerated within the limits of the law. This verbalized, sublimated, and civilized form of aggression presupposes fairness and good sportsmanship. It is the synthesis and conquest of rebellion and subversion. However paradoxical it may sound, democracy is founded on the mutual loyalty of politically opposed groups! You cannot doubt the good motives and intentions of your opponent without undermining the basis for cooperation and successful government. It is most undemocratic to impute disloyalty to the opposition party. History shows that only where there is opportunity to confront and integrate opposing ideas can man eradicate that form of psychological imbalance which gradually turns into a disloyalty to oneself and to the community. Fear of subversion and opposition is often fear of ideas, fear of being identified with certain unacceptable ideas, the fear of betrayal of the hidden part of oneself. Fear of treason will exist as long as loyal opposition is a crime.

Democracy is nonconformity; it is mutual loyalty, even when we have to attack one another's ideas—ideas, which, because they are always human, are always incomplete.

PART FOUR

IN SEARCH OF DEFENSES

THE MOMENT WE BECOME AWARE THAT SPECIAL
POLITICAL PHENOMENA ARE A THREAT TO OUR EX-
ISTENCE, CORRESPONDING INNER DEFENSES DEVELOP
AUTOMATICALLY. WE FEEL REASSURED AS WE DIS-
COVER WAYS TO FACE THE PROBLEMS. THE CLOSING
CHAPTERS OF THIS BOOK DEAL FIRST WITH SOME OF
THE OFFICIAL ATTITUDES AND WITH THE CODE
CREATED TO ENCOUNTER BRAINWASHING, A DANGER
WHICH HAS APPEARED RATHER RECENTLY IN HIS-
TORY. THE FINAL CHAPTER SEARCHES MORE ELAB-
ORATELY FOR THE INSPIRING VALUES WHICH
CHARACTERIZE FREEDOM AND DEMOCRACY. THE
QUESTION OF HOW BEST TO BUILD UP MILITARY AND
CIVILIAN MORALE BECOMES MORE COMPELLING BE-
CAUSE OF THE TREMENDOUS MENTAL PRESSURES
MODERN CIVILIZATION IMPOSES ON MAN.

CHAPTER FIFTEEN

Training Against Mental Torture

The U. S. Code for Resisting Brainwashing

By executive order of President Eisenhower on August 17, 1955, a new code of chivalry was made up governing conduct of American fighting men in combat and captivity.* Six precepts of conduct for combatants were enunciated:

1. I am an American fighting man. I serve in the forces which guard my country and our way of life. I am prepared to give my life in their defense.

2. I will never surrender of my own free will. If in command, I will never surrender my men while they still have the means to resist.

3. If I am captured, I will continue to resist by all means available. I will make every effort to escape and aid others to escape. I will accept neither parole nor special favors from the enemy.

4. If I become a prisoner of war, I will keep faith with my fellow prisoners. I will give no information or take part in any action which might be harmful to my comrades. If I am senior, I will take command. If not, I will obey the lawful orders of those appointed over me, and will back them up in every way.

5. When questioned, should I become a prisoner of war, I am bound to give only name, rank, service number, and date of birth. I will evade answering further questions to the utmost of

---

* Full report in *The New York Times*, August 18, 1955.

my ability. I will make no oral or written statement disloyal to my country and its allies, or harmful to their cause.

6. I will never forget that I am an American fighting man, responsible for my actions, and dedicated to the principles which made my country free. I will trust in my God and in the United States of America.

In the additional report about the recommendations by the Secretary of Defense, it is acknowledged that modern warfare has brought the challenge to the doorstep of every citizen, and that the final front of the cold-war line is in every citizen's mind.

At the same time, a clearly defined code is given telling U.S. prisoners of war how to behave after capture. Although there was a lack of such a code previously, the report states that "American troops have demonstrated through all wars that they do not surrender easily, they have never surrendered in large bodies, and they have in general performed admirably in their country's cause as prisoners of war."

After describing physical attacks on prisoners—death marches, hunger, squalor, cold, torture, disease, and total degradation—the report gives extended attention to all the forms of mental coercion intended to extract false confessions or military information from the soldiers, and to infect them with totalitarian thinking. First, the enemy aimed at the breakdown of the leaders, at confusion of the officers, who so easily influence their soldiers. Then gradually everybody had to undergo the ordeal by indoctrination. The enemy propaganda barrage started full speed. This suggestive attack reached minds not used to highly specialized discussion, minds not informed and rather confused about Communism and its tactics. Inner discrepancies in the reasoning of the man could easily be attacked and reduce him to docile submission.

The report pleads for more extended, skillful training of the soldier (and the citizen) in our basic beliefs and responsibilities, a mental mobilization for the future clash of "ideas" and "wills."

There was a considerable conflict of opinion in the advisory committee to the Secretary of Defense that drafted the code between the hard Spartan view and the more lenient let-them-talk view. The first group maintained that every soldier has to resist to the end;

the latter believed that in the end anybody could be brought into submission.

Nevertheless, all soldiers have to be trained especially to resist and not to be made disloyal to their country, their services, and their comrades. That was the principal reason why this final code of high standards was made up, even though it is recognized that coercion is possible beyond the ability to resist. Yet the psychologist here adds the additional question, Who will judge what is beyond the ability to resist?

The report ends by underlining the fact that the total war for the minds of men is continually going on. The home front is just an extension of the fighting front!

An important point made by the code is that it asks that attention be given to a far more extensive mental battle front. By making it known that the coercive methods of the Communists are well understood by us, the impact and meaning of their cold-war strategy are partly taken away. Finally nobody in the outside world believes them, even though their totalitarian methods may be of use to them for internal propaganda in their own countries. However, we cannot fight indoctrination with mere counterindoctrination.

Letting soldiers sign a declaration that they will never yield to brainwashing has the advantage of at least informing them of what to expect. Yet this knowledge does not protect them against the subtle conditioning by an inquisitor who knows how to circumvent mental obstacles. Time and subtle suggestive penetration can break men's resistance.

Psychologically, a loyalty oath compulsion and a signed declaration do not mean anything in themselves. Only a profound education in mental freedom and democratic awareness can help as a countertoxic. The authorities who ask for signed declarations of loyalty are not enough aware of how much propaganda and persuasive brainwashing and other forms of mental seduction are going on right here in our own society; they are substituting the social and national responsibility for an individual one. It is the moral and political atmosphere behind the man in the hinterland that supplies his mental stamina. The nation is responsible for the mental backbone it trains and transfers to its soldiers in a cold war!

Several P.O.W.'s felt misled by their own government. They had been badly informed about the enemy, in too simple terms of black and white. By showing his good side, the captor could easily arouse suspicion about the honesty of the prisoner's leaders.

From a psychiatric standpoint, it needs to be said again that everybody can be brought to a breaking point regardless of how well-informed and counterindoctrinated he may be. When the enemy wants to persist in his demoralizing methods, he has the means. Alas, the report did not emphasize enough the difficult dialectic dilemma into which many a simple soldier is thrown. For years he has been trained in a society or military group where obedience to the law and conformity to community habits were imprinted on him. Suddenly he has to select and test his own individuality and critical defenses. A cold war asks for a high level of political awareness.

This brings the problem back again to the problem of individual mental vulnerability of persons and to the general problem of morale. Mental courage cannot be cultivated by physical training only. It requires training in mental stamina, in understanding of basic beliefs, and even in nonconformistic thinking. We have to believe deeply in the cause for which we are fighting in order to resist the standpoint of the enemy. It is the strength of conviction that gives moral power!

Indoctrination Against Indoctrination?

An educational concept exists to the effect that conditioning to physical torture will help soldiers to be more immune to brainwashing. In one of the air force bases, airmen had to go through a "school of torture," euphemistically called the School of Survival, in which some of the barbarous and cruel Communist methods of handling prisoners were initiated in order to harden the men against future brutality.* The trainees could stand the ghoulish exercises rather well. However, such a training can condition men to take over, unwittingly, the methods of totalitarianism. It may give a semiofficial green light to enemy tactics by implying that we can do the same. Moreover, such methods may stimulate hidden

* *Time,* September 19, 1955.

sadistic tendencies in both trainer and trainee. Under the disguise of an earnest training need, American youth may be educated in the same sadistic view as their enemies.

The important psychological implication of every form of harsh compulsive training and indoctrination is that it fits into the totalitarian pattern. Moreover, the totalitarian inquisitors don't need to use physical torture in order to uncover the secrets of man's mind, although they may use these methods for their private pleasure. On the contrary, the enemy counted just as much on friendly gestures and special privileges to seduce the hungry, weakened P.O.W.'s into confession. What the inquisitors especially require in order to succeed is that the enemy have a weak personality, that he be a dumbbell with a soldier's need to conform, that he be ridden with anxiety and lacking in patience. The brainwashing inquisitor doesn't need torture. Physical torture will often strengthen resistance against the inquisitor, while isolation alone can accomplish his objectives. The school that teaches only torture and evasion techniques can even arouse latent anxieties and thus, paradoxically, make it easier for the soldier—weakened by his fantastic anticipations—to surrender to brainwashing. The hero at school can become a weakling as soon as he is faced with the real challenge.

It is not so important what the trainee accomplishes during his physical training but what he stands for mentally and spiritually. Does he have a mental backbone? Only this will stand him in good stead during the challenge of prisonership.

The Psychiatric Report About Brainwashing and Menticide

In every report on brainwashing of prisoners of war, several factors that may lead to the accusation of "collaboration with the enemy" have to be taken into account to determine the psychological responsibility of the accused.

Did he surrender mentally under a kind of hypnosis? Can he be made responsible at all; was there a conscious and voluntary collaboration that turned the man into a traitor? Was there cowardice or only spiritual weakness?

Because these questions are so new in our history and often so subtle in relation to the circumstances, it is well to enumerate the fields of interest to be analyzed:

1. *The Accusation.* The psychologist has to study the incriminating facts. We often can see, for instance, in the phrasing of the signed confessions, evidence that the signature was enforced. Some cliché phrases of the enemy can be looked at as gradually wangled out of the head of the victim. For one of the courts I was able to make an analysis of a written confession that was composed of such heterogeneous elements that the process of mental wrestling and gradual giving in of the prisoner could easily be discerned in the papers.

2. *Rumor and mass psychology.* Not all the accusations against a prisoner of war made by fellow prisoners—even when the majority constantly repeat them—may be taken at face value. Under the impact of terror and fear, rumors about special persons are easily communicated. There are personalities who, on the basis of their special character structure, easily become the focal point of rumors. The withdrawn intellectual, for instance, is often accused of consorting with the enemy. When he speaks the enemy's language and can communicate with them, accusations against him can become like a huge mass hallucination.

The investigator has to make a survey of group relations in the P.O.W. camp. The brainwashing enemy tries first to attack the leaders, in order to attack the morale of the remainder of the P.O.W.'s; then he tries to select specially vulnerable personalities for his strategy of mental pressure and ideological conversion.

3. *The personality structure of the accused.* Certain persons, on the basis of their weak ego or their underlying neurotic anxieties, are predestined to give in earlier to mental pressures. To obtain a fair estimate of the individual, intelligence tests and the Rorschach test have to be given, the family background and the religious and ideological foundations of the person have to be studied.

4. *Was the brainwashee well trained to stand the treatment?* What kind of information had been given to the prisoner of war during his training? Did he know enough about the ideological war and the word barrage he might be exposed to? Was he only

prepared for discipline and submission, or also for freedom and nonconforming discussions? Was he only physically trained or also mentally?

5. *The facts of torture.* How long did it take before the prisoner gave in? Did he get drugs? How much isolation? How many hours of interrogation? Were there symptoms of pain and physical illness? Can these facts be verified?

This is only a short survey of viewpoints to be taken into account. They serve to show that with the phenomenon of systematic brainwashing and thought control something is brought before the court that is judicially new. The traditional attitudes toward personal competence, responsibility, and accountability cannot be applied.

The state (the totalitarian system of the enemy) has, in the case of successful brainwashing, taken over, even taken possession of, all psychological responsibility for the obedient acts of persons. Our criminal courts and military courts will have to find new rules of judging those who fell into the hands of such a criminalizing system.

🏴

CHAPTER SIXTEEN

Education for Discipline
or Higher Morale

🏴

The Role of Education

The child's formative years are spent under the guidance of first parents and then teachers; jointly they influence his future behavior. The educational system can either reinforce or correct parental errors and attitudes, either strengthen the child's desire to grow toward freedom and maturity or stifle his need to develop and twist it into the need to resign himself to permanent childishness and dependence.

Since the Renaissance, the ideal of universal scholastic training has made steady gains. But today we unwittingly tend to mold minds into a prefabricated pattern and to give our students the illusion that they know or have to know all the answers. The fallacy of such half-education is that the so-called alphabetics—in contrast to those who cannot read—may become better followers and worse thinkers. The totalitarians, for example, are not against schools; on the contrary, for the more you overburden the mind with facts, the more passive it may become. Intellectual erudition and booklearning alone do not make strong personalities, and in our passion for factual education and the quiz type of examination there lies hidden a form of mental pressure. The awe with which we regard the accumulation of school facts may inhibit the mind so that it cannot think for itself. We must become more aware of the involuntary pressures an educational system can impose on us, and their possibly dangerous effects on the future of our democratic society. The actual strategy of keeping people as permanent students under prolonged supervision is a help to totalitarian indoctrination. For instance, somewhere along the line in some administrative minds, there sprang up the idea that repeated, comparative examinations would increase the quality of the corps of administrators. Instead, infantile anxieties developed related to the fear of this infantile tool of measurement and evaluation: the examination. There is now hardly any administrator who dares to look at reality as the best test of human capacity and human endurance.

The form of education which sets a premium on dependency, which overcontrols the child, which makes a moral appeal through punishment and provoking a sense of guilt, which overrates mechanical skills and automatic learning, this form of education kneads the brain into a pattern of conformity which can easily be turned into totalitarian channels. This is even more the case in regard to the disciplinary training of soldiers. Such rigid education glorifies good behavior far too much; imitation and conformity are approved at the expense of spontaneous creativity, thinking for oneself, and the free expression and discussion of dissenting ideas. Our examination mania forces students into mental pathways of automatic thinking. Our intellectual and so-called objective education overrates rationalism and technical know-how under the delusion that this will keep emotional errors under control. What it does instead, of course, is to train children into automatic patterns of thinking and acting, which are closer to the pattern of conditioned reflexes, of which Pavlovian students are so fond, than they are to the free, exploratory, creative pattern toward which democratic education should be oriented.

Totalitarianism is well aware that youth has a sensitive period during which Pavlovian conditioning may be established without difficulty. Early teachings form nearly indestructible patterns in the child's mind and eventually replace innate instinctual precision. This early Pavlovian automatization of life may itself develop almost the force of an innate instinct. Indeed this is precisely what happens in Totalitaria. Dictators especially organize youth and press them to join disciplinary youth movements.

The paradox of universal literacy is that it may create a race of men and women who have become (just because of this new intellectual approach to life) much more receptive to the indocrination of their teachers or leaders. Do we need conditioned adepts or free-thinking students? Beyond this, our technical means of communication have caught up with our literacy. The eye that can read is immediately caught by advertising and propaganda. This is the tremendous dilemma of our epoch.

In many of our primary schools students are taught in an atmosphere of compulsive regimentation and are imprinted with a sense of dependency and awe of authority which lasts throughout their lives. They never really learn to think for themselves. The scholastic fact-factories, the schools, keep many pupils too busy to think; they may instead educate them into progressive immaturity. As long as people can quote one another and the available "expert" opinion, they are considered well-informed and intellectual. Many schools emphasize what we could call a quotation mania, making the ability to quote the epitome of all wisdom. Yet anyone with an apparently unanswerable logic, anyone who can back up his position with authoritative statements and quotations, can have a strong impact on such a mind, for it can readily be caught and conditioned by emotionally attractive pseudo-intellectual currents. As a matter of fact, in the process of brainwashing the inquisitor makes use of the feeling of confusion his victim gets when he is shown that his facts don't fit and that there are flaws in his concepts. The man who doesn't know the tricks of argument will break down sooner.

I like to distinguish among the intellectuals *quantellectuals* and *quintellectuals*. The former aim for quantity of knowledge and easily yield to any kind of new conditioning. To the quintellectuals, on the other hand, intellect is a quality of personal integrity. Facts are not consumed passively but are weighed and verified. This kind of intellect has a potentiality independent of school education and often school can spoil it.

One of the most amazing cases I ever treated was a typical quantellectual, a doctor of psychology who had just completed his

university education with a dissertation on a psychotechnical subject. He came to me because he was a complete failure in all his
relationships with girls. He wanted this "impotence" to be treated
medically, and at first he rejected any kind of psychotherapy because he "knew all that stuff." In the course of our conversation it
became apparent that his entire scholastic education had bypassed
him. He had gotten A's at school, but the very essence of what he
had studied had eluded him. He had grasped literally nothing about
psychology. He had memorized everything and had understood
nothing. He could quote from every page of the book but explain
none. Every time he had to work out a test or give practical advice,
he went into a panic. It took years of treatment to break through
his rigid, compulsive habits, and to bring him to a point where
he was able to think and feel as a human being rather than as a
machine. At the end of his treatment he started to learn all over
again, reading with greed and fervor what had before been empty
facts.

But he was not the only walking fact-collection I have met. Another one of my patients was a young man who was obsessed with
the desire to accumulate all the learned degrees his university could
deliver. At the time I met him he was a member of a Nazi organization. (Here is an example of the fact that many a pedant has
an affinity with an authoritarian political system.) Even in this
group he provoked hostility because of his search for facts and more
facts, facts only for the sake of facts. His compulsions became too
much for even his totalitarian fellows. He had delusions of grandeur
and had absolutely no emotional relationships at all; both signs
that a psychotic process was going on. But his intellectual capacity
was intact. The son of a scholar, he had lived in constant competition with his father; early in youth he started to read the en-
cyclopedia, and later, in grade school and high school, he was
cheered because of his phenomenal "knowledge." Indeed, he did
know the facts, but he knew nothing else. He knew neither how to
get along with himself nor with anyone else.

These two cases serve to demonstrate how a mechanized educational system, failing to detect even an urgent need for emotional
relationships and a sense of belonging, and placing its emphasis on
learning instead of living, can produce adults who are totally un-

equipped to meet the problems of life, who are themselves only half alive and completely incapable of meeting the challenges of reality. Such men and women do not make good democratic citizens.

One of the most essential tasks of education for mental freedom is to prepare the child for mature adulthood by teaching him to see the essentials and by teaching him to think for himself. There are several fields of interest through which the capacity to think for oneself may be developed—for instance, the field of communication and the science of abstraction. A child's awareness of his own language, of the words he himself uses, as an expressive tool rather than as a set of grammatical rules can lead him to inquisitiveness about other languages and other ways of thinking, and thus may lead him to the ability to think abstractly and to understand relationships. The child's period of greatest sensitivity to foreign languages is when he is about ten—much younger than the age at which we normally teach foreign languages. At this age, too, the child begins to have an active personal interest in words and self-expression. This interest can be used to make language an exciting adventurous exploration instead of a cut-and-dried process of memorization.

Our schools must stimulate inventiveness and self-activity too, through such subjects as carpentry and designing. Creative play with concrete objects also develops the child's capacity to abstract and to generalize, making it easier for him to absorb the abstractions which underlie all mathematics. If, instead of throwing the child into the sea of abstractions he finds in the daily arithmetic drill, we brought him to an understanding of the process of abstraction by carefully graded steps, he would absorb and assimilate what he learned, not merely parrot what he was told. We tend, for instance, to teach mathematical abstractions at too early an age, just as we wait too long to teach language and verbal expression.

History is a subject which is not learned by memorizing facts and dates but through mutual discussion. It has to start with the concept of personal lifetimes and personal history. It is better to give a child a printed report of the history of yesterday and ask for his comments and opinions on it, or better to promote individual thought by letting him search for background information in a library or museum, than to ask him to memorize facts. In this way the learning of history can become an adventure.

We can also revise the system that risks so easily rearing mediocre people who fit into a pattern of mediocrity. Different children must be trained and educated differently. Each one has his own internal timetable; each one will have his own life adjustments. Why should we compulsively do to our children what we would never do to the flowers in our gardens? Every plant is allowed to attain its own natural size. Our current scholastic practice stimulates ambition in a few children, but stifles it in others. Instead of promoting cheating by our rigid examination rules, why do we not allow children to help one another in the solution of common problems? Very often children can teach each other what the teacher cannot.

Think for a moment of the child especially sensitive to the boredom of some of our contemporary schools. He becomes either a conformist—full of good marks and no original thoughts—or a rebel—ripe for the child-guidance clinic of today and possibly for the totalitarian state of tomorrow.

Discipline and Morale

While good morale implies inner strength and self-discipline, it may not necessarily imply a set group discipline in a political or military sense. Good personal morale and backbone were two of the needed qualifications for taking part successfully in the underground during the last war. The partisans, working secretly—now here, now there—relied, in their lonely combat, on their individual initiative and morale as much as, if not more than, on distant leadership and discipline. This is just the opposite of a kind of stand-by morale impelled by blind fear and maintained from a distance, the kind which is obtained in jails or concentration camps, or in a tribe with extreme emphasis on common participation. In the first groups, there was morale without discipline; in the second, discipline without morale. In the same way, there are some officers who can only develop discipline without morale.

Nevertheless, there is usually an inner relation between discipline and morale. Only when a certain amount of initial disciplinary training is given to youngsters or soldiers are they well conditioned for that personal inner strength which is based on self-confidence and trust in the group as a whole, together with confidence in the authorities. Emergency discipline is resorted to during times of stress when there is usually lack of time, with the result that there is not a sufficient period for self-control and adjustment to the group. Only a self-chosen discipline which develops gradually can lay the basis for inner freedom and morale. This rule has been forgotten by many educators. Only this basis of initial, conditioned patterns gives us the confidence to stand on our own.

We all start by introjecting and taking over our morale from others—our parents and educators. The basis of our personal morale is what we internalized from them. The subtle mutual relation between discipline and freedom starts in the cradle under the care of loving and interested and consistent parents. The parents are the first to build morale. The conflict between discipline and morale in a group usually arises when the members are held together by compulsion or necessity. Here the inner coherence will be completely different from that of a situation in which there is a spontaneous loyalty to the group. The aim of all discipline is to develop a better adjustment to the group. In turn, success in identifying with the group develops a stronger ego. From this point on, freedom begins.

A further understanding of these morale-building principles is important for an evaluation of the inner strength or vulnerability of the various cultural groups. We may expect, according to our experiences in psychotherapy, that where too much discipline, or even slavery, prevails, the inner cohesion of the group will be very different from that of a group respecting and holding the individual in high esteem. Yet we have found men even in the armies of totalitarian systems who exemplify high morale. I call to mind those Japanese soldiers who—without any tie with the mother country—stuck to their lonely posts for years after the war, as though the emperor and his generals were still looking at them. This tells us something about the consistent love, security, and dedication they received in the first six years of life.

Discipline and Brainwashing

When we want to train a soldier to resist brainwashing, we have to give him antidotes against mass suggestion. We have to teach him to make up his own answers and to criticize his teachers. We must train him in negative suggestibility and emphasize the courage to reject emotionally pleasant reasoning when it does not seem truthful. Above all, we have to repeat such lessons many times to make a self-confident individual out of a recruit. Against the daily barrage of suggestions, we have to provoke individual criticism. All this has to be done in addition to making the soldier familiar with the concept and implications of brainwashing. In so doing, he will learn, unconsciously, to judge what propaganda is or what it is not—as we all partially do when listening to advertising over the radio. Psychological experience tells us that part of propagandistic suggestions can leak through even alert mental defenses and penetrate our opinions. Anti-brainwashing training has to be done thoroughly and repeatedly. It may appear to be in conflict with rigid discipline; when the teacher and officer knows enough about the subject, however, the student's self-respect is enhanced through identification with the leading officer. True, we see here a change of disciplinary relations, but it offers the real test of discipline in a free, democratic community. A man who has been taught self-esteem and knowledge will stand to the end when the hour of challenge comes.

The change of the war of weapons into a mental cold war requires a change of discipline. The soldier has to *know* not only his rifle, but even more the *sense* of his mission and the *nonsense* of the enemy.

The Quality of the Group and the Influence of the Leader

In every group situation, morale refers to the degree of cohesive strength of the members and to the amount of loyalty toward the group and its goals. Morale may, or may not, imply an understanding of the goals. In Western culture with its subtle pros and cons, a much deeper need for awareness, understanding, and consideration of goals is implied than is called for in a totalitarian state.

In the totalitarian state with its veneration for the strong leader, the threatening loss of coherence—when the dictator or leading group fails—would have a much more disintegrating effect than such failure in a democratic society, whose members usually have reached a higher degree of self-determination and governmental skill. A democracy always finds new leaders ready to take responsibility.

Morale includes the question of how much people can endure physically and mentally, and for how long. Under different kinds of regimentation the limit of endurance will be different. Stand-by morale, based on fear as in prisons, may disintegrate at the least sign of weakness in leader or guard, or when the individuals have not as yet been sufficiently disciplined.

The *kamikazes,* the pilots educated for suicide, were thoroughly indoctrinated with the self-offering ideology; and their morale, as shown in the war with Japan, might be said to have been high—in an Oriental sense. Here discipline and allegiance had become so automatic that life was of no importance either to the individual or to the group. The only thought was to keep going and beat the enemy. This kind of morale is often dependent on obtaining a frenzied desperation—a kind of collective suicidal rage—in pursuit of the national goal.

We are becoming more and more aware of how important leadership is in boosting morale. The leader is the embodiment of the valued human relationships for which we are willing to offer our energy and even, when needed, our lives. Through identification with him we borrow his fortitude. It is not always the official leader who has charge of lifting the morale. Sometimes a sergeant or a soldier may take over this function.

The official leader himself is in a more difficult position. He must be many things that may seem to contradict one another. He must represent paternal authority as well as our ego, our conscience, and our ideals. He must relieve us of our sense of guilt and anxiety, and he must be able to absorb our needs for strength, affection, and dedication—our transference needs, as expressed in psychological terms. He must be able to create group action and motivation and at the same time increase the individual's self-esteem. His doubts may become our doubts; his loss of confidence makes us lose our self-confidence. At times we may want him to be a tyrant so that we can be relieved of our personal resentments and responsibilities. Sometimes we want to compete with him as we competed with our fathers. At other times we want affection from him. The leader must be both a scapegoat and a giant. Our own inner strength will grow, depending on the leader's inspiring and guiding personality. While we may never love him completely, we will use him to grow or decline in our morale.

Yet the individual not only borrows strength from the group and its leader, he also brings his own spirit to it. Even when he is used as a scapegoat to release group hostility, the individual—when he takes it with humor and philosophy—may unwittingly boost the morale of the group. He communicates, as it were, his personal tolerance to others. The black sheep in a platoon is often as much accepted as the beloved sports hero.

In the same way, the group communicates all kinds of feelings to the individual; the process of *morale contagion* is continually going on. Its quality depends on mutual acceptance, friendships, the amount of contagious fear in the group, the quality of interpersonal processes, resistance-provoking qualities in the few, and so on.

Let us not forget that the best morale booster for ourselves is to help to lift the morale of others. When interhuman contact is not allowed, morale is soon lacking. For instance, we heard from several escaped people from behind the iron curtain that their most prominent complaint in the totalitarian system was the feeling of mental isolation. The individual feels alone and continually on the alert. There is only mutual suspicion. The new gospel for those escapees was the ready humane acceptance and contact they experienced in the democratic group, because here was spontaneous enthusiasm and mutual acceptance—even when there was disagreement.

Enumeration of Some Factors Influencing Group Morale

The following factors resulting mostly from military experience may endanger morale:

1. Wrong anticipation of danger; myths and rumors about the enemy.
2. Severe stress; battle fatigue.
3. Poor physical and mental health (flu!).
4. Lack of food, lack of sleep; cold and dirt.

5. Bad leadership.
6. Poor training; lack of skill; overtraining.
7. Poor communication and poor information.
8. Destruction of basic values, lack of faith.
9. Confusion of activities, strife in politics, wrong selection of government.
10. Authoritarian and undemocratic behavior; humiliation.
11. Tyranny; too rigid discipline, also lack of discipline.
12. Homesickness and feelings of estrangement.
13. Internal hostilities, prejudices, persecution of minorities.
14. Thought control and menticide; no right to be an individual, no justice, no right to appeal.
15. No function in the social setting, no duties.
16. Alcohol and sedatives.

The following factors may boost morale:

1. Sound democratic leadership.
2. Well-planned organization with the freedom of improvisation; minimum of red tape.
3. Democratic self-discipline. Do we have faith in our own institutions?
4. Information and unhampered communication.
5. Freedom of religion; moral integrity.
6. Mutual loyalty and mature responsibility; team spirit.
7. Mental alertness; the important psychology of awareness of the problems of our own epoch.
8. A sense of belonging and being accepted.
9. A sense of justice, freedom, and privacy.
10. Confidence in experts ready to give first aid (mental hygiene experts, clergy, Red Cross, Civil Defense, medical first aid).

The Breaking Point and Our Capacity for Frustration

What is the straw that breaks the camel's back? This is a key question in the problem of personal morale. During the Second World War, I treated a fighter pilot who was unafraid of his

dangerous work but who felt unhappy about his personal relationships. Suddenly during an air-raid alert in London, where he was
on furlough, he was struck by utter panic. In normal life he had been
a rather shy and withdrawn young man. Unexpectedly he found
himself in a shelter with a frightened group about him, and he
became contaminated by the fear of other people. The strange
situation found him unprepared and so he broke down. I mention
this point to show again how contagious the atmosphere in a
P.O.W. camp can be.

No one can really tell how he will behave in times of great danger
until it comes to actually facing the test. The true test of reality is
solved in different ways. Many accept the challenge. Some overdefensive, compulsive individuals even welcome the danger. Still
others—who were already unstable—misuse the new situation as
an excuse to break down and let their emotions go. Segal calls the
last group frustrated big-dealers, seclusives, dupes, scared kids,
praise-starved egotists—all having egos that could easily be boosted
by a flattering inquisitor.

In psychology we are aware of the fact that there are two sets
of determinants which bring on mental breakdown: one set consisting of *long-term* considerations which cause a gradual breakdown
of inner defenses, the other consisting of *short-term* factors, the
triggers or provoking factors causing a sudden collapse of the
mental and physical integration. To the first set of factors may belong chronic disease or the many chronic irritations of life. The
second operates by means of a sudden symbolic impact on hidden
sensitivities. A mouse appearing in a girls' class doesn't arouse panic
because of its objective danger. Modern psychopathology has studied the manifold sensitizing occurrences, experienced in early life,
which make people subject to unknown trigger reactions.

Yet, trauma and frustration are emphasized too much as weak-
eners of the personality during its development. As a matter of fact,
the opposite is true. Challenge and resistance to unfavorable influences make the personality. In order to develop greater inner
strength and better ego defenses, the individual has to expose and
traumatize himself. What else is "fair" sport and "fair" competition
but repeated training in morale? Physical training doesn't have to
be "soft." The self-traumatization by trial and error, to which we

unconsciously expose ourselves in encounters during sports, is part of a spontaneous effort toward self-discipline. When the person cannot find strength within himself, he must borrow it from his neighbor and look for strength by proxy. Too great emphasis on dependence or leadership increases this proxy mechanism. Leadership is not exclusively the secret of morale. Identification with the leader may sometimes fortify the person's inner strength, but it may also frustrate his capacity to grapple with his own problems. A frustrating leader may decrease our capacity to tolerate frustration.

Living under too soft circumstances is probably a weakening factor; a recent publication (Richter) on experiences with men under combat stress, and later with rats in the laboratory, have proven that luxury in general influences negatively man's capacity to endure.

Somewhere along the line, good morale means no longer being afraid to die; it means solving that mythological anxiety about death being something dark and obscure; and it means the willingness to accept fate. Accepting fate and duty and responsibility is living in a different way: it is living with the moral courage to stand for moral principles that you have gathered in your life and without which life is not worth living.

The anticipation of bad occurrences can have a paralyzing effect. If one expects people to break down, they may either give in more easily to these false prophets, or, out of hostility, feel boosted in their morale. The press, the radio, television have to be aware of their subtle responsibility as morale-influencing mediums.

It is important to realize that mental prophets expect more panic in others when they themselves feel jittery and insecure. In the last war, there were many sensational forecasts of panic that, happily enough, did not materialize, such as Dunkerque. Man is often mentally much stronger than we expect him to be. Of all the animals, he can suffer most and take danger best—provided he does not weaken himself by his belief in supernatural terror stories nor become unnerved in a cold war.

✠

CHAPTER SEVENTEEN

From Old to New Courage

✠

Who Resists Longer and Why?

What then can give a man strength to resist a menticidal assault? What made it possible for so many thousands to survive mentally and physically the horrors of the Nazi concentration camps and the Communist P.O.W. camps?

The answer is essentially simple. Men yield primarily because at some point they are overwhelmed by their unconscious conflicts. These conflicts, kept under control in normal circumstances, come to the surface under the strain of menticidal pressure. The stronger the inner conflicts and the greater the pressure, the greater the tendency to yield. Men withstand pressure when these conflicts cannot be so easily aroused or have been inwardly overcome.

This simple answer itself contains a clinical paradox. One of the characteristics of severe neurosis, and of some cases of pathological character structure, is that unconscious conflicts are so severe that they are either repressed so deeply that the sufferer is not even vaguely aware of their existence or they are transformed into a set of overt attitudes which are more acceptable to the individual, and therefore easier to handle. If the severe neurotic permitted himself to feel his real conflicts, they would dominate his life completely; consequently he exerts tremendous force to hold down this explosive material. The man who is always rebellious, never growing from healthy rebellion into healthy maturity, may have transformed some basic and profound conflict in his own personality into a chronic resistance against any kind of social demand. Psychiatric examination of returned P.O.W.'s from Korea showed that many of the men who resisted enemy propaganda most strongly were those with a history of lifelong rebellion against all authority —from parents through teachers to army superiors. They were troublemakers wherever they were, among their friends as well as among their enemies (Segal).

This negative side of the coin is only part of the picture. A man with deep self-knowledge, aware of his own inner conflicts and aware, too, of what the enemy is trying to do to him is prepared to meet and resist the attack. I interrogated many people who went through the tortures of Nazi prison and concentration camps. Some were ordinary folk with no political affiliations, some were members of the resistance, a few were psychologists and psychoanalysts. Those who understood themselves, who were willing to accept danger and challenge, and who realized, even faintly, how bestial man can be, were able to stand the harrowing concentration-camp experience. They were not defeated by their own innocent perplexity and lack of insight into themselves and others, but were protected by their knowledge and inquisitive alertness.

There are other factors which play an important role too. My investigations have made it abundantly clear to me that those who can resist, who can maintain their strength under marginal circumstances, never feel that they are alone. As long as they can think of their loved ones at home, as long as they can look forward to seeing them again, as long as they know their families are faithfully waiting for them, they can maintain their strength and keep the unconscious drive to give in from taking over their lives. The love and affection we get and gather in our hearts is the greatest stimulus to endurance. Not only does it provide a goal toward which we can direct our lives, it also gives us an inner assurance and a sense of worth that make it possible for us to keep in check the self-destroying conflicts.

This knowledge of loving and being loved is not limited to love of family or friends. People in whom a religious faith or a political conviction is a deeply rooted, living thing have this same sense of belonging, of being needed, of being loved. Their allegiance is to a whole group or to a set of ideals rather than to individuals. To such people, beliefs are real and concrete, as real and concrete as people or objects. They provide a bulwark against loneliness, terror, fantasies conjured up by the unconscious, and the unleashing of deep-seated conflicts, a bulwark that is as strong as the memory of love. Yet, such mentally strong people form a minority in our conflict-ridden society.

Experience has shown that robust athletes cannot withstand the concentration-camp or the P.O.W. camp experiences any better than can their physically weaker brothers. Nor is intellect alone any real help in fending off the daily assaults on the will. On the contrary, it can provide useful rationalization for surrender. Mental backbone and moral courage go deeper than the intellect. Fortitude is not a physical or intellectual quality; it is something we get from the cradle, from the consistency of our parents' behavior, and from their beliefs and faith. It has become increasingly rare in a world of changing values and little faith.

The Myth of Courage

There is something in the glorious myth of strength and courage that confuses all of us. Physical strength is too frequently confused with spiritual strength. Bravery and heroism are, indeed, needed qualities in battle. Yet analysis of soldiers in combat shows that each one of them has to conduct a constant battle against his own fears. The brave are the ones who can check their fears, who can cope with the paralyzing fantasies that fear creates, and who can control the desire to regress into childish escapism. A man cannot be forced to become a hero, and it is ridiculous to punish him if he is not. It is as pointless as punishing him for bleeding or fainting.

The hero, the man who offers himself up to death for the sake of others, is found more in mythology than in reality. Psychology and anthropology have shown that the hero myth is related to eternal dream images. The hero symbolizes the rebellious new generation, the strong son becoming stronger than the father. He symbolizes, too, our wish to be mature and to take responsibility into our own hands.

We need the myth for the inspiration it offers us. We commemorate with posthumour glorification the heroic feats of the few who have, throughout history, offered themselves up as sacrifices to their comrades or to society. Yet what do we know of their real motives?

During the Second World War, I gave psychiatric treatment to many soldiers. As I spoke and worked with them, I became increasingly conscious of how dangerous it is to stick the simple label "hero" or "coward" on any man. One of my patients, for example, was a boy who had received a high military decoration because he had stuck to a lonely place with his machine gun, firing automatically until the enemy was forced to withdraw. In the course of his treatment, the boy confessed that his apparent heroism was really the result of a paralyzing fear, which had made it impossible for him to follow his commander's order to retreat.

No one can really tell how he will behave in times of danger. Each person will solve the frightening test that reality confronts him with in his own way. Several will accept the challenge and stand up to it. Some overdefensive, compulsive individuals may even welcome this burden as a test of their strength. Still others—whose instability has deep roots in the past—will unconsciously take advantage of a perilous situation to break down completely and let their tears and emotions go.

Freud has directed our attention to the peculiar interplay between external and internal dangers, between frightening reality and equally frightening fantasy. Objective, recognizable dangers often stimulate the mind to alertness and encourage it to set up its inner defenses. But there are subjective panic-creators too—frustration, feeling of guilt, infantile horror fantasies—and these can often be so terrorizing in their effects that all our cultural defenses collapse. Many men who face the test of reality with stalwart courage can be brought to collapse by apparent trivia which somehow touch them in a vulnerable spot.

Another of my wartime patients mentioned previously showed such a pattern. The young fighter pilot, who had flown forty combat missions without any sign of fear or panic, suddenly broke down completely in an air-raid shelter in London. In the course of treatment, it became apparent that this young man was bitterly unhappy about his personal relationships. He did not get along with his commanding officer; he had had a serious quarrel with his girl friend the night before his breakdown. A shy and with-drawn person, when he suddenly found himself in the shelter with a frightened group about him, he became contaminated by the fear in the atmosphere. Weakened by recent unhappiness, he found himself completely unable to put up the inner defenses that had served him so well under the frightening experiences of active war.

Are we to say that he was less of a hero than the much-decorated machine-gunner?

There still lives in all of us an admiration for bravado, for the theatrical display of courage, for the devil-may-care invitation to destruction. We are beginning to recognize now that real courage is different; it is at one and the same time an expression of faith in life and a resignation to death. Courage is not something that can be forced on a man from the outside. It has to come from inside him.

In the reality of modern war—the impersonal Moloch—a man can be easily reduced to a feeling of helplessness and dependency. Personal courage can turn the tide of battle in a hand-to-hand en-counter, but personal courage is no defense against bombs and machine guns. Today, reckless courage, as we have glorified it, is less important than personal morale, faith, conviction, knowledge, and adequate preparation.

A boy of seventeen years of age is drafted into the army. He has spent his entire life in a small town in Texas. He receives training in the routine of army life and the use of his weapons. Soon there-after he is sent to Korea, and almost immediately he is taken prisoner. Now this child has to defend himself against the propa-ganda barrage which well-trained Communist theoreticians daily hurl at him. His education is limited, his background narrow, his political training inadequate. He even tries to escape from his prison camp but is caught. As a result, the enemy's mental hold on him increases. His great disappointment makes him feel trapped. Finally he surrenders and collaborates. How can a military court hold him responsible, and even punishable, for the fact that he finally gave in to enemy propaganda?

This is part of the story of Corporal Claude Batchelor, recently sentenced to twenty years imprisonment for collaboration with the enemy. I would venture to guess that it could have been the story of nearly any American boy of similar background.

After the Second World War, several European countries had to face the difficult problem of how to treat those members of the underground who, after torture by the Nazis, had confessed and betrayed their compatriots. In Holland a Court of Honor was established to judge these special cases. This court reached the following conclusions:

> No man can possibly vouch for it that under no circumstances will he 'confess,' 'cooperate,' or 'betray' his country. No man who has not himself gone through the hell which Communists and Nazis have been so able to organize has any right to judge the conduct of a man who did.
>
> Psychological torture is more effective in many cases than physical torture. This is all the more true of the victim who has above average intellectual background. It seems that intelligence makes physical torture more easily bearable but at the same time exposes one more to the impact of mental torture. Anyone who 'submitted' under such circumstances to the enemy after having given proof of his loyalty, patriotism and courage will suffer terribly because his condemnation of himself will always be more severe than that of any judge.
>
> There is, however, not the slightest reason for shame, nor for considering such a person incapacitated for giving leadership. On the contrary, more than outsiders he will know what superhuman strength is required to resist the subtle methods of mental torture, and more than outsiders he can be helpful to others to prepare themselves for the ordeal as far as that is at all possible.*

The Morale-Boosting Idea

When we look at the varieties of human behavior under extreme and pressing circumstances, we see how easily man can be subdued, and at the same time we see that certain factors seem to

---

* From a letter written by G. Van Heuven Goedhart, U.N. High Commissioner for Refugees, President of the Dutch Court of Honor, which appeared in *The New York Times,* March 15, 1954.

have a positive effect on his morale, keeping him from despair and collapse. When these factors are operative, the spirit revives and people are enabled to live with integrity in spite of dangerous circumstances. There are many such morale boosters—religious faith or a political ideology are among them. Perhaps the most effective is the sense of having some mission and inner goal. This ideal with which a man identifies can be love of the native land, love of freedom or justice, or even the thought of hate and revenge. Whatever it is, at the moment of calamity a guiding idea is as much needed as mere physical strength and endurance. In every case where the individual has learned to withstand danger and to maintain at least some of his normal *esprit* under circumstances of deprivation, want, and brutality, one or more of the morale-boosting factors must have been present.

I do not believe that the inner search for the morale-boosting *regenerative idea* is a conscious function of the mind. Such psychological regeneration is comparable with the physical regenerative processes we see in the body. The body hardly ever gives up its regenerative capacities. Even when a man is dying of cancer, his surgical wounds still heal, the local regenerating forces are still there. The same thing seems to operate on a mental level; in times of confusion, pressure, and exhaustion, man's psychological healing and regenerating forces are still in action. This applies as much to large groups of people as it does to the individual, though in the former, restraining forces remain in action because of intricate interpersonal relationships.

My experiences with people living in the utmost dangerous circumstances showed that very soon after an initial bewilderment the individuals develop an inner need for what we might call mental budgeting. They all display observable clinical symptoms indicating that this process of regaining their self-assertive resistance is going on. When they first come to the prison camps, for instance, they show complete passivity, surrender, and depersonalization, but soon a guiding idea begins to grow out of their need to understand fate, their need for protective intercommunication and adherence to some common faith, for building something for the self. We can detect this favorable change in mood by the way every prisoner makes his own corner a place of security, even when it is only a dirty wooden bunk. He begins to rearrange the few things he has; he builds his own nest, and from it he begins to look out into his miserable marginal world.

When the prison-camp inmate finds friends whose faith and strength of character are greater than his, his life becomes more bearable to him. Through mere association with others he can better face the horrors without. Mutual love and common hate, both may be equally stimulating. Renewed human contact changes his inherent fear into confidence in at least one other person. When this grows into some identity with an active, working team, the temporary loss of inner strength is gone. When he does not find such a group or personality to identify with, the prison guard and his foreign ideology may take over.

It must be said that the stimulating morale-boosting idea is nearly always a moral idea, an ethical evaluation—faith in goodness, justice, freedom, peace, and future harmony. Even the most cynical dictator needs the help of moral ideas to raise the morale of those submissive to his regime. If he cannot give them at least the illusion of peace and freedom in addition to prospects for future wealth, he reduces them to dull apathetic followers. At the entrance of the Nazi concentration camps were large signs bearing the cynical slogan: *Arbeit macht frei* ("Work makes man free"). This may not have fooled the inmates, but it gave the German people outside the camps a way of justifying their inhuman behavior. The need for moral justification, which is felt by even the most ruthless tyrants, proves how deeply alive these ideas of morality are in man. The more a man lives in marginal and torturous situations, the greater is his need for supportive moral values and their stimulating action.

In general we may say that there are three influences under which the unbearable becomes bearable. Again, in the first place, one must have faith; this can be simple faith in religious or ethical values, or faith in humanity, or faith in the stability of one's own society, or faith in one's own goals. In the second place, the victim must feel that in spite of the disaster which has overtaken him and turned him into an outcast, he is wanted and needed somewhere on this earth. In the third place, there must be understanding, not sophisticated book knowledge but simple, even intuitive, psychological understanding of the motivations of the enemy and his deluded drives. Those who cannot understand and are too perplexed break down first.

Anti-brainwashing training has to be done very thoroughly. It is true that inner defenses can be built against thought control and against the daily barrage of suggestions. With the help of good and repeated instruction, people can be made familiar with the concepts. Perceptual defenses are then built up; we learn to detect the false propaganda and we do not listen to it. Even though part of the propagandistic suggestions leak through these perceptual defenses and creep unobtrusively into our opinions (all advertising is based on this leakage), it cannot be stressed enough that full knowledge of the enemy's methods gives us more strength to resist.

Several psychologists have told me how, under the frightful circumstances of life in the Nazi concentration camps, they felt sustained by their science. It gave them perspective and made it possible for them to see their own suffering from a greater distance. It was the philosophical attitude of the inquisitive mind that fortified their inner strength.

Still, there are only a few stories of those who could not be broken down by the process of Communist brainwashing. Such a hard-boiled revolutionary as the Spaniard El Campesino, for one, was able to stand it (Gonzales and Gorkin). He knew the tricks of the totalitarians. It is also possible that they might not have thought him important enough to waste too much time and effort on him; after all, he could always be sent to a concentration camp to waste away.

It must be repeated that any kind of illicit group formation in the camps—no matter how dangerous—immediately gave the individual a sense of being protected. Most of those who resisted cooperation and group membership and worked on their own succumbed to despair and defeat. Those who betrayed their comrades usually did so after they had gone through a long period of isolation, not necessarily enforced, but often caused by their own peculiar character structure.

Human contact with a trusted source is needed more than bread to keep the spirit of freedom and belonging alive. During the Second World War the anti-Nazi underground lived on the daily radio news from free England. Even now there are people in enslavement and distress who live on the few communications we are able to transmit to them. The Voice of America and Radio Free Europe have a tremendous morale-boosting function in countries where the totalitarian air leads to despair.

In our present-day fight against brainwashing, intelligent preparation for what the prisoner has to expect and simple understanding of the enemy's tactics are the greatest aid. In the first place, this will undermine the enemy's political strategy; nobody will believe his deceitful accusations. In the second place, victims of brainwashing will no longer suffer from the paralyzing bewilderment of those who are suddenly caught by an unfamiliar situation. Perhaps, too, we should advise our soldiers under duress to confess too much, to confuse the inquisitor and to take over the enemy's strategy of confusion, lying, and deceit to bring him to frustration. This suggestion was also made by Rear Admiral D. V. Gallery of the United States Navy.* In cases where victims of menticide have done this, the inquisitors have often begged their victims to become rational again; the torturer himself was disturbed and upset by the feigned craziness of his victim. Of the greatest importance is the victim's awareness that other people know and understand what is happening, that there is a home front that is acquainted with his lonely struggle and torture.

If he does succumb, he should know that others understand that he cannot be held completely responsible for his behavior. His brain wanted to resist, his mind wanted to say no, but in the end everything in his body acted against him. It is an eerie and strange experience—awareness of the fact that against one's will, one has lost the freedom of mental action. It is an experience which enough pressure can make familiar to most men.

Are the effects of brainwashing only temporary? There is a difference between young people whose thoughts are still likely to be molded into permanent patterns of thinking and adults whose patterns are already formed by a free education. In mature people, brainwashing is an artificial nightmare they can often shed the moment they return to free territory. In some, it may leave long-lasting scars of depression and humiliation, but gradually the spell subsides in an atmosphere where freedom reigns.

* *The Saturday Evening Post*, January 22, 1955.

During and directly after the Second World War, those members of the resistance who had lost their bearings under the influence of the Nazi terror made it necessary for psychiatrists to face a new problem, that of a temporarily changed personality. Obviously the terror in prisons and concentration camps had not only made meek collaborators of a certain few, but they came out of their ordeal as lost souls, full of guilt and remorse and unable to face themselves as valid citizens. Even the honorable official exoneration of responsibility granted to them by a special court was not always able to repair their self-esteem. Before accepting themselves they had to go through a slow and difficult psychological process of undoing the nightmarish mental confusion into which they were thrown. During psychotherapy several of them had to recall and experience once more the terror they had suffered: their initial struggle to resist the mental dinning of their inquisitors, the gradual paralysis of will, their final surrender. It was a subtle inner battle between their feelings of guilt and the wish to reassert themselves. Emotional outbursts were followed by thoughts of suicide as a final flight from their shame. After they had vented their pent-up emotions, the therapist was able to convince them that everybody has his physical and psychological limits of endurance. From this point on, they could express themselves freely as independent human beings with a mixture of both negative and positive qualities.

In one case of a young man who had spent years in a concentration camp after a thorough brainwashing by the Nazis, the process of rehabilitation lasted nearly two years. The victim emerged from it without mental scars, and was even strengthened by his bitter experience.

I am convinced that in the case of prisoners who were for years in a totalitarian prison and were consequently politically conditioned, a cathartic, psychotherapeutic approach will help them to find their old inner selves once more. Threats and aggressive discussions would only be a continuation of the same coercive brainwashing process their jailors used. The best therapy for them is the daily contact and exchange with the free, democratic world, as we have seen proven in so many cases of ex-prisoners of the totalitarian machine. Free air is for them the best therapy!

For the millions of children who from the cradle are pressed into the framework of mental automatization, no such option for freedom exists. For them there is no other world, there are no other beliefs; there is only the all-consuming totalitarian Moloch, in whose service every means and every deed is justified.

Brainwashers are very naive in thinking that the enforced reformation of the mind—the transformation of capitalist prisoners into Communist propagandists—will be permanent. For the first few weeks after their return to a normal environment, the ex-prisoner will speak the language he has been "taught." He will recite his piece, but then, and often suddenly and surprisingly, his old self comes back. If the victim has a chance to investigate and examine the Communist propaganda and accusations, the whole artificial nightmare will fall away. For this reason, the jailers are careful not to dismiss all their converts at once. A few must stay behind as hostages to assure that those who are released will not expose the whole plot and thus endanger their friends in jail. Those who do tell the truth on their return home feel guilty because their revelations may expose the hostages to even greater torture.

I have been fascinated by a peculiar character trait that makes for courage and endurance. I called it in my study on the problem of time the *sense of continuity,* the awareness that our experiences *now* are not only chained to our experiences from the past, but also to our image and fantasy of a future. We live in a world where we accept too much of the actual occurrences, without asking why and for what all this happens. Those who think of planning for the future are sneeringly called utopianists, as if the idea of Utopia had not always sprung from human yearning. Our ancestors believed in the future, the coming of Christ, the coming of the messiahs, the Kingdom of God. They anticipated and worked for a better epoch. The people in the concentration camps who believed in a future, who believed in a plan, who could see their actual calamity as a small chain between past and future, could endure better their temporary suffering.

I had the privilege of knowing people who belonged to the few kernels of strength and who were able to do more than exist passively and borrow strength from others. They were able to live courageously under the extreme stress of the Nazi concentration camp. They accepted the camp and the persecution as a challenge to their minds. Physical pain did not touch them. The abnormal circumstances stimulated their spirit; they lived beyond the circumstances. The morale of these people inspired others; they lived by fortifying and helping others. They accepted the Spinozistic *amor fati*, the love and acceptance of fate. They are a living proof that the mind can be stronger than the body.

The New Courage

Philosophy and psychology have made us aware of new challenges and new courage. Socrates, over two thousand years ago, considered bravery a spiritual courage which goes far beyond the courage of physical battle. A soldier can be aggressive and have contempt for death without being brave. His rashness can be a suicidal foolhardiness inspired by a collective elan. This may be the panicky courage of the unaware primitive infant in us.

There is also a spiritual bravery, a mental courage that goes beyond the self. It serves an idea. It asks not only what the price of life is, but also for what that price is being asked. It asks for a hyperconsciousness of the self as a thinking spiritual being.

It is only comparatively recently that spiritual courage has been esteemed. Socrates' notion has taken a long time to seep into our thinking. It was only after the Reformation that the heroic struggle of the lonely battling personality gained value. To defend your own dissenting opinion courageously, even against the pressure of a majority opinion, acquired a heroic color—especially where nonconformism and heresy were forbidden. Gandhi's quiet and stubborn campaign of passive resistance is today considered more courageous than the bravery of the soldier who throws himself into the ecstasy of battle. Spiritual bravery is not found among the conformists or among those who preach uniformity or among those who plead for smooth social adjustment. It requires continual mental alertness and spiritual strength to resist the dragging current of conformist thought. Man has to be stronger than the mere will for self-protection and self-assertion; he has to be able to go beyond himself in the service of an idea and has to be able to acknowledge loyally that he has been wrong when higher values are found.

Indeed, there is a spiritual courage that goes beyond all automatic reflex action. Man is not only a mass, a piece of kneaded dough; he is also a personality. He dares to confront the human masses as he confronts the entire world—as a thinking human being. Consciousness, alert awareness are themselves a form of courage, a lonely exploration and a confrontation of values. Such courage dares to break through old traditions, taboos, prejudices and dares to doubt dogma. The heroes of the mind do not know the fanfare, the pathetic show, the pseudo-courage of exaltation and glory; these brave heroes fight their inner battle against rigidity, cowardice, and the wish to surrender conviction for the sake of ease. This courage is like remaining awake when others want to soothe themselves with sleep and oblivion. Totalitarian ideology is able to blackmail man through his inner cowardice. It threatens him into surrendering his innermost convictions in exchange for glamour and acceptance, for hero worship, for honor and acknowledgment. Yet the true hero is true to his ideals.

Only when people have learned to accept individual responsibility can the world be helped by the combined efforts of many individuals. Don't imitate the master, don't merely identify with the leader, but if you do conform, accept his lead with the full recognition of your own responsibility. Such heroism of the spirit is only possible if you are the master of your emotions and in full control of your aggressions.

The new hero will not be recognized because of his muscles or aggressive power, but because of his character, his wisdom, and his mental proportions.

Intimate knowledge of bravery dethrones most of the popular notions about it as an exalted fascination. Psychological knowledge fosters new forms of courage, demanding exhausting labor, the labor of thought rather than the easy work of recklessness.

I cannot take any other option than for this enduring courage of life, courage that no longer embodies the magic attraction of suicide and decline. Courage should be the vivid faith in, and the alert awareness and the sound consideration of, all that moves life.

Such courage accepts the great fear behind all the mysteries of life and dares to live with it.

The Nazis were very much aware of the existence of unbendable heroes among their victims, whose faces could not be changed, whose minds could not be coerced. They called their calmness and stubborn will physiognomic insubordination, and they tried to kill these heroes as soon as they were discovered. Happily, the jailers had many blind spots when it came to detecting spiritual greatness.

When the war was over, most of these heroes disappeared modestly into the crowd after their mission was fulfilled, leaving leadership to the more sophisticated politicians.

CHAPTER EIGHTEEN

Freedom—Our Mental Backbone

The totalitarian state is continually driving out man's private opinions and convictions. For the police state, thinking is already acting. The inner preparation for action as expressed in trial action —thought—is not accepted. Innate doubt and the trials and tribulations of thought adaptation are denied. Inbreeding destructive thought is one way to undermine the community. Not trusting the liberty of thought and free expression of opinion is even more dangerous; the natural destructive desires are repressed to that uncontrollable realm of the mind that may explode more easily into action. The verbal expression of a destructive thought however often partly conquers that thought, and renders it less potent. Here lies the actual paradox! Condemning antisocial thought—thought not yet put into action—provokes a short circuit of explosive action!

Every piece of logic may have its dangerous implications: inquisitional murder took place in the service of high ideals. If we cannot gamble with the innate good sense of man, a free and peaceful society are impossible, a democracy is impossible. Moral culture begins and ends with the individual. Only the cult of individual freedom, individual possession, and individual creativity makes man willing to curb instinctual desires and to repress destructivity. Man is not only a social being. Somewhere away from the crowd and the noise, he has to come to grips with himself and confront his

God and nature. In order to grow, he needs reserve and isolation and silence. In addition to his mechanical devices and machines, he needs to get back to nature, to camp out-of-doors by himself. Somewhere along the line, he has to be the maker of some of his own tools, as a shoemaker or a healer or a teacher. Without being thrown on his own and knowing loneliness, man is dwarfed, he is lost among the waves of overpowering human influence and a sea of coercive probabilities.

The Democratizing Action of Psychology

The deepest conviction of the power of psychological understanding came to me in my protracted mental struggles with a man who held membership in a totalitarian organization. He came to me for psychological advice during the Nazi occupation of Holland, and I knew that I had to be careful to avoid discussing politics with him; in those days free expression of opinion could be severely punished, and my patient would have reported me if I had said anything "suspicious."

However, as my therapy of passive listening liberated him from his personal tensions, the patient became more humane. He developed an increasing respect for the individual personality as such, and sometimes grew very critical of the Nazis' callous treatment of human life and human dignity. As time passed, he dissociated himself more and more from his totalitarian political friends. This was indeed courageous, for, especially at that time, the turn from collaboration toward nonconformism was usually interpreted as high treason. In his last visits before we agreed that he was cured, we spoke of our mutual faith in the dignity of the individual and our confidence in the decisions of the mature adult as to the path of his own interests.

Does psychology really exert a democratizing influence on the authoritarian and totalitarian spirit? The case I have just cited would seem to indicate that it does. On the other hand, we know that Goebbels's propaganda machine applied psychological principles to hypnotize the German people into submission. Hitler, too, laid down his psychological artillery barrage to spread panic throughout Europe.

In Nazi Germany, all psychoanalytic treatment was controlled by psychology's own *Führer,* Goering's brother. Certainly the science of suggestion, hypnosis, and Pavlovian training can be used to enlist cowardly, submissive followers for a program of despotism. These uses of psychological knowledge are perversions of both the principles and the purposes of psychology. Intrinsic in the psychological approach, and above all in psychoanalytic treatment, is an important element that fosters an attitude diametrically opposite to the totalitarian one.

The true purpose of psychology, and especially of its mental health branch, is to free man from his internal tensions by helping him to understand what causes them. Psychology seeks to liberate the human spirit from its dependency on immature thinking so that each man can realize his own potentialities. It seeks to help man to face reality with its many problems, and to recognize his own limitations as well as his possibilities for growth. It is dedicated to the development of mature individuals who are capable of living in freedom and of *voluntarily* restricting their freedom, when it is indicated, for the larger good. It is based on the premise that when man understands himself, he can begin to be the master of his own life, rather than merely the puppet either of his own unconscious drives or of a tyrant with a perverted lust for power.

As we have said earlier, every man passes through a stage in his own development of greater susceptibility to totalitarianism. This usually occurs during adolescence when the pubescent becomes aware of his own personality—the authority within himself. In not accepting this responsibility, he may look for a strong leader outside the home. At an earlier age—in infancy—the more unconscious patterns of compulsion and automatic obedience are laid. With the advent of his new sense of selfhood, the youth begins to oppose the adult authorities who previously directed his life.

Becoming conscious of the entity we call ego or self or *I* is a painful mental process. It is not a matter of chance that the feeling of endless longing, of *Weltschmerz,* is traditionally connected with adolescence. The process of becoming an autonomous and self-growing individual involves separation from the security of the family. To achieve *internal democracy,* the adolescent must separate himself from his protective environment. In so doing he is not merely intoxicated with his sense of growth and emancipation, he is also filled with a sense of fear and loneliness. He is entering a new world in which he must henceforth assume mature responsibility for his actions. At that time he may become an easy prey for totalitarian propaganda. A personal grudge against growing up may lead him to forsake the struggle for personal maturity.

This problem is particularly acute in Western society not only because of the real ideological-political battle we have to face, but also because our ways of raising children may emphasize this problem. Whereas primitive groups impose some measure of social responsibility upon the child early in life and increase it gradually, our middle-class culture segregates him completely in the world of childhood, nursery, and schoolroom, and then plunges him precipitously into adulthood to sink or swim. At this turning point, many young people shrink from such a test. Many do not want a freedom that carries with it so many burdens, so much loneliness. They are willing to hand back their freedom in return for continued parental protection, or to surrender it to political or economic ideologies which are in fact displaced parental images.

Alas, the youth's surrender of individuality is no guarantee against fear and loneliness. The real outside world is in no way altered by his inner choice. Therefore the youth who relinquishes his freedom to new parent figures develops a curious, dual feeling of love and hate toward all authority. Docility and rebellion, submission and hate live side by side within him. Sometimes he bows completely to authority or tyranny; at other times, often unpredictably, everything in him revolts against his chosen leader. This duality is an endless one, for one side of his nature continually seeks to overstep the limits which his other, submissive side has imposed. The man who fails to achieve freedom knows only two extremes: unquestioning submission and impulsive rebellion.

Conversely, the individual who is strong enough to embrace mature adulthood enters into a new kind of freedom. True, this freedom is an ambiguous concept since it involves the responsibility of making new decisions and confronting new uncertainties. The frontiers of freedom are anarchy and caprice on the one side and regimentation and suffocation by rules on the other.

If only we could find an easy formula for the mature attitude toward life! Even if we call it the democratic spirit, we can still explain more easily what democracy is not, than what it is. We can say that our individualizing democracy is the enemy of blind authority. If we wish a more detailed, psychological explanation, we must contrast it with totalitarianism. Our democracy is against the total regimentation and equalization of its individuals. It does not ask for homogeneous integration and smooth social adjustment. Democracy, in comparison with these aims, implies a confidence in spontaneity and individual growth. It is able to postulate progress and the correction of evil. It guards the community against human error without resorting to intimidation. Democracy provides redress for its own errors; totalitarianism considers itself infallible. Whereas totalitarianism controls by whim and manipulated public opinion, democracy undertakes to regulate society by law, to respect human nature, and to guard its citizens against the tyranny of a single individual on the one hand and a power-crazy majority on the other. *Democracy always fights a dual battle.* On the one hand, it must limit the resurgence of asocial inner impulses in the individual; on the other, it must guard the individual against external forces and ideologies hostile to the democratic way of life.

The Battle on Two Fronts

The inner harmony between social adaptation and self-assertion has to be re-formed in every new environment. Each individual has to fight over and over again the same subtle battle that started during infancy and babyhood. The ego, the self, forms itself through confrontation with reality. Compliance battles with originality, dependence with independence, outer discipline with inner morale. No culture can escape this inner human battle, though there is a difference in emphasis in every culture and society and in every family.

The combination of internal and external struggle, of a mental conflict on two fronts, renders the Western ideal of an individualized democracy highly vulnerable, particularly when its adherents are unaware of this inherent contradiction. Democracy, by its very nature will always have to fight against dictatorship from without and destructiveness from within. Democratic freedom has to battle against both the individual's inner will to power and his urge to submit to other people. It also has to battle against the contagious drive for power intruding from over the frontiers and so often backed up by armies.

The freedom toward which democracy strives is not the romantic freedom of adolescent dreams; it is one of mature stature. Democracy insists on sacrifices which are necessary to maintain freedom. It tries to combat the fears that attack men when they are faced with democracy's apparently unlimited freedom. Such lack of limitations can be misused to satisfy mere instinctual drives. However, because democracy does not exploit man by myth, primitive magic, mass hypnotism, or other psychological means of seduction, it is less fascinating to the immature individual than is dictatorial control. Democracy, when it is not involved in a dramatic struggle for survival, may appear quite drab and uninspiring. It simply demands that men shall think and judge for themselves; that each individual shall exercise his full conscious ability in adapting to a changing world; and that genuine public opinion shall mold the laws that govern the community. Essentially, democracy means the right to develop yourself and not to be developed by others. Yet this right like every other, has to be balanced by a duty. The right to develop yourself is impossible without the duty of giving your energy and attention to the development of others. Democracy is rooted not only in the personal *rights* of the common man, but even more in the personal *interests* and *responsibilities* of the common man. When he loses this interest in politics and government, he helps to pave the road to power politics. Democracy demands mental activity of a rather high level from the common man.

What the general public digests and assimilates in its mind is, in our new era of mass communication, just as important as the dictates of the experts. If the latter formulate and communicate ideas beyond the common grasp, they will talk into a vacuum. Thus they may permit a more simple and even an untrue ideology to slip in. It is not enough that an idea is only formulated and printed; we have to take care that the public can participate in the new concept.

The mystery of freedom is the existence of that great love of freedom! Those who have tasted it will not waver. Man revolts against unfair pressure. While the pressure accumulates he revolts silently, but at some critical moment it bursts into open revolt. For those who have lived through such an outburst, freedom is life itself. We have learned this especially in the days of persecution and occupation, in the underground, in the camps, and under the threat of demagoguery. We can even discover it in the totalitarian countries where nonetheless the terror, the resistance goes on.

Freedom and respect for the individual are rooted in the Old Testament, which convinced man that he makes his own history, that he is responsible for his history. Such freedom implies that a man throws off his inertia, that he does not cling arbitrarily to tradition, that he strives for knowledge and accepts moral responsibility. The fear of freedom is the fear of assuming responsibility.

Freedom can never be completely safeguarded by rules and laws. It is as much dependent on the courage, integrity, and responsibility of each of us as it is on these qualities in those who govern. Every trait in us and our leaders which points to passive submission to mere power betrays democratic freedom. In our American system of democratic government, three different powerful branches serve to check each other, the executive, the legislative, and the judiciary. Yet when there is no will to prevent encroachment of the power of one by any of the others, this system of checks, too, can degenerate.

Like adolescents who try to hide behind the aprons of parental authority rather than face mature adulthood, the individual members of a democratic state may shrink from the mental activity it imposes. They long to take flight into a condition of thoughtless security. Often they would prefer the government, or some individual personification of the state, to solve their problems for them. It is this desire that makes totalitarians and conformists. Like an infant the conformist can sleep quietly and transfer all his worries to Father State. When the intellectuals lose their self-control and courage and are possessed only by their fears and emotions, the power of those with prejudice and stupidity gains.

Since within each of us lie the seeds of both democracy and totalitarianism, the struggle between the democratic and the totalitarian attitude is fought repeatedly by each individual during his lifetime. His particular view of himself and of his fellow men will determine his political creed. Coexisting with man's wish for liberty and maturity are destructiveness, hate, the desire for power, resistance to independence, and the wish to retreat into irresponsible childhood. Democracy appeals only to the adult side of man; fascism and totalitarianism tempt his infantile desires.

Totalitarianism is based on a mechanized narrow view of mankind. It denies the complexity of the individual, and the struggle between his conscious and unconscious motivations. It denies doubt, ambivalence, and contradiction of feelings. It simplifies man, making him into a machine that can be put to work by governmental oil.

In every psychoanalytic treatment there comes the moment when the patient has to decide whether or not he will grow up. The knowledge and insight he has gained have to be translated into action. By this time he knows more about himself; his life has become an open book to him. Although he understands himself better, he finds it difficult to leave the dreamland of childhood, with its fantasies, hero-worship, and happy endings. But, fortified with a deeper understanding of his inner motivation, he steps over into the world of self-chosen responsibility and limited freedom. Because his image of the world is no longer distorted by immature longings, he is now able to function in it as a mature adult.

Systematic education toward freedom is possible. Freedom grows as the control over destructive inner drives become internalized and no longer depend on control from the outside, on control by parents and authorities.

It is the building up of our personality and our conscience—ego and superego—that is important. Nor can this development be brought about in an enforced and compulsive way as tyrants and dictators try to do. We must develop it through free acceptance or rejection of existing moral values until the inner moral person in us is so strong that he is able to go beyond existing values and can stand on his own moral grounds. The choice in favor of freedom lies between self-chosen limitation—the liberation from chaos—and the pseudo-freedom of unconscious chaos. To many people freedom is an emotional concept of letting themselves go, which really means a dictatorship by dark, instinctual drives. There is also an intellectual concept of freedom, meaning a limiting of bondage and unfreedom.

In order to become free, certain outside conditions must be prevented from hampering this moral development of self-control. We have to become increasingly aware of the internal dangers of democracy: laxity, laziness, and unawareness. People have to be aware of the tendency of technology to automatize their minds. They have to become aware of the fact that mass media and modern communication are able to imprint all kinds of suggestions on our brains. They have to know that education can turn us either into weak fact-factories or strong personalities. A free democracy has to fight against mediocrity in order not to be smothered by mere numbers of automatic votes. Democratic freedom requires a highly intelligent appraisal and understanding of the democratic system itself. This very fact makes it difficult for us to advertise or "promote" it. Furthermore, inculcating democracy is just as dangerous as inculcating totalitarianism. It is the essence of democracy that it must be self-chosen, it cannot be imposed.

The Paradox of Freedom

Freedom and planning present no essential contrasts. In order to let freedom grow, we have to plan our controls over the forces that limit freedom. Beyond this, we must have the passion and the inner freedom to prosecute those who abuse freedom. We must have the vitality to attack those who commit mental suicide and psychic murder through abuse of liberties, dragging down other persons in their wake. Suicidal submission is a kind of subversion from within; it is passive surrender to a mechanized world without personalities; it is the denial of personality. We must have the fervor to stand firmly for freedom of the individual, for mutual tolerance and dignity, and we must learn not to tolerate the destruction of these values. We must not tolerate those who make use of worthy ideas and values only to destroy them as soon as they are in power. We must be intolerant of these abuses as long as the battle for mental life or death goes on.

It cannot be emphasized too strongly that liberty is only possible with a strong set of beliefs and moral standards. This means that man has to adhere to self-restrictive rules—moral rules—in order to keep his freedom. When there is lack of such internal checks, owing to lack of education or to stereotyped education, then external pressure or even tyranny becomes necessary to check unsocial drives. Then freedom becomes the victim of man's inability to live in freedom and self-control.

Mankind should be guaranteed the right *not* to hear and not to conform and the right to defense against psychological attack and against intervention in the form of perverted mass propaganda, totalitarian pressure, and mental torture. No compromise or appeasement is possible in dealing with such attitudes. We have to watch carefully lest our own mistakes in attacking personal freedom become grist for the totalitarian's mill. Even our denunciation may have a paradoxical effect. Fear and hysteria further totalitarianism. What we need is careful analysis and understanding of such phenomena. Democracy is the regime of the dignity of man and his right to think for himself, the right to have his own opinion— more than that, the right *to assert* his own opinion and to protect himself against mental invasion and coercion.

When the United Nations has devised rules curtailing menticide and psychological intrusion, it will have insured a human right as precious as physical existence, the right of the nonconforming free individual—the right to dissent, the right to be oneself. Tolerance of criticism and heresy is one of the conditions of freedom.

Here we touch on another crucial point related to the technique of governing people. There is a relationship between overcentralization of government, mass participation, and totalitarianism.

Mass participation in government, without the decentralization that emphasizes the value of variation and individuality and without the possibility of sound selection of leaders, facilitates the creation of the dictatorial leader. The masses then transfer their desire for power to him. The slave participates in a magic way in the glory of the master.

Democratic self-government is determined by restraint and self-limitations, by sportsmanship and fairness, by voluntary observance of the rules of society and by cooperation. These qualities come through training. In a democratic government those who have been elected to responsible positions request controls and limitations against themselves, knowing that no one is without fault. Democracy is not a fight for independence but a mutually regulated interdependence. Democracy means checking man's tendency to gather unlimited power unto himself. It means checking the faults in each of us. It minimizes the consequences of man's limitations.

The Future Age of Psychology

Let me repeat what I said at the very beginning of this book. The modern techniques of brainwashing and menticide—those perversions of psychology—can bring almost any man into submission and surrender. Many of the victims of thought control, brainwashing, and menticide that we have talked about were strong men whose minds and wills were broken and degraded. But although the totalitarians use their knowledge of the mind for vicious and unscrupulous purposes, our democratic society can and must use its knowledge to help man to grow, to guard his freedom, and to understand himself.

Psychological knowledge and psychological treatment may in themselves generate the democratic attitude; for psychology is essentially the science of the *juste milieu*, of free choice within the framework of man's personal and social limitations. Compared with the million-year span of human existence and evolution, civilization is still in its infancy. Despite historical reversals, man continues to grow, and psychology—no matter how imperfect now—will become one of man's most powerful tools in his struggle for freedom and maturity.

BIBLIOGRAPHY

"Admissibility of Results of Lie-Detector and Truth Serum Tests" (Oklahoma Court), *Journal of American Medical Association*, Vol. 133, 1951.

Ahrendt, H., *The Origin of Totalitarianism*. New York, Harper & Brothers, 1950.

Almond, G. A., and others, *The Appeals of Communism*. Princeton, Princeton University Press, 1954.

Asch, S. E., "Opinions and Social Pressure," *Scientific American*, Vol. 193, 1955.

Ashby, W. R., *Design for a Brain*. New York, John Wiley & Sons, Inc., 1952.

Aspaturian, V., "What Do the Communists Mean by 'Peaceful Coexistence'?" *The Reporter*, 1955.

"Automation Is Here," *Democratic Digest*, 1955.

Baschwitz, K., *Du Und Die Masse*. Amsterdam, Elsevier, 1937.

Bauer, R. A., *The New Man in Soviet Psychology*. Cambridge, Harvard University Press, 1952.

Beck, F., and Godin, W., *Russian Purge and the Extraction of Confession*. New York, Viking Press, Inc., 1950.

Beer, M., "The Battle for Man's Rights," *United Nations World*, 1950.

Bergler, E., *The Battle of the Conscience*. Washington, D. C., Washington Institute of Medicine, 1948.

—— *The Superego—Unconscious Conscience*. New York, Grune & Stratton, Inc., 1952.

Boeree, T. A., *The Sinister History of Christiaan Lindemans, Alias King Kong.* Unpublished manuscript.

Bonhoeffer, W., and Zutt, G., "Uber den Geisteszustand des Reichstagsbrandstifters Marinus Van Der Lubbe," *Monatschrift für Psychiatrie,* Vol. 89, 1934.

Burney, C., *The Dungeon Democracy.* New York, Duell, Sloan and Pearce, 1951.

Byfield, R. S., *Logocide, The Fifth Weapon.* New York, Privately printed, 1954.

Cantril, H., Gaudet, H., and Herzog, H., *The Invasion from Mars.* Princeton, Princeton University Press, 1940.

Commager, H. S., "The Real Danger—Fear of Ideas," *The New York Times Magazine,* June 26, 1949.

The Convention on Genocide. Lake Success, N. Y., United Nations Department of Public Information, 1949.

Dicks, H. V., "Observations on Contemporary Russian Behavior," *Human Relations,* Vol. 5, 1952.

Dobrogaev, S. M., *Speech Reflexes* (translated and digested from the Russian). New York, National Committee for a Free Europe, 1953.

"Document on Terror," *News from Behind the Iron Curtain,* Vol. 1, 1952.

Dooren, L., *Dr. Johannes Wier.* Salten, Holland, De Graafschap, 1940.

Ferenczi, S., "Stages in the Development of the Sense of Reality," in *An Outline of Psychoanalysis.* New York, Modern Library, 1925.

Frazer, J. G., *The Golden Bough.* New York, The Macmillan Company, 1947.

Freud, A., *The Ego and the Mechanisms of Defense.* New York, International Universities Press, Inc., 1946.

Freud, S., *Basic Writings.* New York, Modern Library, 1946.

Fried, J. H. E., *Les Méthodes et les procédés du fascisme.* [Paris], United Nations Educational, Social and Cultural Organization, 1949.

Fromm, E., *Escape from Freedom.* New York, Farrar & Rinehart, Inc., 1941.

Gallery, D. V., "We Can Baffle the Brainwashers!" *Saturday Evening Post,* 1955.

Gilbert, G. M., *The Psychology of Dictatorship*. New York, The Ronald Press Company, 1950.

Gonzales, V., and Gorkin, J., *El Campesino: Life and Death in Soviet Russia*. New York, G. P. Putnam's Sons, 1952.

Haggerty, J. J., Jr., "Think or Die," *Collier's*, 1955.

Heiden, K., "Why They Confess," *Life Magazine*, 1949.

Heller, E. L., "Thought I'd Never Get Home," *Saturday Evening Post*, 1955.

Herling, G., *A World Apart*. New York, Roy Publishers, 1952.

Heron, W. *Time*, 1954.

Hershey, B., "The Sick Men Who Rule the World," *The Nation*, 1949.

Hill, G., "Brain-Washing: Time for a Policy," *Atlantic Monthly*, 1955.

Hitler, A., *Mein Kampf*. Boston, Houghton Mifflin Company, 1943.

Hook, S., "Why They Switch Loyalties," *The New York Times Magazine*, Nov. 26, 1950.

Horsley, Gantt W., "Bolshevik Principles and Russian Physiology," *Bulletin of the Atomic Scientists*, Vol. VIII, 1952.

Hsu, F. L. K., "Suppression Versus Repression," *Psychiatry*, Vol. XII, 1949.

Hunter, E., *Brain-Washing in Red China: The Calculated Destruction of Men's Minds*. New York, The Vanguard Press, 1951.

────── "Government by the Insane," *The Freeman*, 1953.

Huxley, A., *The Devils of Loudun*. New York, Harper & Brothers, 1952.

────── *The Doors of Perception*. New York, Harper & Brothers, 1954.

Jong, L. de, *The German Fifth Column in the Second World War*. Chicago, The University of Chicago Press, 1956.

Kafka, F., *The Trial*. New York, Alfred A. Knopf, Inc., 1937.

Kalme, A., *Total Terror*. New York, Appleton-Century-Crofts, Inc., 1950.

Karp, D., *One*. New York, The Vanguard Press, 1953.

Kayman, G., "Forensic Psychiatry," *American Journal of Psychotherapy*, Vol. VIII, 1954.

Kisker, G. W., *World Tension: The Psychopathology of International Relations*. New York, Prentice-Hall, Inc., 1950.

Krugman, H. E., "The Role of Hostility in the Appeals of Communism in the United States," *Psychiatry*, Vol. I, 1953.

Lassio, S., "La Verité sur la condamnation du Cardinal Mindszenty," *Le Figaro*, 1950.

Lasswell, H. D., "The Strategy of Soviet Propaganda," *Proceedings of The Academy of Political Science* (Columbia University), Vol. XXIV, 1951.

Lea, C. H., *The Inquisition of the Middle Ages*. New York, The Citadel Press, 1954.

Lehmann-Haupt, H., *Art Under a Dictatorship*. New York, Oxford University Press, 1954.

Leites, N., and Barnart, E., *Ritual of Liquidation*. Glencoe, Ill., Free Press, 1954.

Little, A. M. G., "Pavlov and Propaganda," *Problems of Communism*, Vol. II, 1953.

London, T. D., "The Scientific Council on Problems of the Physiological Theory of Academician I. P. Pavlov: A Study in Control," *Science*, Vol. 116, 1952.

Luther, R. H., *American Demagogues—Twentieth Century*. Boston, Beacon Press, 1954.

MacDonald, D., "The Lie-Detector Era," *The Reporter*, 1954.

MacDonald, J. M., "Narcoanalysis and Criminal Law," *American Journal of Psychiatry*, Vol. 111, 1954.

Malinowski, B., *Magic, Science and Religion*. New York, Doubleday & Company, Inc., 1954.

Mayo, C. W., Speech before the Security Council of the United Nations, Oct. 26, 1953.

"Médecine, quatrième pouvoir?" *Esprit*, 1950.

Meerloo, J. A. M., "Die Abwehrreaktionen des Angstgefühls," *Zeitschrift fur die gesammte Neurologie und Psychiatrie*, Vol. 133, 1931.

—— *Conversation and Communication*. New York, International Universities Press, Inc., 1952.

—— "The Crime of Menticide," *American Journal of Psychiatry*, Vol. 107, 1951.

—— *Delusion and Mass-Delusion*. New York, Nervous and Mental Disease Monographs, 1949.

—— "Democracy and Fascism Within Us," in *Total War and*

the Human Mind. New York, International Universities Press, Inc., 1945.

—— "International Law and Morality," *New Europe*, 1945.

—— "Living by Proxy," *American Journal of Psychotherapy*, Vol. II, 1953.

—— "The Monument as a Delusional Token," *American Imago*, 1954.

—— "Morale," *Military Review*, 1954.

—— "The Psychology of Treason and Loyalty," *American Journal of Psychotherapy*, Vol. VIII, 1954.

—— "Television Addiction and Reactive Apathy," *Journal of Nervous and Mental Diseases*, Vol. 120, 1954.

—— "Thought Control and Confession Compulsion," in *Explorations in Psychoanalysis*. New York, Julian Press, Inc., 1953.

—— "Treason and Traitors," in *Aftermath of Peace*. New York, International Universities Press, Inc., 1946.

—— *The Two Faces of Man*. New York, International Universities Press, Inc., 1954.

Miller, W. L., "Can Government be Merchandised?" *The Reporter*, 1953.

Mitscherlich, A., and others, *Doctors of Infamy: The Story of the Nazi Medical Crimes*. New York, Henry Schuman, Inc., 1949.

Moloney, J. C., "Psychic Self-Abandon and Extortion of Confessions," *International Journal of Psychoanalysis*, Vol. 36, 1955.

—— "A Study in Neurotic Conformity: The Japanese," *Complex*, 1951.

—— *Understanding the Japanese Mind*. New York, Philosophical Library, 1954.

Newman, C. L., "Trial by Jury Outmoded," *Science News Letter*, 1955.

"No Bands Playing: Colonel Arnold's Story," *Time*, 1955.

Pavlov, I. P., *Conditioned Reflexes and Psychiatry*. New York, International Publishers Company, 1941.

Peck, D. W., "Do Juries Delay Justice?" *The New York Times Magazine*, Dec. 25, 1955.

"People v. Leyra," *North Eastern Reporter*, Second Series, 1951.

Piaget, J., *The Language and Thought of the Child*. New York, Noonday Press, 1955.

Prychodke, N., *One of the Fifteen Million*. Boston, Little, Brown and Company, 1952.

Razran, G. *Science News Letter*, 1954.

Reik, T., *Gestandniszwang und Strafbedürfnis*. Zurich, Internationaler Psychoanalytischer Verlag, 1925.

—— *The Unknown Murderer*. New York, International Universities Press, Inc., 1949.

"Report on Vogeler," *The New York Times*, April 29, 1951.

Richter, C. P., "Civilized Life Affects Combat Stress," *Science News Letter*, 1954.

Ross, L., "Red China's Dope Peddlers," *The New Leader*, 1954.

Rostow, W. W., and others, *The Dynamics of Soviet Society*. New York, New American Library, 1954.

Rousset, D., *The Other Kingdom*. New York, Reynal & Hitchcock, 1947.

Rud, F., "The Social Psychopathology of Schizophrenic States," *Journal of Clinical and Experimental Psychopathology*, Vol. 12, 1951.

Samuels, G., "American Traitors," *The New York Times Magazine*, May 22, 1949.

Santucci, P. S., and Winokur, G., "Brainwashing as a Factor in Psychiatric Illness: An Heuristic Approach," *Archives of Neurology and Psychiatry*, Vol. 74, 1955.

Schultz, H. H., *Das Autogene Training*. Stuttgart, Georg Thieme Verlag, 1934.

"The Schwable Case," *The New York Times*, March 10-11, 1954.

"The Schwable Case," *The Reporter*, 1954.

Segal, H. A., "Initial Psychiatric Findings of Recently Repatriated Prisoners of War," *American Journal of Psychiatry*, Vol. 111, 1954.

Shipkov, M., Bulletin of the State Department [Washington, D.C.], 1950.

Siegel, V., "College Freedoms Being Stifled by Students' Fear of Red Label," *The New York Times*, May 10, 1951.

"Soviet Expunging West's Psychiatry," *The New York Times*, Oct. 16, 1951.

Spence, K. W., and Farber, I. E., "Conditioning and Extinction as a Function of Anxiety," *Journal of Experimental Psychology*, Vol. 45, 1953.

Sperling, G. E., "The Interpretation of the Trauma as a Command," *Psychoanalytic Quarterly*, Vol. 19, 1950.

Strassman, H. D., and others, "A Prisoner of War Syndrome: Apathy as a Reaction to Severe Stress," Paper read at American Psychiatric Association, May 9-13, 1955.

Swift, S. K., *The Cardinal's Story*. The Macmillan Company, 1949.

Taylor, A. J. P., "The Judgment of the Diplomats," *The Saturday Review*, 1954.

Taylor, E., *The Strategy of Terror*. New York, Houghton Mifflin Company, 1942.

Tyler, D. B., "Psychological Changes During Experimental Sleep Deprivation," *Diseases of the Nervous System*, Vol. 16, 1955.

Universal Declaration of Human Rights. Lake Success, N. Y., United Nations Department of Public Information, 1949.

Vogeler, R. A., *I Was Stalin's Prisoner*. New York, Harcourt, Brace & Company, Inc., 1952.

Waelder, R., "Authoritarianism and Totalitarianism," in *Psychoanalysis and Culture*. New York, International Universities Press, Inc., 1951.

Walker, R. L., "Psychological Control" in *China Under Communism*. New Haven, Yale University Press, 1955.

Weissberg, A., *The Accused*. New York, Simon & Schuster, Inc., 1951.

West, R., *The Meaning of Treason*. New York, Viking Press, Inc., 1947.

Weyl, N., *Treason*. Washington, D. C., The Public Affairs Press, 1950.

Wier, Johannes, *De Praestigiis Daemonum*. Basel, Per J Oporinum, 1563.

Winokur, G., "Brainwashing, A Social Phenomenon of Our Time," *Human Organization*, Vol. 13, 1955.

—— "The Germ Warfare Statements," *Journal of Nervous and Mental Diseases*, Vol. 122, 1955.

Wortis, J., "Some Recent Developments in Soviet Psychiatry," *American Journal of Psychiatry*, Vol. 109, 1953.

Yen, M., *The Umbrella Garden*. New York, The Macmillan Company, 1954.

Zimmering, P., and others, "Heroin Addiction in Adolescent Boys," *Journal of Nervous and Mental Diseases*, Vol. 114, 1951.

INDEX

313

ABOUT THE AUTHOR

DR. JOOST A. M. MEERLOO was born in 1903 at The Hague, Netherlands, where he received his early education. His M.D. was earned at Leyden University (1927) and his Ph.D. at the University of Utrecht (1932). Between 1928 and 1934 Dr. Meerloo served as teacher and staff psychiatrist in several hospitals; in the latter year he entered private practice in psychotherapy and psychoanalysis at The Hague, serving also as psychiatric consultant to the Royal Court and to governmental agencies. Under the Nazi occupation of the Netherlands, Dr. Meerloo was able to observe at firsthand the methods of mental torture and forced interrogation described in this book.

In 1942 he narrowly missed death at the hands of the German occupation forces in the Netherlands and escaped to England, where he served as a colonel, chief of the Psychological Department of the Netherlands Army. For two years before he came to the United States in 1946 he was High Commissioner for Welfare for the Netherlands Government, acting also as adviser to SHAEF and UNRRA. Dr. Meerloo was decorated with the Distinguished Service Cross in 1943. Since settling in New York, he has taught in several schools and conducted the private practice of psychotherapy and psychoanalysis; he became a citizen of the United States in 1950. He is an honorary member and fellow of several professional societies.

His writings include thirteen books, among them *Total War and the Human Mind, Patterns of Panic,* and *The Two Faces of Man,* and more than two hundred articles in both learned and popular journals. He is also distinguished as an editor and is a well-known book reviewer. *The Rape of the Mind,* his fourteenth book, draws upon his experiences and intimate knowledge of what extreme mental pressure can do to the human mind.

CPSIA information can be obtained
at www.ICGtesting.com
Printed in the USA
LVHW040457130723
752370LV00001B/1